Manhook

Copyright © 2005 Ken Ratcliffe
All rights reserved.
ISBN: 1-4196-0807-X

To order additional copies, please contact us.
BookSurge, LLC
www.booksurge.com
1-866-308-6235
orders@booksurge.com

KEN
RATCLIFFE

MANHOOK

2005

Manhook

Pam,

He saw that face
And he lost all
Control.

[signature]

CONTENTS

ACKNOWLEDGEMENTS

To my many friends who supported me by being kind to the early revisions, I thank you. Heartfelt thanks to Melissa Lassor who pointed me to Iowa where I was further encouraged at the Writer's Workshop by Wayne Johnson, a talented writer and dedicated teacher. To my zany friend and collaborator, Bill Stevens, thank you for your lens on life. To my brilliant, young editor, Erin Dionne, who encouraged me to push my characters to the point of discomfort—you're a shooting star.

The behavioral descriptions of the Tungara frog were excerpted from an article by David Berry, *Why everything may not happen for the best,* October 16, 2003, *International Herald Tribune.*

An excellent reference for would-be and practicing entrepreneurs can be found in, *Entrepreneurship: Back to Basics,* authored by Gordon B. Baty and Michael S. Blake, *Beard Books.*

To Christine—
After all these years, I'm still full of smit.

PROLOGUE

Hal Brauner, the CEO of Allied Computer, sat behind his aircraft carrier-sized desk shaking his head at his V.P. of Human Resources.

"Do you believe that?"

Laurie Wells predicted earlier how the meeting would end but gave the boss credit. "You were right. We didn't have to fire him. He quit on his own."

"What a screwball," Brauner said. "If he waited another week I would have let him go with severance. I should have canned him when he missed the sales forecast again and trashed the stock."

"Hal, once he told you he was under psychiatric care, he tied our hands. He would have claimed a breakdown caused by his dismissal and sued us."

"I know, I know. What a conniving bastard." Brauner bolted up, pounding the desk. "He barges in here, quits, and says it's my fault that the stock is down." He slammed a palm with the back of his hand. "He's the one who hasn't delivered. It's always someone else with him."

"I think he's nuts," she said, throwing the keys to Lutz' company car into her briefcase.

"And what's with the electric fish? How many times has he told me about that?" He mimicked Lutz' omniscient air: "Hal, did you know that an electric fish eats only the tails of other electric fish?" He snickered as he backed against the edge of the desk. "Fruitcake."

"Well, your team will be delighted to be rid of that know-it-all." She walked to the boss to shake his hand.

He grinned. "Yeah, tell them I shit-canned the jerk."

She shook her head at Lutz' accusations on the way to the door.

"And get rid of that pompous-ass controller of his."

She turned with a smirk. "You want Phil out?"

"Yeah, I'm tired of that punk nipping at my pant leg. Move him out."

"My pleasure," she said.

YOU'RE IT!

August, 1999

L utz entered the doctor's waiting room just before noon and pressed a button on a coffee table as he sat. *Bzzzzzzzzzzz.* The psychiatrist was prompted in his inner office to close the current session, exit that patient through a door to the corridor and prepare for the next—a system with a built-in misery shield.

Minutes later, the door opened and a handsome, sinewy doctor with thick black hair, nodded to Lutz. "Bob, come in."

Lutz resented that a man at least five years older than he could have such a formidable, slicked-back coiffure—forcing his own thinning, grey-speckled mop into hideous contention.

Dr. Felton moved to his desk and scribbled in a folder while Lutz entered and sat in his normal chair, a dark blue upholstered piece more suited to a living room. It was all too formal for Lutz. A 19th century painting of a horse-mounted aristocrat hung on a dark, rich-looking wood behind his desk. A picture to the right matched in mood: a pack of young hounds was gaining on a frenzied fox. Dark green wall-to-wall carpeting completed the décor, all of it clinically irrelevant, Lutz thought; merely buoyant to the doctor's hourly ransom.

Felton closed the folder and sat across in trained silence— poised in his cardboard cut-out elegance—unwilling to initiate talk.

Lutz smiled. "I did it."

An eyebrow twitched. "Pardon?"

"I quit."

Felton managed his surprise. "I thought we agreed to talk about it further before you acted."

"Did it yesterday."

"Were you positive with your boss?" If he were wearing glasses, he would have peered over the top of them.

"Very." Lutz said, letting his eye contact stray.

Felton opened the folder and scanned notes from their last session then closed it and studied his patient. "Why yesterday when we had planned to discuss it further today?"

"Timing," Lutz said.

Felton nodded, though not in agreement with the reason. "A decision of this magnitude…is it really about timing?"

"Yeah," Lutz said, his jaw firm. "There's a time to noodle and a time to act."

"Have you been taking your Zoloft as prescribed?"

Lutz squinted at him. "Why? You think I quit on an impulse?"

"We did agree to spend one more session—this one—talking about it."

Lutz sat back and dismissed him with a look. "Well, that's not going to happen."

"We had planned this, Bob. You were to do it next week."

"Whatever," Lutz said, flicking an imaginary bug from atop his fly.

"And your wife was okay with this?"

Lutz shook his head with disgust. "Not really. But Pat didn't have to go to that office every day. I got home yesterday in a taxi; it was pouring like hell and she had all the windows open." He looked at the ceiling then back at the doctor. "She's smoking again. Imagine, ten years off the butts, now she's sneaking them in the house."

"What's going on?"

"She's been jumpy lately; says I make her nervous." Lutz picked at a cuticle, stalling, not wanting to shoulder any more blame.

"She's upset with you," Felton declared.

What's with this guy? Lutz spoke to the paintings. "She didn't want me to leave Allied. She said I didn't think it through. That it happened all too fast."

That was Felton's position, too.

Lutz returned his gaze to the doctor, "You know I hate that place. How I don't believe that Allied's been operating on the up and up."

Felton nodded. "And I thought that we had agreed to script a brief, professional letter of resignation today." He paused to pursue his patient's wandering eyes and brought them back. "Together."

Lutz spread his hands. "It didn't get done. What's the big deal?"

Felton leaned forward. "It's a pattern. You need to get in touch with the anxiety that forces you to act before fully assessing the repercussions."

"What do you mean?"

"You made an important decision against her wishes. Should there have been a more explicit agreement before you went forward with the resignation?"

He waved off the doctor. "That's not my makeup. We've talked about that."

At the last session, he told Felton how Pat bugs him. How she'll nag him to run an errand and how he sees himself stuck behind a geezer driving with a dozen eggs loose on the floor; and how he moans in a checkout line as a dead guy counts out change. How people don't anticipate, don't plan, just drive around blocking the movement of others; and how he eventually refuses to go.

"So you accepted the position at iCare?"

Lutz nodded, holding his smile. "I start Monday."

Felton said, "I thought you and Pat would first spend time away?"

Lutz' pulse quickened. "They need me now."

"Can you see why Pat would be upset with that?"

Lutz, unnerved by Felton's piercing green eyes, looked down and massaged his temples before popping up to lecture the ceiling. "She gets no vote. At the end of the day, I'm it!" He put his head back down in thought and stared at the floor before sitting up. "Ever play tag in grade school?" He said, forcing a calmer tone. "You tagged a kid and said, 'You're it'! And he was 'it' until he could tag someone else?"

"Sure," Felton said.

"Well I got tagged in my twenties and I'm still it. I'm fifty years old and there isn't a soul around to tag. And Pat? What does she know about making money? I'm the rainmaker. I'm it!"

"You said she would be willing to downsize...live a simpler life."

Lutz flicked a wrist to dismiss him again. "They *all* say that. Stick them with a sensitive guy making twenty grand. They want a sweeter man who will pay more attention? Give them 'Mr. Feminineside'. A little time in that lifestyle and they'll want the big hitter back."

"So this is about money."

He gave the doctor a 'where have you been?' look. "Of

course it is. I need to get Janie through college and have enough to retire. It wasn't going to happen at Allied. This is my brass ring."

"Did you get the stock options you asked for?"

Lutz let a small, crooked smile escape. "Yes, the million shares."

"You must be pleased."

The smile was now fully out and pulling at his face. "This opportunity has legs...there's a lot of upside in the deal."

"And a lot of risk," Felton countered.

Lutz shook him off. "We do the IPO in two years. I sell half the shares. Say iCare goes out at thirteen bucks a share. I make a profit of twelve per share times five-hundred thousand—a gain of six million bucks." He beamed.

He didn't volunteer that iCare's position in the Internet sector was fraught with risk. Industry pundits warned that a correction would force Internet valuations down to more realistic levels. (One Wall Street analyst projected "realism" at pennies.)

Lutz continued, "It doesn't stop at a gain of six. The company performs and the stock heads north." He sat back, buoyant, running upside numbers in his head.

"Are you prepared for less of an outcome?"

He squinted at the psychiatrist. "Huh?"

"What if the company doesn't go public?"

Lutz reddened. "That's not going to happen."

"Well what if it does?"

He glared at Felton. "What is it with you today?"

"Sorry?"

"Why are you so negative? You hassle me about resigning a few days early and now you're challenging me over the iCare deal."

"I'm trying to help you set expectations," Felton said.

"No you're not. You're rubbing my nose in my decision. You think I made this move without thinking it through. It's part of a pattern."

Felton watched Lutz fidget with a pen that he took from his shirt pocket. "Do you think that maybe I move fast because I know that I'm not going to get any help?" He held the pen as a projectile and stabbed the air. "That no one ever coached me."

"When have you needed coaching and not gotten it?"

"I'm not talking about you. I'm talking about my old man." He returned the pen to his pocket with a headshake. "He was the crassest guy I have ever known. I swear; he spent so much time with his fellow firefighters, he forgot how to talk. One time, in high school, I use his car, and I'm leaving the house with my date. He's cutting his little shit-patch of lawn with a push mower and yells to me: 'Don't be out all night playin Johnny Stinkfinger! Get your ass home!' Do you believe that?"

Felton's eyes widened though he tried not to react.

"The girl was mortified." His eyes bugged at the doctor. "And he was always whacked on Canadian Club."

Felton glanced at the folder. "You said he was a binge drinker."

Lutz nodded and sat back. "Whenever he was home. He slept at the station house most nights. In fact, we preferred it that way. Off shift he was a tough guy to be around. Didn't say much until he got into the hooch, then he got nasty. My mother said it was because of things he saw on the job." Lutz looked over at the paintings then back to the doctor. "The only time he showed any tenderness was when I was six or seven. He came into my room one night—after a fire—wearing all his gear. His face was black with soot. 'Bobby,' he said, 'I stepped in the dog.' I said, 'Pop, what dog?' My old man started crying, 'I stepped in him, Bobby'." He looked down and balled his fists. "I don't want to talk about this."

Felton watched him doodle in the carpet with the tip of a shoe.

He looked up with determination. "I'll make this iCare thing work; I want that goddamn money."

"Bob, you have proven yourself already. Look at what you have accomplished. Take it slow and you should be fine." Felton opened the folder. "You started with fifty milligrams and six weeks later went to seventy-five." He studied his patient. "I'd like you to increase your daily dosage to one-hundred milligrams."

"Why?"

"You're increasingly agitated. Plus, it will help you to think more clearly."

"Great." He pointed into his lap. "Talk to the little guy."

"You're still having decreased libido?"

"Yeah," Lutz said, with a look meant to assign blame to the doctor, "If I don't pee, I don't touch it."

Felton spoke while he continued to write, "One-hundred is how we should proceed." He looked up. "And again, no alcohol."

Lutz said, "Alright. Can we move on?"

Felton was back into the folder, scribbling. "So now you'll take two pills daily."

"Alright!" The tips of his ears warmed as he glared at the doctor.

Felton put it aside.

Lutz said, "Do you know that 13% of Americans are over sixty five? And by 2030, that number goes to 20%?"

Felton nodded, "It's a crisis that the health care industry is little prepared for."

Lutz reacted with enthusiasm. "That's good for us. With the high cost of assisted living, the market for iCare's system will be enormous. Tens of millions of people."

"So, what did you say to your boss?"

"Huh?"

"When you resigned. What did you say?"

Lutz said, "Why are you going there?"

Felton watched him brush an imaginary speck from his pants. "I told him that I didn't think he was doing such a great job."

"Did you say any of the things we rehearsed at our last session?"

Lutz said, "Not really," and returned a toe to the carpet.

"Why?" Felton said.

Lutz looked up. "Because I needed to cough up a giant hairball."

"Was that productive?"

"Yeah," he said, and took Felton through Allied's pervasive management style, one that chose harmony over results. How people would be gone tomorrow because Brauner ducked decisions today..."HR is supposed to recruit the very best. Instead, they protect the very worst. I need them to recruit sales people. Do they? No, they're busy working on a dress code for Casual Fridays. I say, 'what do you people work on next: Fuck-around Tuesdays?'"

Felton interrupted. "What did your boss say during the discussion?"

"Huh?"

"Was he threatened by the things you said?"

He shook his head at the doctor. "I told you I didn't want to talk about that." Then he droned on, citing more malfeasance—all examples of poor planning followed by dismal execution.

***

"…and HR wanted us to coach poor performers, but…
Bzzzzzzzzzzz.
Lutz stopped. "You're next nut is here."
"We need to wrap up," Felton said.
Lutz puffed a stream of air in relief and started to stand.
Felton went for the folder. "One other thing."
Lutz sat.
He scanned through it. "You've been under my care for six months. This is the second increase in your medication. Most patients stabilize at fifty milligrams." He looked up. "Today's increase moves you to the high side of recommended dosage."
"Then don't do it," Lutz said, matter-of-factly.
"You are increasingly anxious. I would normally prescribe an anti-anxiety solution, perhaps a mild sedative, but I'm concerned with your drinking."
Lutz grasped the arms of the chair and began to rise. "Are we done?" He didn't care about Felton's response. He moved to the door then turned to offer a disapproving glance before leaving.

***

Minutes later, while Lutz was headed home, Felton was on the phone with his ex-wife. "Grace, I'm not going to beg. This could have significant impact on my practice and the future of our daughter. Have some compassion, for God's sake."
"Then you should have thought of that before you continued on with your little problem."
"Come on, Grace; help me out."
"You bastard, Laurence! Don't do this to me. You already lost a wife over this; why not a practice?"
"I'll pay you back within sixty days; I promise. I'm

into a big billing cycle and the insurance companies will be reimbursing faster starting this month."

"Last time was the last time, Laurence. I *told* you that. I don't know why you expect this of me."

"Grace...Jesus, help me out." He picked up the racing form and slapped it back down on the desk. "I swear; this is the last time."

iCARE

Lutz felt like a kid that first Monday morning, inches taller and a year smarter, heading off in crisp new corduroys to start the school year. With big-business politics now out of the way, he would personally shape a culture that acknowledged initiative and rewarded results.

He parked his wife's Volvo wagon in the iCare lot and counted the cars. *Twelve.* By the end of the week he would see to it that all employees were in by 8:00 AM, within an hour of his arrival.

He walked briskly to the aging one-story brick building for his first real taste of Internet culture and was met in the lobby by a pert redhead. "Good morning, Mr. Lutz. I'm Lillian, your assistant." She shook his hand firmly. "Welcome to iCare."

"Hello, Lillian." He flashed a quick grin at her then saw that nothing had changed since his meeting with the Chief Engineer on his first and only visit. The place looked like teenagers were in charge. Papers were strewn on every surface, and cardboard boxes—some broken down and flattened; others half-full—cluttered the floor and the top of file cabinets. The boss of this hovel—an over-developed and under-dressed receptionist—struggled to attach plastic tabs to olive green file folders, the tip of her tongue peeking from alternate corners of her mouth to supervise.

He smirked at Lillian. "Did she quit grade school to work here?"

"No, Rosemarie completed her first year of college. She took a sabbatical to join us full-time."

He walked to the receptionist who was wearing a halter top and no bra. "Rosemarie, how are you? I'm your new CEO."

Snap-snap-pop. "Nice ta meetya."

"Please don't do that."

"Huh?"

"Snap your gum," he said.

Lillian stepped around him, her back to Rosemarie. "She's a good kid. I'll talk to her."

"Terrific," he said, walking away. "And tell her to put some clothes on."

Lillian chased after him, not sure if he had seen his corner office during the interview process. He entered the small confines—*too small for a CEO,* his immediate thought—and eyed the decades-old wooden desk. "Nice to see you kept the Goodwill furniture for me."

Lillian moved around him and pushed on the top of the oaken mass to prove its sturdiness. "We bought it second-hand at Marty's for fifty dollars. They threw in the chair."

He shrugged at the image of the ergonomic chair he left behind at Allied. "I guess it will do." He put down his briefcase and rubbed his hands together briskly, anxious to dive in. "Bring in the employee files so I can go through their performance reviews."

She looked at him. "Huh?"

"Performance reviews," he repeated. "I want to see who's been put on a get-well program. You know, so I can coach them." He smiled at her. *Out the fucking door.*

"There are none," she said.

"There are no underperformers?"

"No," she said, with cheeks flushing to match her strawberry hair. "No performance reviews."

He squinted at her.

"The guy before you didn't have time for them. He'd take us out for a beer and let us know how we were doing."

"You're kidding me?"

She smiled. "No. That's how they do it in start-ups."

He shook his head and she left, anxious to do so.

He took out a new notebook that he had purchased on Saturday. He would catalogue all relevant information, like he did when he was a kid managing his bug and snake collections. His high school biology classmates nicknamed him "A to Z" because he knew the taxonomy of most living things.

Each section of the notebook would contain a strategy for building iCare into a powerhouse. In the first, he wrote: *Acquiring People*. His job as CEO would be to recruit a team that could take the company forward. He drew three columns and printed 'Marketing', 'Sales' and 'Finance' across the top. *Shit!* He ripped the page from the notebook, crumpled it and scanned the office. "Lillian, could you get me a waste basket? *Please!*"

"Yes, sir," she called from her desk.

He wrote 'Marketing' and 'Finance'. Sales would be his job. No one could close deals like he could.

Taking a company public was a true test of an executive, requiring skills across all business disciplines. Who is your competition and how do you block them from entering your space? Is the business model sustainable? The CEO must be a big thinker in all areas. Lutz believed he was such a man— one who could synthesize the organization into a well-oiled machine. *Brauner was wrong that he lacked the discipline to develop a plan and stick to it.*

Lillian forced a smile a step before poking her head around the corner. "Professor Maltbie's office just called to say he's on his way. He wants to talk to you."

"Great," Lutz said.

Maltbie, an angel investor who put up the seed money to launch iCare, was a professor of economics at the M.I.T. Sloan School. Lutz interviewed with him over dinner and marveled at his fine mind, good humor and capacity for drink. Lutz continued to fill his notebook with attributes important in each of his new hires then closed it and put it towards the corner of the desk. He started to stand, then reached over to square it with the edges.

"Lillian?"

"Yes," She called.

"Bring me the iCare business plan."

She appeared in the doorway trying to finesse the question by being overly cute. "Huh?" She said, batting her eyelashes.

He frowned. "You're kidding me."

She brushed her skirt.

A voice rescued her from behind. "Lillian, oh Lillian, oh Lillian my love." She turned to a bear hug from a short, disheveled man with white hair, bushy eyebrows and a suit made of chalk.

"Professor, how nice to see you."

He put a hand to his eyes. "I continue to be blinded by the aura of you."

She poked his arm playfully. "Oh, stop," she said.

"You know, Mrs. Maltbie isn't feeling well these days. Should she unfortunately pass, perhaps we should seek a merger."

Lillian wagged a disapproving finger at the rotund little man. "I'm going to call her."

The professor gasped into his palm. "Oh, dear," he said, and cackled.

Lillian flapped a hand, brushed by him—an arm extended to ward off another hug—and closed the door behind her.

Lutz stood. "Professor, so nice to see you again."

The professor offered his hand. "I can't say how pleased I am that you decided to join us."

Lutz shook it firmly. "It's a wonderful opportunity."

"Yes it is." Maltbie smiled and took a seat as he scanned an index card and returned it to his pocket.

Lutz reached for the notebook.

"No need for you to write anything down," Maltbie said. "There are only a few things I want to go over."

Lutz smiled and pushed the notebook aside and sat, then rose to square it with the corner of the desk before sitting again.

"The first is why I believe iCare to be an enormous opportunity. Are your parents alive?"

Lutz shook his head. "My father passed two years ago, but my mother is still with us."

"One day you may want to have in-home care for her. Where would you go?"

Lutz waved a hand. "I'd ask around; make a few calls."

"And whom would you call?"

Lutz furled his brow. "A hospital? Maybe a social worker?"

Maltbie was bouncing his legs on the balls of his feet. "Do you know why our medical system is inefficient?"

Lutz shook his head.

"The free market doesn't work for healthcare because

corporations foot the bill. Employees don't pay for it so they don't demand quality. I mean, why don't we expand entitlements and have industry pay for worker nourishment as well." Maltbie stood, walked to the door, opened it and twirled a finger at employees milling around the coffee area. "We already subsidize the vending machines. Let's proceed and bring food right into the worker's kitchen." He slapped a knee. "We'll PopTart their kids!"

Lutz was being entertained and smiled broadly.

The professor sat. "Elderly rat packs scour the nation—making a shambles of our medical system—gumming appointment books across the land. And if homebound, they'll demand in-home companionship from visiting nurses. Do you know why?"

Lutz said, "Because they can?"

"Yes. Yes," Maltbie said, slapping his knee again. "It's free. They're monopolizing the caregiver supply, turning them into babysitters. Underperforming nurses are causing disequilibrium in the health-care labor market. Everyone loses save the senior who is delighted to have an RN prepare her tea." The professor shook his head in amusement.

Lutz stared bug-eyed at the animated professor. *I finally have a mentor.*

Maltbie continued, "Meanwhile, the seniors with serious ailments can't get access. And their kids—baby boomers in a financial position to do something—can't navigate the maze."

Lutz, anxious to contribute, said, "Because the system is fragmented."

"*Exactly.*" Maltbie stood and clapped. "And we will *not* wait for the pols to fix the problem. We'll privatize the system and push the haves to the front of the line."

"Professor, isn't that somewhat elitist?"

Maltbie's eyes grew. "You've got a problem with privatization?"

Lutz smiled. "Not at all."

"Splendid. So, let's plan our attack. First: do the market research to find out how many boomers want to move a parent to the front of the quality-care line. Find out where they live and how much they're willing to pay."

Lutz was agitated with the assignment. *What does he think I was planning to do?*

"Point two: we need a qualified channel to exploit this opportunity. There are a number of home-care franchises springing up but they're not accredited. They can cook and clean, but can't give the elderly as much as an aspirin. We talked about our efforts with the VNA during your interview."

Lutz nodded.

"The VNA's powerful brand is woefully underutilized. They're so focused on the needy that they can't grasp the economic value of the helping hand. Their revenue comes mostly from hospital referrals and is Medicare and Medicaid funded—where Uncle Sam pays fifty cents on the dollar."

"So they lose money on every home visit," Lutz volunteered.

The professor grinned. "We'll connect them to those who can afford to pay. We'll enrich the VNA with bigger margins so they can attract and retain competent nurses. Everybody wins."

Lutz eyed the notebook, anxious to record a plan of attack.

Maltbie spoke to the window. "Do you know why we picked you as CEO over the other candidates?"

"No," Lutz said, hoping to hear Maltbie run on about Lutz' years at Allied.

"Because of your sales background. We have made little progress in our talks with them. They're very nice people, but Florence Nightingale couldn't spell *profit.*" Maltbie turned and pointed at the phone. "You make a call to the head of the VNA in Plymouth and you will have carved a turkey and trimmed a tree before you get one back." His cackle returned. "They are totally intimidated by the concept of Internet based home-care management; afraid there isn't adequate security over patient confidentiality."

Lutz shook his head. "What are they afraid of?"

"HIPAA," the professor announced. "A patient confidentiality law they *must* conform to...with serious consequences if they don't. Our engineers are working on encryption software that will secure the Internet transactions. Your predecessor didn't know how to sell against their objection in that area. You can."

Lutz smiled. "I appreciate your confidence."

"Point three," Maltbie said, returning his gaze to the window. "We're running out of money."

Lutz sat up. "Sorry?"

"We have slightly north of three-hundred thousand dollars and a run rate of eighty thousand per week. I cap my investments in start-ups at one-million." He turned back to Lutz. "I've already put that amount in and don't intend to violate that rule."

"Four weeks of cash?" Lutz said.

"That's it," Maltbie said. "So, you're focus will be to raise the next round of financing."

A rush of heat found his face. "But I was told in the interview process that the next round was imminent."

"That you were. But I received a call this morning from

our potential investor notifying me that he was no longer in a position to move forward."

Lutz sat up, indignant. "But I left a nice paying job with the understanding that we would receive the cash to operate for at least the next year."

The professor, hands in his pockets, spoke to his shoes. "If I had known of this unfortunate occurrence at the time of my offer, I certainly would have informed you."

"Unfortunate occurrence?" Lutz said, moisture forming in his palms. "That's what you call four weeks of cash and no prospects for funding?"

"Again," the professor said, "I apologize."

"What about Goldman Sachs? I thought they were interested in investing?"

"Oh, maybe in a later round, but not this one." Maltbie reached into his shirt pocket, smiled weakly, and handed Lutz a slip of paper. "Goldman gave me this referral. Good day." He walked to the door, opened it and shuffled from the office.

Lutz heard Lillian's syrupy voice. "Come back to see us soon, Professor."

"Yes, yes. And next time I shall bring an indecent proposal." A cackle faded towards the debris in the lobby.

***

What the Christ is happening to me? This could be the shortest tenure in the history of capitalist man. First day on the job and I'm toes up.

Lutz, head in sweaty hands, saw the events of the last week flash by. Why didn't he sit tight at Allied until all elements of the iCare deal were in place? He could have toughed it out a while longer. *I need to slow down...think things through. Shit!*

He reached for the notebook and started a new section: *Raising Capital.* He looked at Maltbie's scribbled note with the telephone number of Jack Reese at Broadline Ventures. He muttered to himself, "slow down; slow *fucking* down," then spun in his chair, grabbed the phone and started dialing.

***

A few miles away in his office, Felton had ended an unpleasant phone discussion with a Boston art dealer and was into another one with a contact in New York City. He looked up at the painting that was the topic of discussion. "You can't be telling me that it's worth forty thousand. I paid more than that three years ago."

"Doctor, you asked for my professional opinion. I know that particular artist, and that is what it will fetch, give or take."

"And tell me again why it hasn't appreciated like the other."

"Because it is a southbound view of a northbound horse."

"So," Felton countered with agitation. "A horse's ass is still art."

"Yes sir," the dealer said. "But in this market, it is foremost a horse's ass."

BROADLINE VENTURES

Jack Reese was responsible for the poor performance of three organizations in the past two years, the last a devastating stint at Pierce Foods. Within a month of his taking an executive post—a position that his wife, Helen, had pressured her co-owner brother into providing—his wanton behavior with a promising sales intern would effect his ouster. The young lady, badly bruised from a rough sex interlude, was frightened of Reese and demanded a transfer to a safer venue. Reese would not respond to her claims and was summarily dismissed by David Pierce. When other women in the Pierce Foods organization came forward with similar claims, Reese took residence at a Pittsburgh four-star hotel to await his divorce settlement and plan his new career. At a Capital Formation seminar sponsored by the hotel, the featured speaker from London, a savvy banker, Sumner Shanes, touted the riches flowing from the New Economy. At the close of the seminar, Reese approached Shanes with an invitation to dinner, during which, the banker, plied by top vintage Bordeaux, related the frustrations of raising money in Europe.

***

"I raised over two hundred million for Charter Bank last year and less than ten percent of that found the VCs on the West Coast," Shanes said, shaking his head. "The other ninety percent sits in municipal bonds returning single digits." He shrugged and poured another glass of wine. "Let's just say that my European friends are less than pleased with Charter's performance."

Reese said, "Why doesn't the bank invest more in start-ups?"

Shanes sat back with a chuckle. "You're joking."

Reese shook his head. "Seriously, why aren't they putting the money to work?"

Shanes eyed the businessmen at the next table and leaned in discreetly. "Because they don't know how. They're bankers."

Reese's expression signaled that he was not at all familiar with what top end investment bankers do. The bankers he had met, until today, wanted him to open a checking account.

"They don't have a clue how to assess technology and operational needs. They're bean counters." Shanes brushed the sleeve of his Seville Row suit. "The VCs who understand Internet economics don't want their money. They can't spend what they've got."

Reese shook his head, poured the last of the wine into Shanes' glass and signaled the waiter.

Shanes continued, "Look at Yahoo! Two years after they go public, their market cap is ten billion." He shook his head. "Do you believe that? And Charter missed riding Amazon and eBay, too. Disgraceful." He put a thumb down to trash his colleagues before reaching for his glass.

Reese leaned forward. "I just came into a substantial sum. I'd like your advice on where to put it."

Shanes looked towards a wall of glass and took in the high-rises on the skyline. "Out there," he said with a wave.

"Pittsburgh?" Reese said.

"No." A palm pushed towards the window. "Further out. Boston."

"What's in Boston?"

"Only the largest base of universities and government labs in the nation," Shanes replied with a snooty air. "Where do you think the Internet was invented?"

Reese smiled and moved his chair in.

"The West Coast VCs don't have the bandwidth to look at deals outside of the valley. There are plenty of comparables in the Boston area looking for funding. Inject money and management into those deals and move through the IPO window quickly." He winked at Reese. "It's the second mouse that gets the cheese."

The waiter hurried to the table with another bottle, two new wine glasses and menus. He uncorked it and started to pour into a new glass when Reese said, "Hey," and tapped his. The waiter stopped to top off Reese's glass, did the same for Shanes, and left with the clean glasses.

Shanes continued, "I've been watching East Coast VC behavior throughout this boom; they're much too risk averse. Opportunities are right under their noses but they don't act." He pointed at Reese, his thumb extended. "Bad trigger fingers."

Reese said, "So, you raise the capital and my firm will put it to work."

Shanes sat back with a wry half-smile. "How many people do you have in your firm?"

Reese moved his chair in again. "Two," he said.

Shanes smiled. "Two?"

"Yeah," Reese said. "You and me."

Shanes shook his head. "And what makes you think I would give up a Vice Presidency with Charter Bank—and a nice salary, I might add—to start an investment firm with a guy I met today?"

Reese puffed his chest. "Because I've got a million dollar sign-on bonus that says you will."

Shanes laughed. "You're going to give me a million bucks to quit my job to raise money for a new venture firm? What do you know about investing in start-ups?"

"You raise a hundred million in Europe and I'll manage the portfolio back here. You can then be the judge of what I know and what I don't."

Shanes poured for himself and smiled at Reese. "One million, huh?"

"Yes," Reese said. "And a cut of profits made from the investments."

Shanes squinted at Reese. "You're serious."

"Very," Reese said.

Shanes looked away and chuckled to himself before returning to study Reese. "I'll need to think about it."

"What's to think about?"

His pompous air returned. "For starters; how about a twenty year career in banking and that nice annual salary I mentioned."

Reese leaned in. "Try this sometime: get a fistful of new hundreds, spread 'em out and go down on it like you're eating pussy." He sniffed the air. "It's full of great smells." He leaned closer, his jaw tight. "*Fuck* the bank." He topped his clenched fists. "You know that ring around Saturn? Our planet's got one, too. Ours is filled with cash." He raised his butt from the chair and thrust an imaginary stick at the ceiling. "We'll punch a huge fucking hole in it!"

Shanes, eyes wide, looked up at the cash flowing from the ring then at the businessmen who were smiling at Reese's display. "Ah, I don't know," he said.

Reese turned sarcastic. "We're in the biggest economic

boom of all time and you raise money to put into munis. Kind of a fucking joke, huh?"

Shanes dropped his eyes.

"I'm serious about this." Reese reached in his suit jacket for his checkbook, wrote one out and handed it across. "Cash it and you've accepted my offer." Shanes held it in both hands and stared in awe.

The waiter returned. "You are ready to order, gentlemen?" He looked at Reese.

"Yeah." Reese picked up the menu, scanned it and put it down. "I'll have the bald eagle," he said, calm and serious, casually scanning the surrounding opulence.

The waiter snatched the menu from the table—his forehead furled—studied the specials, then flipped it over to search the back side.

Reese slapped the table and roared. "I'm just fucking with you, pal. Bring us a carafe of chilled *Stoli* and a couple ounces of Beluga." He smiled at Shanes. "That okay by you?"

"Sure," the banker said, his eyes full of twinkle.

***

When the check cleared, Reese finalized an office lease, ordered high-end furniture and placed ads in the *Wall Street Journal* for top-tier MBAs. Shanes had resigned from Charter Bank and was handing out Broadline business cards to his former European clients. The Dutch put in the first twenty-five million; the Germans followed with forty and the Brits made up the rest.

***

"Look at that son of a bitch go!" Reese squeezed a racquetball in each hand as he watched live quotes on his office monitor. America's stock exchanges sizzled, with technology stocks fueling the flame. Academicians were stymied by the new math. Value theory held that an enterprise's wealth was in its stream of profits. But New Economy companies were selling at gigantic multiples to revenue, with no profit in the plan and no plan to make profit.

The intercom: "Mr. Shanes calling from London."

Reese hoped the meeting in Boston was still on. He was anxious to meet the Goldman Sachs people to build a relationship that would get Broadline into future deals.

"Sumner, how are you?"

"Great, Jack. What, another new secretary?"

"Yeah, the other one quit. Didn't like how I operate." He grabbed his crotch. "This one's been trained."

"Listen, I told you about that start-up in Cambridge."

"Yes, iCare."

"Well, Goldman called and said they weren't going to invest in this round. It's too early-stage for them. They threw us a bone but want in on the next round if the thing takes off."

"How much money is iCare looking for?" Reese said.

"They need to market to baby boomers once the software is ready. It will be expensive. Goldman loves the concept of Internet-based home care for the elderly. Hey Jack, we're getting older."

"Tell me about it." Reese squeezed the racquetball and punched it into his abs.

"They think it's a real opportunity—if iCare can execute. Their engineering guy is evidently pretty smart and has designed encryption software that could make their solution unique."

"What's your bottom line?" Reese said.

"I think it's a hell of a first pitch to take a swing at. We could hit this one out of the park."

Reese stood and jingled change in his pocket as he paced. "How do you see the follow-up rounds going?"

"The rule is to raise a round of financing every six months at double the value. If we fast track it, we could be at an IPO in eighteen months with a six-hundred percent gain. And once we take it public, it could double or triple on the first day of trading."

Reese went back to his desk to peck at his calculator. "So, our six million could go to a hundred million inside two years," he said, knowing that the majority of that gain would find his pocket.

"I like that number," Shanes said with nonchalance, pooh-poohing their potential wealth. "They just hired a new CEO, Bob Lutz. In fact, he starts today. He was a top-level exec at Allied Computer. Real experienced."

Reese said, "I'll give him a call and set up a meeting." The secretary came in, put a memo on his desk and winked. He smiled at her short skirt and whore hose as she sashayed to the door.

"Great," Shanes said. "*Ciao.*"

Reese hung up and leaned back in his chair. Getting a guy out of a huge corporation like Allied was a plus. But, did this Lutz guy have any understanding of how these deals work? And the real test: did he have any balls?

He rose, walked to the window and looked down at the courtyard below. A young woman was sitting on a bench with an ice cream cone. He was immediately engaged by her focus on the licking process: how she tamped the vanilla top before swirling her tongue to collect the softened flavor. He squeezed and the racquetball exploded.

The intercom: "a Mr. Lutz for you on line three."

Well-well. He walked over and punched the button. "Jack Reese."

"Mr. Reese, I'm Bob Lutz, CEO of iCare."

"How are you?" Reese said, opening a desk drawer for a new ball.

"One of our board members suggested I call you."

"Yes." He squeezed.

"Said your firm might want to invest in us."

"I heard Goldman was currently looking at you guys," Reese said, smiling into the phone.

"Yes...ah...they're currently kicking the tires."

No they're not. "My partner says you're in health-care."

"Yes. We have some pretty aggressive goals in our business plan."

Reese said, "Can you send it to me?"

"Huh?"

"The business plan. I'd like to see it."

"Oh, ah...sure," Lutz replied. "But I was hoping that you'd come to Cambridge to meet with me in person to go over it."

Reese looked at his desk calendar. "How about next Friday?"

"Ah...yuh...yes, that would be perfect."

Reese took a pen from his shirt pocket. "How about the afternoon—two-thirty?"

"That would work."

"Address?"

"Huh?"

"What's your address?"

"Oh...yuh. 138 Kendall Square. Do you know Cambridge?"

"Yes." Reese squeezed and watched a muscle ripple from his wrist.

"See you then."

Click.

Reese hung up, bounced the ball on the desk, and smiled. "Nervous fucker," he muttered, and moved to the window to watch her again. She pushed the tip of the cone into her mouth, followed by a little suck on a fingertip. He loved the oral fixation of this young generation of women. If she were there tomorrow doing the lick thing, he would mosey on down and introduce himself. He looked over at a black, leather couch and smiled. "Janis," he called.

The secretary appeared in the doorway—her legs apart, unladylike—a hand on a hip, snapping her gum through a smile.

"Close the door," he said.

PHIL

L utz was at his desk Wednesday morning staring at the notebook. He had slept fitfully the night before after downing a bottle of wine and a vodka nip he had hidden in the garage. He had a week left to complete the funding pitch, adding in a full day to rehearse. He opened the notebook, reviewed yet another revised outline, and started writing.

At eight o'clock, Lillian appeared in the doorway, wearing a pretty flowered dress and matching yellow hair band. "Good morning."

"Morning," Lutz said, without looking up.

"I told the employees that I was going to take you around and introduce you," she said, forcing a nervous smile.

He looked up at her briefly then down at the notebook, made an erasure and swept it away with the side of his hand.

"But you stay in your office with the door closed and never come out."

"I'm working on the business plan. It has to be completed by next Friday."

"Can you meet them today?" She said.

"No. I'll be working on the plan."

"They'd really like to meet you."

"Get out," he said, still writing.

"I'm not kidding." She nodded at the top of his head. "They really would."

"No." He looked up. "I meant get out of my office."

She gasped into her hands and backed out the door and closed it.

He reached into the briefcase and brought out a book, *An Entrepreneurial Primer,* and opened to the first chapter.

Your business plan communicates your aggression to investors and employees. It is your battle plan for deploying arms and materiel.

He went through the checklist provided by the author and started writing.

At ten o'clock, Lillian tapped softly on his door and peeked in. "There's someone here to see you."

"I'm busy," he said, not looking up, and continued writing.

"He said you'd be happy to see him." The boyish-looking visitor pushed past Lillian, smiling. "Bob," he said.

Lutz stood and smiled broadly. "Phil, what are you doing here?"

"They let me go. I spent yesterday negotiating with Laurie Wells. I got three months severance."

"Good for you," Lutz said, and moved around the desk to shake his hand.

"She offered me one month's pay. I said, 'three', and reminded her of my grasp of accounting." He winked at Lutz. "She must have gone straight to Brauner because she was back with a check from Payroll by the end of the day." He tapped his shirt pocket.

Lutz clapped his pleasure with Phil's craftiness.

Phil Breen, at twenty-eight, was a whiz-kid. Numbers sang to him. He would snicker at how management executed tirelessly on a bad plan. His mantra for cost reduction: *Screw the three martini lunches—look at headcount.* He would marvel at how competitors could outsell Allied with half the number of people.

"Phil, I could really use your help with the business plan."

Phil grinned as he pulled a chair over to Lutz' desk and rolled up his sleeves. "I'm yours."

Lutz called to Lillian, "Bring in some coffee for my Chief Financial Officer." He opened his notebook to the first section, *Acquiring People,* and next to 'Finance' put a checkmark, then looked at Phil. "We've got a problem, partner."

"What's that?"

"We've got four weeks of cash."

Phil frowned. "Did you know that when you took the job?"

"Not really," Lutz said.

"You don't have to pay me." Phil tapped his pocket again. "Any prospects?"

"Yes. A guy from Broadline Ventures is coming next Friday." He looked down at the notebook. "That's why I have to get this done."

Phil said, "Never heard of Broadline."

"They're out of Pittsburgh. They just closed a new fund and have a lot of money to invest."

"How much do we need?"

Lutz said, "Our spending is accelerating. And we need a dozen more engineers."

"What's the valuation?"

Lutz gave him a puzzled look. "Huh?"

"How much is iCare worth?"

Lutz shrugged. "I don't have a clue. We don't have any revenue, just a million lines of code written since iCare's inception. What's that worth?"

Phil smiled. "In this market, anywhere from zero to a hundred million."

Lutz shook his head. "And all those years schlepping bags through airports for a couple hundred grand a year."

Phil sat back and looked at Lutz. "Do you know what the cosmetic industry sells?"

Lutz studied him. "Beauty?"

"No." Phil smiled. "Hope."

Lutz squinted at him.

"That's what our plan has to project."

"Hope?" Lutz said.

"The biggest form of such: greed."

Lutz sat up and rolled a finger for Phil to continue.

"We need to show a market sizing. Show the demographics of an aging population and how a deteriorating medical system is struggling to keep up; and how people with dough will go around the system to secure better care."

"You should have been here yesterday to meet the professor."

Phil said, "Who?"

"An angel investor and board member. He's going to love the way you talk."

Phil grinned. "We start with a view from thirty-thousand feet and assess the market size, drop down to twenty thousand and identify potential customers, go to ten to find out where they are, and then land in their wallets."

Lutz smiled at Phil. "Fuckin A."

"I'll need an office with an Internet hook-up to do the research."

Lillian walked in, discreetly eying Phil before placing the cup of coffee on the desk.

"Lillian, get Phil an office with a high-speed Internet connection."

"Sure." She stole another glance at the handsome newcomer before leaving.

While reaching for the cup, Phil turned his head to check her out as well. He jostled it and coffee spilled onto the notebook.

"Shit," Lutz said, and started ripping out pages.

Phil jumped up. "What are you doing?"

"I'll have to re-write this."

"Ah, geez, Bob." Phil left to get some napkins from Lillian.

He returned and dabbed at the mess. "I'll do some what-if scenarios to scope the possible revenues. Then we'll 'Old Maid' the VC and let him pick the card with the highest projection. What's his name?"

"Jack Reese."

Phil looked at his watch. "I'll see you in the afternoon with the first pass on the sizing," and left.

Lillian came in with more napkins and began wiping the desk. "He's cute," she said.

"Maybe to you." Lutz showed her a real smile for the first time. "To me, he's beautiful."

Lillian bounced on a toe, turned and left his office, leaving the door open.

Lutz opened his notebook, made four columns and wrote *thirty thousand* above one, *twenty thousand* over another, and *ten* then *wallet*. He sat back, adjusted his chair and wrote for the next three hours until Lillian poked her head in. "You have a call from a Brad Torgerson. He said it's important."

What the hell does he want? Torgerson was Lutz' best friend for forty years. He met him in grade school after Lutz saw him playing 'Punching Bag' with the school bully. Torgerson was the bag, and Lutz jumped in and took the majority of blows on his behalf. Unfortunately, the trend continued throughout their teen and adult lives, with Lutz intervening for his friend too many times.

He picked up. "Hey, Torg, how'd you find me?"

"I called Pat for your new number." Torgerson's voice cracked. "Bobby, I need to talk to you. Can I come by?"

"What is it?"

"I can't tell you on the phone."

Lutz fanned the pages of his notebook. "Is it Ellen?"

"No," Torgerson said. "Much worse."

"Can it wait?"

"Til when?"

He looked at his watch. "Late afternoon. How about the bar at the Sheraton?"

"Okay. But hurry." Torgerson hung up.

The last time he intervened on Torgerson's behalf, Lutz had his nose altered—along with the majority of fingers he had raised in defense. Torgerson's business had a setback and he needed temporary financing. Unable to convince the local bank, he moved down the lending chain and found a bottom feeder. When the thug continually pressured Torgerson for payment, Lutz paid him a visit in Boston's North End—not the best neighborhood for confronting a guy named Rizzo.

Lutz sat back, rubbed his knuckles, and then ran a finger over the knob that marked the bend of his nose. His friend didn't sound so good.

CANDIRU

(*Vandella cirrhosa*) scaleless parasitic
catfish found in the Amazon River Region. A
translucent eel-like fish that feeds on blood.
-Encyclopedia Britannica

L utz entered the *Pub* just after 5:00 PM. Wooden
stools—likely the ones he and Torgerson had fallen out
of years earlier—could seat a dozen or so people. Peanut
shells covered the floor.

Torgerson was seated in the back at a table formed by
a scarred slab of redwood attached to an enormous pedestal.
Lutz waved and walked to him. The ashtray teemed from
Torgerson's dogged commitment to chain-smoking.

"Hey pal...been here long?" Lutz reached for his pal's
dead-fish handshake.

"A couple hours. Thanks for coming." Worry tugged at
Torgerson's face. His baggy eyes sank into cheekbones normally
masked by poor diet and a sedentary life.

Lutz looked him over as he pulled out a chair. "Good
weight loss or bad?"

"*Horrible.* I'm in the shit."

"You were upset on the phone. What's up?"

Torgerson started telling how a building boom had
forced him to hire more employees and how good people are
impossible to find. "The renovation business is up fifty percent

over last year. I turn down loads of jobs. I can't get good people."

Lutz said, "Is it Ellen?"

"What?"

"Why you look so awful. How many pounds have you lost?"

Torgerson studied his belt buckle, "I dunno. Twenty?" The top of his comb-over didn't match the brown on the sides. The sun had assigned it a reddish hue. "I can't eat no more. She's makin me crazy."

"How is Ellen?" He figured Torgerson had little patience for hot flashes.

Torgerson's eyes widened. "On the phone." He grabbed his beer. "She's on all the time."

Lutz turned to look for the waitress, couldn't get her attention, and returned to his friend.

"And when she's not, she's cryin."

"Depressed?"

Torgerson nodded. "I can't sleep at all."

"Not *you*. Ellen. You should encourage her to see someone."

"Yeah, I guess."

Torgerson sat back with his beer and sighed.

"So, what's up?"

Torgerson looked at a couple sitting a few tables away and moved his chair in. "If I don't put somebody on the horn to call my accounts, they don't pay. Then I'm in the shit when I gotta pay *my* bills." He looked like he was fighting tears as he drained his beer, put it on the table and tapped his shirt pocket for another smoke.

"Torg, what is it?"

He put up his hands. "Don't yell at me."

Lutz said. "I don't yell at you."

"Yes you do," he insisted. "Lately, you do."

"I promise."

Torgerson cranked his head and fumbled with his cigarettes until one slid into his palm. He lit it and forced a nervous cough. "I'm havin a collection problem so I hires this girl to call overdue accounts. Never seen a kid with such balls."

Lutz flagged the waitress, pointed at his friend's bottle of beer and held up two fingers.

"Half my overdue accounts are now current. Pushy... real pushy. And smart as a whip." He touched the end of the ash to the top of the bottle. "Now I'm noticin she's kinda cute."

He's involved with a woman at work.

"One day after work she drops by my office in a pair of tight dungaree shorts and invites me to the employee softball game—and I go."

"You played softball?" He smiled at the image of Torgerson chasing a ball, a hand on the buckle of his drooping pants.

"Hey, I gave it a try." Torgerson watched an annoyed Lutz look towards the bar again. "And after the game, we're in a bar drinkin boilermakers. She can throw 'em down for a small kid." He shaped little mounds in the ashtray and avoided Lutz' probing eyes.

"Look at me.

Torgerson eyed the floor.

"How old is she?"

Torgerson's eyes scanned Lutz then headed down again. He shifted to collect his answer. "Twenty-three," he mumbled to the ceiling.

"Twenty-three! I've got a Walkman older than that."

He shook his head and smiled at Torgerson, impressed. Lutz liked young women: the bright eyes, the taut skin and the playfulness that moved them to quick, natural smiles.

"She asks me to go back to her place for a nightcap. Y'know, it's on the way. And it goes from there."

Lutz leaned in to hear more.

Torgerson pulled on his cigarette. "We get there; she says be quiet, her roommate's asleep and she gets pissed if woke up. She makes a highball and grabs me a beer and puts on a Johnny Mathis record. We're slow dancin and kissin and stuff."

He was picturing Torgerson with his hands on her ass, grinding away, when the waitress interrupted the thought with beer. Lutz took in half the bottle on his first swig, wiped his chin, and said, "Chances Are?"

"Chances are what?"

"The Johnny Mathis record," Lutz said with impatience. Was it the album, 'Chances Are'?" Lutz wondered why a twenty-three year old would play music from that era. "Never mind," he said. "You didn't do it, did you?"

"Wait," Torgerson said, his eyes growing. "She goes into the bedroom, comes back, sticks her tongue out and wiggles it at me. She was really cute when she did that. A little white pearl is sittin on her tongue. I ask her why it doesn't fall out." He stuck his tongue out like a kid being checked for a sore throat. "She takes the thingy out and shows me a hole in her tongue. Then she puts the stem through her tongue again and screws the pearl on top. Keeps it there when she does the wiggle thing."

"That's tongue jewelry," Lutz said. "Lots of kids have those." He remembered the battle with his daughter Janie before she went off to college and his refusal to let her pierce any skin. Pat refereed a compromise and he okayed a small ankle tattoo.

Torgerson leaned in. "We're dancin real romantic when she stops in the middle of the 'Twelfth of Never', takes my hand, leads me to the couch and gives me a little push. My arms are up so I won't spill my beer. Then she kneels down between my legs and starts fiddle-fuckin with my belt and takes it out. She grabs it Bobby, looks at it then—you know, down she goes." Torgerson sat back and closed his eyes. "She's rollin that pearl around so I gotta come right away." He opened his eyes and jerked his head side to side. "I'm lookin around for somethin so she can get rid of it, but I can't reach nothin by now."

Lutz moved his chair in again.

"But she don't need nothin. It's gone. She looks up and says, 'Thank You, Mr. Torgeson'."

"Geez." Lutz wiggled in the chair. "Then what?"

"I told her to call me Brad."

"No, how'd you get home without Ellen suspecting something?"

To any other person, dialogue with Brad Torgerson would be immensely entertaining. But Lutz was annoyed by his friend's inability to get in front of a discussion and struggled to be patient.

"Ellen don't know anythin about this, and that ain't the problem." Torgerson put a hand to his throat and grimaced.

"What's she doing?"

"She makes me jealous so I'll give her a commitment. Last time I go, there's a motorcycle out front. I figure it's her roommate's boyfriend's bike so I go up to the second floor, knock, and this huge black guy opens the door. I lose it."

Lutz shook his head. "Didn't you know she had plans with this guy?"

Torgerson jerked a shoulder. "She told me to drop by."

Lutz leaned in. "She's playing you."

Torgerson looked at him, surprised. "No she's not."

Lutz sat back and nodded with certainty.

"Bobby, stop!" He reached for his beer, sipped, and put it down. "So, I get in my truck and go to a bar. Listen to the jukebox for a couple hours, all confused." He looked dreamy-eyed at Lutz. "I think I'm in love."

"What!?" Lutz put his hands on the table and glared. "She goes down on you once and you're in love?"

Torgerson sat back. "No. Not once—at least a dozen times. Plus I've been nailin her."

"I thought she's worked for you for a couple of months. How long have you two been doing it?"

"We just had our one-month anniversary. I bought her a card and a box of candy."

Lutz drained his beer and signaled the waitress.

"Torg, do you know what a candiru is?"

Torgerson shrugged ignorance. "They from Australia, too?"

"No, they're tiny parasitic fish that live in the Amazon. You skinny-dip and take a leak; they track the urine and swim up your urethra. It opens these barbs like an umbrella (Lutz formed a claw with his hand) so it sticks in there. They have to cut your dick off to get it out."

Torgerson's eyes widened. "No way!"

"I tried to get one for my fish tank when I was a kid, but they were illegal."

"Why you tellin me this?"

"You need to be careful. Have you been wearing protection?"

Torgerson, his mouth agape, said, "No. I figured she's clean."

Lutz furled his brow. "You *figure* she's clean?"

Torgerson moved his hand above the table. "Her desk is always neat. She's classy. Wears nice clothes...outfits that match and stuff."

Lutz exhaled, studied the ceiling for a moment, and leaned in. "You pick up something; you could give it to Ellen."

"I don't wanna talk about it," Torgerson said, glancing over at the couple.

Lutz watched his friend flatten the mounds in the ashtray before he pressed. "She's playing you if she wanted the biker there. She wants something. Do you ever drop in when she's not expecting you?"

Torgerson shook his head. "Not anymore. There's *always* somebody over. She says he's her bud. I don't trust her. I drop by another time and the black guy's there *again*...watchin cartoons."

Lutz held the instinct to verbally attack. "What's this commitment thing she wants?"

Torgerson hesitated before replying, "She wants me to leave Ellen."

Lutz sprang. "She's trash. Get a hold of yourself. You leave Ellen; you'll lose everything, including your business."

Torgerson extended his arms. "*See*, you're getting mad, Bobby. Just like I said you would."

Lutz stared at the ceiling then returned with a calming tone. "Listen to me. You said you don't trust her. You can't live like that."

"I *know*, but something about her is special."

Lutz leaned forward, reeking of wisdom. "Because you've been intimate. Guys can't whack it more than once without getting involved. With those types, a dick is a dick."

Torgerson sat up and glared. "What types?"

"Forget it," Lutz said, taking another beer from the waitress.

"Last night I go over to her place to talk—the guy's there *again*. She says it's platronic, he's like a brother."

"That's *platonic*," Lutz said. "Maybe they *are* just friends."

"Well this friend of hers is killin me and I know she's doin it because I won't commit. I'll have to ditch Ellen. My kids'll hate me. I can stop callin but I still have to work with her."

"You call her from *home*? What if Ellen listens in?"

"We used to talk every night. She's real smart. Tells me books I should read to round me out. Ellen thinks I'm doin paperwork in my office. There's no extension upstairs, so she can't listen in."

"Cool it," Lutz said, after a swig. "Too risky. Does she ever call *you*?"

"Only on my business line." Torgerson sagged in the chair. The shoulder seams of his shirt rested on his biceps, his turkey neck protruding from the gaping collar. "Come up with a plan," he said. "You're good at that."

Lutz knew that his friend wasn't capable of crafting an escape. Ellen's a nice person and he had to protect her. Brad's foolishness will destroy her.

"I'll lose my family. You gotta *help* me."

"You'll lose more than that. You live in The People's Republic of Massachusetts. She'll get half your assets."

His jaw dropped. "*Half?* She hasn't worked in thirty years."

"That's the law. It's a partnership."

Torgerson's face soured. "She's my partner?"

"You divorce Ellen; you'll end up in a one room flat drinking cheap wine out of a Welch's jelly glass." Lutz glanced at the couple at the next table before leaning in. "And *don't* start hiding money."

"What do you mean?" Torgerson said.

"Remember Johnny Johnson, the guy who owned the chain of Dunkin' Donut shops with his wife?"

"Ain't he in prison?"

Lutz nodded. "One morning, he drops in on his newest shop, goes in the kitchen and discovers the new baker with his cruller in the missus, beats the snot out of the kid and storms out."

"They put him away for that?"

"No. He comes up with a scheme to stretch out the marriage while he siphons cash. I saw him a few years ago in a bar—a hooker on each arm. Said he was spending his wife's half on pussy."

"Get out," Torgerson said, tapping his pocket on the way to his beer.

"So, J.J. works the register and doesn't ring all the sales. With five shops, he's skimming ten grand a week."

Torgerson said, "He gets caught?"

Lutz nodded. "It's difficult to skim in a donut franchise. The franchisor ships in the raw dough each week and they track it. When a franchisee reports sales, they know if all the dough is accounted for. They do the same checks on coffee."

Torgerson scratched his head. "Ain't that something?"

Lutz fought a roll of his eyes. "But J.J. buys dough from a third party. Headquarters can't figure out why his sales are down so they check dough shipments against his sales and can't find a thing."

"How's he get caught?"

"Broads," Lutz said.

"The hookers?"

"Nah. He's nailing two chippies at work and one gets jealous...calls Dunkin' Donut headquarters and invites them in for a look-see. Long story short—they call the Feds and J.J. does time."

Torgerson's head swayed in distress. "Aw, why'd you tell me that story? My girl wouldn't do that to me."

Lutz rubbed his knuckles then signaled for the bill.

He would develop a rescue plan. The girl was a con artist and needed to be removed from Torgerson Construction. Torgerson wouldn't do it. Lutz would confirm what she wanted and extricate her.

"Okay, I'll go see her, see what she wants."

Torgerson's misty eyes widened. "She wants *me*."

Lutz gripped his knees. "Goddamnit! Can't you see she's setting you up?"

Torgerson was more saddened than alarmed by Lutz' claim. He cared for his young girlfriend and was afraid to lose her affections.

Lutz said, "What's her name?"

Torgerson leaned in to answer. "Valerie," he said. "Valerie Quinn."

Lutz sat back, hands to his cheeks. "Ooh, an *Irish* floozy."

Torgerson sank. Lutz had wounded him.

He touched Torgerson's arm, "Sorry".

Torgerson was suddenly encouraged. "Bobby, maybe I should talk to her at work tomorrow, huh? Ask her to see you. What should I say?"

"*Listen*. Don't say anything to her at work. Get her off somewhere where she can't cause a scene. This young lady's been around the block and won't go away quietly."

"What block? She's not a hosebag. She said she only uses the pearl on me. We can work it out."

"Torg, what's happening to you? One minute you say she's choking you, the next you want to be a couple."

"I know. I'm breakin down. You *gotta* help me."

"She's setting you up," Lutz repeated.

Torgerson shook his disagreement. "You see everythin as a businessman."

The waitress handed Lutz the tab. Torgerson had two beers before Lutz arrived. "Are you okay to drive?"

"Yeah."

Lutz handed him the tab. "You pick it up, I'll get the tip." Torgerson rose and headed towards the waitress. Lutz dug in his pocket and put fifty cents on the table.

Outside, Lutz massaged support into his friend's bony shoulder as Torgerson fumbled through baggy pants for his keys. "It's going to be okay, pal."

"I'll tell her you want to talk. How should I tell her what for?"

"Say I'm your close friend and I've got a proposition. And do it off the premises. Take her out for a drink. Then call me at the office Monday. Don't call me at home."

Lutz followed him back to the highway ramp and processed possible escape scenarios for his friend. During his career he had observed the stupidity of men who received inordinate attention from nubile underlings. His sample size of Allied executives who risked families to engage in youthful fascination pointed to a certain fact: when a cute little tart dives face-first into an older guy's lap, it's about money.

FATAL ATTRACTION

Phil walked into Lutz' office the following Monday morning. "I surfed the Internet all weekend. Look at this." He handed over a bulging folder.

"Hey, thanks for giving up your weekend. I appreciate it."

"No problem," Phil said. "You're gonna like it."

Lutz leafed through the file that Phil had categorized, with sorts of demographics by region. "You got all this off the Net?"

"Yeah, but I need to get more information on 'boomers'. You go through the folder." Phil started to walk away, turned and grinned. "Look at the spreadsheet; the numbers are enormous."

Lutz spent the morning poring through the folder making notes and smiled at each factoid that supported the iCare opportunity. Lillian brought him a sandwich at noon, left and closed the door.

Phil came back hours later. "We can place ads through AARP. A lot of people get the magazine when they turn fifty. I called their circulation department to get ad rates. It's quite reasonable." He smiled. "Did you know that many boomers are now that age?"

Lutz sat back and smiled at him. "You are one smart bastard."

Phil gloated. "Thanks, boss."

There was singing in the lobby. "Lillian, oh Lillian, oh Lillian, my love," followed by a cackle then Lillian's chirp: "Professor, back so soon?"

She brought the smirking academic into Lutz' office.

"Professor," Lutz said. "So nice to see you again."

Maltbie was bouncing, anxious to entertain. He looked at Phil. Bob stood, "Professor, meet iCare's new CFO, Phil Breen."

"Well you're a fine looking young man," Maltbie said. He shook Phil's hand and looked over at Lillian. "Keep away from my girl." He winked at her.

"Professor, I would never cheat on you," Lillian said, walking a safe distance around him to exit.

"Phil worked for me at Allied," Lutz said. "We made quite a team."

"Splendid... Alphonse and Gaston. Don't let any fly balls drop between you."

Lutz smiled. "Phil is very thorough, as am I."

Maltbie's lower lip quivered: a sign of impending humor. "I heard over dinner last evening that two of my Sloan peers have been nominated for the Worthington Prize. The $500,000 cash prize is awarded annually to the top theory or treatise in economics. It's quite prestigious, you know." He fought a broader smile. "Just a rung beneath the Nobel." He coughed. "I do find it ironic, however, that a paper titled, *The Allocation of Scarcity in Impoverished Nations,* would garner such a generous prize." His face reddened as he fought for control. "Each year, the Economics Department has a poetry contest with the distinguished Professor Rawlings winning the last three." He reached into his pocket and brought out a cocktail napkin. "Last evening, with added inspiration from a fine

digestif, I believe I reached new heights of poetic punditry."
He studied the napkin. "Do you mind?"

Lutz' hand invited him to recite.

***

Scarcity, paucity
With increased velocity
Swollen black bellies and bellicose eyes
Oh Malthus! Dear Malthus!
Come back and help us
You must drive our limo
To the Worthington Prize

***

Lutz said, "That's powerful irony, Professor."

Maltbie shook his head. "Such pompous asses. I can't wait
to submit it." He returned the napkin to his pocket. "Actually,
I came today for another purpose." Lutz looked at Phil. "He
should stay," the professor said. "That referral I gave you last
week?"

Lutz nodded.

"Have you contacted him?"

Lutz smiled. "I called him right after you left. He's
coming this Friday."

"Splendid," Maltbie said. "I did research on Mr. Reese.
He's a newcomer to venture capital. Did you know that?"

"No," Lutz said.

"Be careful. He'll be looking to hit a home run. And, he
has less than a glorious past."

Phil furled his brow at Lutz.

"I won't bore you with sawings from the rumor mill. But,
be careful in negotiations." He reached into the inside pocket

of his suit jacket for a document that was folded lengthwise. "Here," he said. "The missus and I will be on a cruise for the next six weeks. I have given you signatory authority to move forward on the term sheet."

Lutz stood to receive it. "I appreciate your confidence, Professor."

Maltbie said, "There are a number of venture firms entering the market to exploit the start-ups. And many are less than ethical in their means. You know, looking for a quick buck. Be careful," he repeated.

Lutz nodded at Maltbie and looked at Phil, who was nodding also.

The professor clapped his hands. "So, tell me straight, my friends. Do I unseat Professor Rawlings?"

"I believe you will, Professor," Lutz said, and stood to escort him to the lobby.

"Sit," Maltbie said. "Miss Lillian will see me out." He shuffled out of the office.

Lutz studied Phil. "What was that all about?"

"A message to watch your back," Phil replied. "I'll do some sniffing to check out this Reese guy," and he left.

Lutz continued working through the folder, when Lillian appeared in the doorway.

"Yes?" Lutz said.

"It's Brad Torgerson."

He waited for the door to close before picking up to hear how the meeting with Valerie had gone.

"Hey pal, how'd it go?"

"Not good," Torgerson said. "I took Valerie for a drink last Friday night. She said she won't meet with you."

"Why not?"

"She wasn't real happy about me bringin you into this.

'Stay out of it', she said. She was pissed that I even told you about her."

Lutz reached for his notebook and a sharp pencil. "What reason did you give for me wanting to see her?"

"I told her that you were my best friend. You were worried about me and you might be able to help us out of the situation."

Lutz sat back. "And?"

"She started yellin...'what situation'? So I told her that she couldn't work for me if she kept doin the black guy."

Lutz stood and paced. "*Why* did you say that? What if she claims sexual harassment? You could be sued."

"For what?" Torgerson said.

"She could say you fired her because she wouldn't do it with you anymore. Watch what you say. She's in a position to hurt you."

Torgerson coughed into the phone. "She already hinted about doin somethin like that. I'm in the shit."

Lutz said, "She did? What did she say?"

"She says she's doin a great job and needs the money. She didn't mention a lawyer, but she's a smart cookie."

Lutz shook his head and gestured to the window. "You were supposed to say I was your friend and I had a proposition for her. You were to arrange a meeting and I'd take it from there. How could you screw *that* up?"

"I'm sorry... it's, you know... when I'm around her, I lose it. I practice all day what I'm gonna say. Then over the drink, I freeze."

Lutz opened the notebook. "Can't you convince her to see me?"

"She wants you to leave it alone. Said, 'tell him to give it a flippin rest'."

He had anticipated such a reaction and went to the page where he had listed actions under NEXT STEPS. "What if I drop in on her, pull her aside and go through my proposal?"

"You think that's a good idea?"

"Where does she hang out?"

"She's in a dart tournament in a few weeks. She practices after work."

Lutz rolled his eyes. "Where and when?"

Torgerson said, "What?"

Lutz blew a burst of frustration through the phone. "What were we just talking about? I could drop in on her at dart practice. *Where* the fuck—and *when?*"

"Why are you mad at me again?"

"Because you're not keeping up. This is important. C'mon."

A match was struck and Torgerson exhaled into the phone. "Well, I know that Thursday night she'll be at a place called Frosty's, a bar on the New Hampshire border. She leaves work every day at 6:00, so figure around 7:00. Can you go? Huh? Will you go see her? And go easy. What are you gonna say?"

"I'll work it out." He looked in the notebook at a notation he had made: WARN HIM. "But first let me ask you something (he used a calmer tone; not wanting to freak Torgerson). You ever see the movie with Michael Douglas and Glenn Close about a weekend affair Douglas has when his wife is away?"

"Nah."

"Well, he meets this woman, nails her, then gets his wits about him and tries to end the affair." It was the most chilling movie Lutz had ever seen—*Fatal Attraction,* where Close stalks Douglas, even shows up at his office. In the final scene, she breaks into his house and boils his daughter's pet rabbit on the stove (Lutz' calm had left him and he was now talking faster and louder). "Everywhere Douglas goes, she goes. She won't let the guy end it. Eerie as hell." He stood and began to pace. "Then she ends up in his freaking house! I won't go into what she does...something about the daughter." He paused for a reaction: Torgerson's breathing was more labored.

He continued, "He...comes...home...and there's this pot on the stove and..."

"Awww...*shoot*, Bobby. Valerie's not like that. She wouldn't come by the house. She's not a nut case. Why you tellin me this?"

"*Hey*. Calm down. I want to know what we're dealing with. How do you know she's not going to flip out?"

Torgerson's breathing developed a wheeze. "She's a nice person...she wouldn't hurt me."

"What if she decides to tuck a legal document up your ass? I need a sense of her before I can put together a plan. I'm doing what I've been trained to. I'm a businessman. I cover bases."

Torgerson moaned, "Why's this *happenin* to me?"

Lutz sat. "Because you're a nice person and you're being taken advantage of." *And you're weak.*

"If you go see her, what are you gonna say?"

"Let me ask you something. Did you do a background check on her when she was hired?"

"Yeah, we check all employees for criminal records or if they've ever had their pay garnisheed. They're around property and need to be bonded."

"Did she check out okay?"

"I think so," Torgerson said.

"But you're not sure."

"Personnel checks it, Bobby. Nothin was ever said to me."

"*Make* sure. And go through her file yourself. Don't let anybody know what you're doing."

"I'm tellin you. She's a good kid. She's clean."

"Another thing," Lutz said.

"Yuh?"

"Were you alone with her at her place after that first night?"

There was silence then a nervous cough before Torgerson replied. "Twice."

Lutz stood, tugged on his underwear and sat. "Any drugs?"

"No," Torgerson said.

"Did she ever allude to drugs; hint that she was a user?"

"Nope."

"Any joints in the ash trays?"

"She doesn't smoke."

Lutz thought, *She smoked you.*

"And that black friend of hers."

"What about him?" Torgerson said.

"What does he do?"

"About what?"

"Jesus, for a *living.* Did she ever mention his job?"

"As a matter of fact, she said he has his own business, something to do with stealth. He works with electronics."

"Do you know his name?"

"No."

Lutz looked in the notebook at another reminder: KB. "Have your security firm do a background check. Tell them he submitted an application for employment."

"Why'm I doin all this?"

"We're looking for dirt. Nothing moves negotiations along faster than a nasty past."

"I don't follow. What's the black guy's past have to do with Valerie?"

"Have you ever heard of the game, *'Six degrees of Kevin Bacon'*?"

"Yeah," Torgerson said, "he's the actor who was in a movie with someone who was in a movie with someone else. Right?"

"Exactly!"

The line went silent then Torgerson said, "I still don't get it."

"If we play *'Six degrees of a black man,'* we might find something in his past that we can trace to Valerie to force her cooperation."

"Like what?"

"Perhaps the black guy's a felon who knows a felon whose felonious friend has something we can pin on her."

"I don't want you to hurt her."

"Torg, I'm not going to. Why would I do such a thing? I'm looking for leverage...something to make her more cooperative."

"Okay. I'll get to work."

"*Wait,* I'm not done." Lutz wiggled in the chair.

"What?"

"You said that you were alone with Valerie at her place on two other occasions."

Torgerson didn't respond.

"Did you have sex with her?"

Torgerson exhaled before replying, "Yeah."

"Anything kinky?" Lutz stood again, pinched his crotch and began to pace.

"What do you mean?"

He cradled the phone in his neck and held out his hands in measurement. "Any sex toys or the like?"

"What the *hell* are you talkin about?"

"Did she perform or suggest the performance of an act that could be judged lewd and lascivious?"

Torgerson said, "Geez, you sound like a lawyer."

Lutz rolled his knuckles on his fly then sat. "Well did she?"

"It depends on what you mean by kinky?"

"I'm talking about anything outside the realm of ordinary."

"Ordinary for Ellen?" Torgerson asked.

He slapped a palm to his forehead. "I'm not talking about marriage. I mean *real* sex."

"Oh," Torgerson said.

Lutz pressed, "C'mon, anything?"

"Well, last time she wanted to handcuff me to the bed, wet me down with Witch Hazel and sprinkle me with baby powder. She said it feels like snow flakes."

"Did you let her do it?"

"Nah, I was worried she'd leave me there."

"And the other time?"

"What?"

Lutz gestured to the air. "Anything strange...out of the ordinary?"

"Not really."

"Are you sure?"

"*Yeah.*"

Lutz pinched his crotch again. "What was she wearing?"

"Huh? Why you askin me this?"

"*What* was she wearing?"

"*Nothin.* We were doin it. She was naked."

Lutz kept at him. "Did she take off her clothes, or did you disrobe her?"

"I took her panties off."

"Okay...good." He went back to sit. "What color were they?"

"*What?* Bobby, c'mon. I'm not answerin any more questions."

"Okay." Lutz looked in the notebook for more action items. "Here's what I'll need from you before I drop in on her tomorrow night."

"Okay," Torgerson said.

"First, the background check. Confirm that there's nothing in her past that we can use. Ditto for the black guy after you find out his name." He put a checkmark next to VALERIE and another on BLACK GUY.

"How I do that?"

Lutz groaned at the ceiling. "Figure it out!"

Torgerson's breathing signaled frustration from yet another assignment.

"Third, confirm place and time for dart practice." *Checkmark.* "Then call me back with the answers and set up a time when you can drop by the office to give me the money." Checkmark number four went next to CASH.

"What money?"

"I'll need two grand in hundreds," Lutz said.

"Why?"

"Just do it. I'll talk to you later. Bye."

Lutz hung up. *Red thong. She was wearing a red thong.* He stood and squared the notebook to the corner of the desk, tucked his shirt in and headed for the door. He stopped, ashamed at his grilling of Torgerson. This was not the time for titillation. A tramp was dragging his friend into madness. He would execute a rescue and bail out his friend as he always had. He was good at cleaning up the messes of others.

ROAD TO FROSTY'S

Thursday morning, Lutz relented and toured the building with Lillian to meet the employees. He stayed in the lab for an hour with the founder of iCare, Hank Hinckel, looking at the different screen shots his team had designed. "I don't like that one," Lutz said to Hinckel.

"Why?" The head engineer said.

"You need softer colors: pinks, blues; colors that are caring. Nurse colors."

"Nurse colors?" He frowned at Lutz. "Wouldn't that be white?" He looked over at the rest of the engineers for support. "We can't do a website in white."

Lutz pointed at the monitor. "Well, you're certainly not going to use those reds and purples there: bruise colors; the wrong ones to attract the elderly, wouldn't you think?" He scanned the faces of the engineers who were nodding in deference. "Why don't you do it in black?" He smirked and poked the corner of the screen. "And put Dr. Kevorkian up there."

Hinckel shrugged. "Yeah, I suppose."

Lillian rolled her eyes and tapped Lutz' arm. "We should get back."

Lutz said to the room, "Thanks guys," and left with Lillian who turned to Hinckel on the way out and made a face.

***

Torgerson called later in the morning to report on the items Lutz had assigned. "Valerie will be at Frosty's tonight at 7:00. She's got other plans so won't be there long."

"Okay," Lutz said and reached for the notebook. "I'll be there— 7:00 sharp."

"You sure this is a good idea, just droppin in on her?"

Lutz turned the pages. "Hey, she won't see me voluntarily."

"Ah...I dunno, Bobby. I don't feel so good about this."

"The problem won't disappear on its own," Lutz said, brushing the page with the side of his hand. "Let's get this behind you."

"She's gonna be pissed."

"Did you go through her file?"

Torgerson exhaled a puff into the line. "Yeah, like I said, she's clean."

"Are you sure?"

"*Yeah*, only a speedin ticket."

"Any luck on the black guy?"

"I called Stealth Security in New Hampshire and got a recorded message; says he's Samuel Prigget, President of Stealth."

"How do you know that Samuel Prigget is the black guy?"

"His voice was deep like the guy in the Verizon ads."

Lutz sat back and rolled his eyes. "Is the name Prigget enough to do a background check?"

Torgerson coughed. "How many black guys you think are in New Hampshire?"

Lutz nodded to himself. "What else did you find out?"

"He's clean except for an aggravated assault in New Jersey in '95. Hell of a background—Special Forces. Moved back to

New Hampshire after the service. Owns his business." He hacked again. "You still gonna go see her tonight?"

Lutz turned to a new page. "Give me directions."

"Easy. Head west on Route 2 and look for the old drive-in theater off on the left. Real ugly—sticks up over the trees. We took the Sistrunk sisters there once, remember?"

Lutz remembered all of the ladies he was intimate with and his passionate reaction to each. "No, I don't," he insisted.

"Take 212, the exit after the drive-in, and head northwest for exactly sixteen miles. It's a windy road so give yourself enough time. Frosty's is on the right, across from a junkyard on the New Hampshire line."

"Got it," Lutz said. "Have you got the money?"

"I went to the bank this mornin—hundreds like you said. What are you gonna to do with it?"

Lutz drew a three-dimensional dollar sign and scrawled next to it: AND BULLSHIT WALKS. "Bring it by this afternoon." Lillian appeared in the doorway. "Torg, I gotta go."

***

Torgerson pestered Lutz on the phone twice more: the first time wanting him to abort the plan, and then calling to make sure he was going through with it. He came by the office at mid afternoon with typed directions and an envelope with the money, noting on the directions: *7:00 SHARP! GO EASY!*

***

Lutz planned on an hour drive and left the office at 5:45 to have time to observe the bar and drive around for an escape route should his proposal require a hasty exit.

He would free his friend by using business fundamentals

learned as an executive. He was zealous in his belief of the pitch: how marketing could sway a slow believer.

Torgerson called again just before Lutz left the office. "You can't miss her," he said. "She's real cute—blond with a really cute pony tail; goes half-way down her back. Five-two and a hundred pounds soakin—really cute."

Lutz put the envelope in an inside pocket of his sport coat. He would offer cash up front followed by payments linked to her behavior. *You do this; we'll do that. Connect the dots, Kitten.*

He planned to open negotiations with a thousand-dollar offer and use the other grand to close the deal if she balked. She should accept the payments if Lutz skillfully pitched them as buoyant to her future.

The cash would buy her silence and agreement to not pursue a sexual harassment claim. There was no guarantee that she would never confide in the affair—most young women, like all men, can't keep it to themselves—but Lutz would push for an agreement to not litigate, secured later by her signature on a formal release. He would insist on this before additional payments began.

Quinn could receive up to two grand tonight then monthly payments after she signed the release. *Not a bad deal for a hosebag.*

Though she was just twenty-three, Lutz figured her for a street-smart, trailer-trash survivalist, who would be quick to grasp the proposal's merits. He would respect the surroundings. Customers could challenge him if she made a scene.

***

Off he went to solve his friend's problem. A depressed economy showed as he left the more vibrant Massachusetts and entered the Granite State. The architecture of the Bay

State—saltboxes intermixed with garrison colonials on an acre plus—morphed into small bungalows on weedy roadway lots. One dump had a pink flamingo plugged into the dirt next to a rusted Studebaker; he figured it for some kind of gallows-humor practiced by the downtrodden. Motor homes appeared at random, none part of a planned trailer park community.

A sign, *"Danger: Moose Crossing,"* appeared and he recalled teasing a New Hampshire motorist who had an *I Brake for Moose* bumper sticker and was informed that it is the moose that initiates the collision. The animals require huge amounts of sodium and will visit roads to lick the remnants of rock salt. They panic easily and rush to self destruction. He muttered through a snicker, "Like Torgy".

His mind raced with imagery of the bar as he nervously patted his nose knob with the tip of a finger.

A road sign announced the border town of Wrenford, New Hampshire. The hometown of Frosty's was three miles ahead. He pulled onto the shoulder and stopped to organize his thoughts and reaffirm the syntax and demeanor he would use on Quinn. He was Brad Torgerson's concerned friend and wished to speak with her. He would be tactful, sensitive to her refusal to meet, and was here as Brad's envoy: "to seek a solution to your problem." He decided that 'envoy' was too formal and would use 'best-buddy' in his opening pitch.

He reached for the package purchased before getting onto Route 212. The small brown bag contained two vodka nips and a pack of Juicy Fruit. He looked in the mirror—saw it clear behind—twisted open a nip, drank it and continued on.

He would explain to Quinn that he didn't know the cause of their conflict and was concerned with his friend's ability to function in his business. *Business* would be emphasized to keep Ellen's name out of the discussion. What was Quinn's motivation? Why a young, attractive woman would provide repeated delights to his ordinary friend required an answer. She had to be maneuvering for financial gain.

He would be assertive but not too, suggesting she would be ill advised to continue her employ at Torgerson Construction. He would say, "Brad is very pained by this matter, and for him to see you every day would be far too upsetting."

If Quinn voluntarily separated from Torgerson Construction and signed a release, finances would support her transition. He would then offer the thousand as a good-faith first payment.

Lutz feared the venue. Negotiation seminars teach the concept of 'patch': always deal on your own turf. Do it in the office where you can manipulate who attends, where they sit, even lower your opponent's chair to gain a power position. But, with Quinn adamant that she would not meet with him, he had to have the discussion in her gin joint.

He saw the junkyard. Beaten cars rested atop one another in a dusty graveyard, their innards awaiting transplant to more functional frames. He wondered if his dad's old Hudson Hornet could be in there. The car's digital clock said 6:48 PM when he saw the sign:

Bienvenue

...Welcome to New Hampshire

The bar was to appear on his right but did not. However, over pines in the distance he saw what appeared to be the Northern Lights. He continued slowly to the source and saw a parking lot that was likely over-lumined for security. In front of the entrance sat five Harley-Davidson motorcycles in a row of intimidation.

Shit! A biker bar.

He continued past the barroom searching for possible

escape routes, veered at a fork, and the road abruptly ended in front of a ramshackle barn. *Moron! Not this way!*

Side roads were out—too dangerous. Should he be pursued down a side street, it could dead-end, trapping him. His portable phone with 911 pre-loaded sat next to the paper bag on the passenger seat. Useless, it displayed *'searching for connection.'*

Plan, goddamnit. He rubbed his hand.

He parked, pointing the car south for a quick escape and watched two guys approach the entrance and shuddered at the one wearing a chain across his chest.

He tossed the sport coat in the back seat after removing the envelope, counted the money—sure he was not being watched—and folded ten bills into each pant pocket. He drank the second nip, stuffed it under the passenger seat, ate a piece of Juicy Fruit, then opened the car door and stepped out.

He checked the door to be sure it remained unlocked, then duck-walked around the car and ran a hand over each tire, inspecting. *Quinn, you poor girl...here comes a raid on Entebbe.* He mussed his hair, stood, and staggered into a new balance then walked briskly to the steel door to Frosty's, grabbed the handle with both hands, pulled, and stepped in.

PIXIE

U.S. Airway flight #2287 originating in Pittsburgh landed at Boston's Logan airport at precisely 7:00 PM and taxied to a stop. Jack Reese stood in the first class cabin, opened the overhead compartment and removed his overnight bag. He smiled at the attractive woman occupying the seat next to his. "My card if you should have a change of heart." She took it with blatant disinterest and turned away. "I'll be staying at the Charles Hotel in Cambridge." She looked out at the tarmac and shook her head.

Reese hated holier-than-thou women: the missionary types who screwed with the lights out. He knew she was a prude from the way she responded to his initial hello. He enjoyed playing with her during the flight, using crude innuendo to crawl her skin.

He was first off the plane and moved past security to the transportation area. A chauffer, wearing what looked to be a bus driver's cap, held a sign: *BROADLINE.* Reese shoved his bag at him. "Let's go, Kramden."

"This way sir," the driver said, and hurried in front. They strode to a limousine at the curb, the driver opened the door and Reese went in. When the driver opened the trunk to place the bag inside, Reese spun around and yelled. "Open the fucking thing—*lay* it out! There's a suit in there."

The driver hurried to enter and start the ignition, put it into gear and said, "The Charles?"

Reese said, "Yeah."

"Welcome to Boston. We have beautiful evenings this time of year."

Reese bolted forward in the seat. "Cut the fucking tour guide!"

The driver didn't respond. His head spun side to side to navigate the airport's exit maze.

Reese didn't have to be at iCare until 2:30 the next afternoon so he planned to spend the evening carousing and playing with his catch through late morning. He had tried to coax a Pittsburgh prostitute into accompanying him on the trip but she refused, making an excuse to avoid his punishing ways.

Reese said, "Where do you find puss in this town?"

"Sir?" The driver said to the mirror.

"Where do I go to meet fancy women?"

"Oh," the driver said. "There are very lovely ladies to be found at the bar in the Copley or the Regal Bostonian."

"Where are those joints?"

"The Copley's just off the Pike and the other is at Faneuil Hall, not far from your hotel."

"You gonna drive me there?"

"Sir?"

He took out his money clip, peeled a hundred dollar bill off the top and threw it over the seat. "Let's try the Copley first."

"Certainly." The driver, now thoroughly enthused, smiled at the mirror.

They exited off the Mass Pike, navigated a series of one-way streets and pulled in front of the Copley Plaza. Reese opened the door. "Stay right *fucking* here. I won't be long."

He entered the bar, a Boston relic formed in rich woods

and shiny brass, and saw two women seated together, laughing and drinking pink cocktails. He approached with a swagger, kneading his abs with his knuckles. "Ladies, ladies. Now what could possibly be in those drinks that would make them such a pretty pink?" He went to the brunette who sat next to a buxom blond.

"Mine's a Cosmopolitan," the brunette said. "It's pink from cranberry. Want a sip?"

He tasted the drink. "Hmm. Not bad. He stepped back and ogled her. "And I bet you're all pink inside, too."

The brunette said, "Huh?" She looked down, shocked, while the blond giggled.

He moved three seats over and sat next to the blond. "And what's your name?" He took her hand and kissed it softly.

"Pixie," she said.

"Trixie?"

She slapped his hand. "You heard me."

He put on the charm. "And how does a girl get a name like Pixie? Could it be that pretty little turned up nose?"

She blushed through her makeup. "My real name is Gloria."

He stepped back to eye her then moved in and tapped her thigh with the back of his hand. "Pretty solid there, Blondie. How do you keep in such good shape?"

"I work out," she said. "Aerobics."

"Well, you've really tightened yourself up." He looked around the front of her to wiggle his eyebrows at the brunette, who looked away.

Pixie smiled, leaned back in her chair and looked him up and down. "You're not in such bad shape yourself. You look like a Marine." He ran his hand quickly through his buzz cut then extended his arm. She squeezed his bicep. "I love men with big arms." She bent forward to giggle in her drink.

He leaned into the bar again to speak around the blond. "Honey, do you know the difference between Sales and Marketing?"

The brunette sat back, full of disinterest.

"Sales is when I tell you I've got a big dick."

Her shoulders jumped and she sat up.

Reese chuckled at her reaction. "And Marketing is when Pixie here tells you that I'm hung." The blond slapped the bar.

"I think it's time for you to move on," the brunette said. "You can take that square jaw and military cut down to Parris Island."

Pixie said, "Aw, come on, Christine. He's just trying to be funny."

"He's a pig," the brunette said.

"Let me make it up to you, Christine, and pay for your drinks." He took out his clip and Pixie eyed the roll. He peeled off a fifty and threw it on the bar then put his hand on the inside of Pixie's knee and gazed in her eyes. "You sure are a pretty one."

She lowered her eyes exposing more of the robin's egg coloring caking her lids.

"Who does your makeup?" He stood back to admire the brilliant hues on the rest of her face.

"I do." She giggled and reached for her drink.

"I *love* that look," he said. "Want to have a champagne dinner with a rich guy?"

"Sure," she said, after a goodly sized gulp.

Christine spoke to the mirror above the bar. "Pix, you're supposed to give me a ride home."

He took out the roll and peeled another fifty and threw it on the bar. "Your cab fare, Chrissie."

"Pix," she said to her drink. "You don't know this guy."

Reese moved around Pixie and pushed against the brunette. He ran a finger slowly down the back of her neck. A chill tightened the skin across her back. He put his cheek against hers and whispered, "You're the one I prefer. Be my nasty little princess." She stiffened.

He returned to Pixie. "Collect your things, sweetheart. Our limo is waiting."

Pixie stood and draped a sweater over her shoulders, picked up her purse, then wiggled in her dress and tugged at the hem. "Okay," she said, "but first I gotta pee."

A GIRL LIKE YOU

Blazing light from the parking lot flashed through the open door placing a smoky penumbra around the bar straight ahead. There were bums standing, bums on stools, and a pot-bellied bum behind the bar serving. Lutz pulled the door closed with two hands, turned and scanned the room for immediate threats. The menagerie was too invested in low-life banter to notice him.

The décor was *Nouveau-firetrap*, with a leak-stained plywood ceiling and graffiti walls of knotty-pine encasing a few thousand feet of squalor. The place smelled like something was rotting inside the walls and eating its way out. Butts formed a mosaic in the floor and his shoes tore from the linoleum when he shifted to observe the remainder of the pit.

To the right was a row of booths the length of the wall. Across from the booths was a dartboard. In the far corner was a jukebox.

He moved in to order, holding his breath against enough man-made fumes to drop a canary from its perch. "Bud," he said, to the ape behind the bar. He considered buying a round of beers for the boys then cautioned himself: *Don't get too friendly.*

He retreated quickly, wiping the beer bottle with a cocktail napkin, and spotted her. A petite, pony-tailed blond held a dart and inched her toe along a strip of duct tape. A huge black guy had a muscular arm around her waist and pulled at her—laughing, bouncing and pointing to the floor claiming some sort of infraction. She laughed, slapped at his arm, and twisted away. It was Quinn. She had a nice figure, just like Torgy claimed. Taut buttocks, snug in pink panties, peeked from cut-offs when the black guy jostled her.

He looked for a discreet booth in the row of four where he could isolate her, drifted towards it and sat. He turned slowly to the left. She noticed him, but didn't react. She watched the black guy shoot then walked to him, grabbed his arm and spoke into his elbow. He turned and studied Lutz before nodding. With a feathery pirouette on a tiny sneaker she approached.

"Well-well," she called, "You wouldn't happen to be my boss' buddy?"

"Hi. Miss Quinn?"

"S'me," she said.

"I'm Bob." He stood and offered his hand, which she refused. He sat, showing little reaction to being rebuffed.

"Didn't Brad say I wasn't interested in meeting you?"

"Let's talk," he said, and motioned to the other side of the booth.

She was pretty—*very* pretty—with an oval little face framed by evenly shaped bangs. Indigo eyes beamed from a clear white background. Although she was just twenty-three, he expected to see signs of a punishing lifestyle. He studied her face. A sprinkling of light golden freckles settled on her cheeks and the top of her nose. She had the skin of a teen and confidence of a woman, a combination rarely found in hellholes.

"Miss Quinn, please don't be put out by my coming here."

"Valerie," she insisted.

He nodded. "I'd like some of your time."

She looked over at the black guy before sitting, biting at her lip to stifle a smirk.

"Can I get you a beer?"

She raised a full bottle at him while maintaining sharp and confident eye contact.

He couldn't tell if she sported the pearl, and fought the image of her little face bobbing in Torgerson's lap, the ponytail swaying to his guttural rhapsody.

"This is quite a place," he said.

"Yeah, we stay quiet about it; keeps the crowds down."

He smiled. "Brad says you're quite a dart player."

"Not that good." She looked over at the black guy. "Not as good as Satch."

He continued to smile at her.

She said, "So, what do you want?"

"Huh?"

"Why are you here?"

"Brad said you didn't want to see me. I decided to come anyway...see if you'd agree to talk."

"Yeah, he told me you were coming."

"Brad did?"

She said, "Yeah, just before I left work."

That weakling.

"He begged me to talk to you, said you were a good guy...I can trust you."

He nodded.

It was starting well. She was at ease in the presence of a professional man many years her senior. Torgy was right about 'a hundred pounds soakin'. Her eyes were bright and intelligent.

"Well thanks for showing," he said. "This must be difficult."

"No problem." She squinted at him. "What do you mean, difficult?"

"He told me about the problems you two are having and... I...I hope you understand...we're good friends."

She peered into her lap and shook her head. "He's the one having problems. I'm real worried about him."

He was pleased that she was concerned for his friend.

"What's *with* him?" He said.

She shrugged. "Maybe that's something you can help me with. He's been freaky."

He nodded agreement. "When did it start?"

"He's been absolutely nuts lately—getting more and more possessive. Guys from your generation are wicked control freaks, huh?"

He played with the napkin.

She looked at him and he keyed on the depth of blue in her eyes. "He's always giving me grief about my friends, who I'm hanging with and whether I'm sleeping with other guys. It's none of his business. I don't ask him what he does with his wife, do I?"

He was careful to show no reaction.

She continued, "Why should I let him dictate where and with whom I play? I want to be with him, but not *only* him. And he can't *handle* it."

He was impressed with how she spoke.

"Is that why you think he's upset?"

"Yeah, mostly. He thinks I've got something going on with Satch. I told him we're just friends. He's using Satch as an excuse. He wants me to stop seeing *all* guys. I'm not going to do that," she said, her eyes narrowing.

He shrugged.

"He caused a hell of a scene at my place the other night."

"*Oh?*" He sat up as if it were new information.

"He dropped by and Satch was there. Brad went crazy."

It's good that Torgy leaked my visit. She's being open.

"Valerie, if I may…Brad has an awful lot to lose if he continues this relationship with you. Please don't be offended by what I just said."

Her jaw fell. "*What?* I'm not forcing him to be friends with me."

He shook his head. "I'm sorry…I didn't mean…"

She said, much too loudly, "Do you think I'm using him—that I'm going to hurt him? That's why you're here, eh? Well, you've got that wrong, Mister."

His head swung to the bar then snapped back.

"Brad is very upset," he said. "I'm just trying to help. Please tone it down."

She leaned in and glared. "Tone *what* down? What did he tell you? Something about me and other guys?"

He wanted to bristle back at her but didn't. "Yes. And he feeling pressured about things."

"What things?"

"Marriage," He said.

"Oh, *please.*" She rolled her eyes, reached for her beer and smirked at him. "What about his marriage?"

"Are you putting pressure on him?"

She jerked her head, "C'mon. He's the one who wants more."

He thought, *Torgy's in deeper than I thought.*

"Listen," she said. "I owe Brad. He took a chance on me." Her hand re-introduced the hovel. "I could *never* get a job like that in Cow Hampshire."

He agreed internally, projecting the remainder of the Granite State as an extension of Frosty's.

"We're good friends," she said. "I care about him."

He leaned in. "So why is he so upset?"

She rested her cheeks in her hands. "He wants more of a commitment."

He kept a neutral expression. "How so?"

She shook her head. "I just went through that. He doesn't want me to see other guys. He even offered to get me my own apartment."

"That was nice of him," he said, his tongue briefly finding an inner cheek.

"Yeah, he'll pay the rent and think he can drop by anytime." She looked for his reaction and got none. "I know how men think."

He took a swig from his beer. *That's exactly how men think.*

She continued, "Then I'd have to sneak around. What if I wanted a guy to stay over? Brad will *freak.* He wants me to himself."

He didn't get the new-age concept of 'staying over'. He didn't get to stay over with Pat until after the honeymoon.

She said, "He's getting really bad. You need to get him under control."

He held a smile. *Me? You're the one on the joystick.* "How did you two get involved?"

She brushed the air. "I just fell for him. He's a nice man."

He nodded agreement.

"He does nice things for people. He's been paying Clara Ringston's rent since her husband died. She was left with three little kids; one a special needs child. Brad never bugs her about paying the money back. He says they're advances, but never docks her pay."

"That is nice of him to do that," he said.

"I could tell you other stories: how he helps out the employees, not just with money, but with advice. We adore him." She reached for her beer and chuckled, "And he's a *very* funny man."

Lutz didn't find Torgerson humorous lately, though he was hysterical in high school.

She sipped and put the bottle down. "There's this UPS guy who delivers every morning. He's got this funny walk… kind of a waddle."

"Like a penguin," he said.

"Yeah…kinda. Well, Brad is sure to be in the area and will fall in behind the guy and walk exactly like him." She smiled broadly showing small, evenly shaped teeth. "Last week, Emily, an older lady who sits next to my desk, wet her pants. Now she leaves the area whenever the guy shows. She can't take it." She slapped her leg.

What a wonderful, natural laugh she had. Their meeting was going better than he thought it would. And she was genuinely fond of Torgerson. But, enough of this. It was time to move on his plan.

"So, what do we do?" He said, shifting in the booth.

"About what?"

"About Brad's behavior. I'd like to get my old buddy back." He shifted again and awaited her reply.

She watched him and sighed. "I like him so much more when he's happy. He's such a different person lately."

"I'll say. And the weight loss. Phewww."

"I know," she said. "I'm so worried for him."

"So, what do we do?" He lifted one buttock slightly and tilted his head, eying her mouth, waiting for the answer.

She continued to study him, squinting, processing his movements.

When he shifted again, she sprang.

"What are you doing?"

"Huh?"

"Why are you leaning over like that? Like you're trying to look in my mouth? Stop with that."

He was always sensitive to where he looked when talking to an attractive female—focusing on the nose, rarely at the mouth, never staring in her eyes. Cute women were always on the lookout for seductive intentions so he stayed mid nose to upper lip. *Damn.* It had been unconscious: the awkward, twisted, angular search for the "thingy".

"What is it with guys? Did Brad say something about my pearl?" She shook her head. "What else did he tell you?"

He brushed at a shirtsleeve, trying to collect himself. "Ah…nothing really," he said. "Just that you two have been having relations, or… a …a relationship, I mean…and—"

She stopped him, "What kind of relations? Is that why you were staring at my mouth?" She folded her arms and glared at him before reaching for her beer and sitting back. "Guys can't keep anything to themselves. The whole world has to hear about it. What's that all about?"

He wanted to tell her that it was a guy thing; that Torgy meant no harm by telling how he polishes her pearl. *I also know you dig Johnny Mathis.* "Brad didn't tell me anything other than you two were intimate… and that he was very, very fond of you."

"Seal it!" She sat up stiffly. "Why did you want to see me?"

He was about to start his pitch when her dart mate, who had circled to the bar area to observe them, rushed from behind and forced his way into the booth. His muscular thigh and forearm crunched Lutz against the filthy wall. He felt a sharp pain in his right shoulder and moved his head towards the force to look into a huge charcoal face.

"Is this guy a problem, Val?" Satch said into Lutz' mouth.

"Whoa...easy! Let him up," she said. "It's okay."

Lutz feared such a confrontation and, if witnessed by the bikers, the possibility of escalation.

"Back off Satch. It's okay...everything's okay," her tone soothing. "Why don't you get us three beers from Frosty? Mr. Lutz and I are having a discussion. Everything's fine." She waved him away. "Go...go."

Satch addressed Valerie while pointing an accusatory thumb at Lutz. "So this is the friend of the dude who was talking shit at your place." He measured Lutz. "Why you here, fuckwad: *Pro*nunciation, *e*nunciation, jibber-jabber or truth?"

"Truth!" Lutz said.

He moved back into Lutz' face. "I'll fuck you up, Elmer. What's your game?"

"Nothing...*really*. I'm just trying to talk to Miss Quinn."

Lutz attacked his pocket for beer money. The bikers were less than fifty feet away. He had put one grand into each pant pocket so that Quinn wouldn't see what he was prepared to offer. He reached for his beer change, and the folded hundreds spewed onto the table. Valerie eyed the denominations and lunged in with a stern whisper, "*Never* flash a roll like that in here."

He snatched the money from the table and dug in his pocket again, found a smaller bill and thrust it at Satch, who smiled, snapped it, and headed to the bar to turn Lutz' largesse into beer.

They were left to continue their discussion.

"He's a good guy," she giggled, amused by his reaction to Satch. "He keeps an eye on me."

He clutched his shoulder. "Why'd he call me Elmer?"

"Ha!" She slapped the table. "Elmer Fudd. He adores Bugs Bunny."

He shook his head. "What are you doing in this place? It's dangerous."

She put him off with a flick of her wrist. "These are my people. My dad was a biker. Most guys in here are harmless. I know who the mean ones are. I stay over here and ignore them but they send over beers and try to get me drunk."

He rubbed his left hand.

She continued, "See that jackass at the bar...the guy with the red bandana?" She nodded over his left shoulder.

He feigned scratching his shoulder with his chin to steal a glimpse of the guy.

"No, *don't,*" she whispered through a clenched jaw. "Don't...be...so... *obvious.*"

He snapped back to look at her.

"That's Eddie Markey, a parolee from Riker's Island. He choked a guy for eating one of his beef jerkys. The guy didn't ask if he could have one."

"*Where* were his manners?" Lutz said.

"They say the guy was near death when the bouncer pulled Markey off. A real bad act, that one. Satch swears he's gonna have a piece of him someday."

"And the bartender. Is that Frosty?" he said, not showing that he was disturbed by her story.

"In the flesh," she said.

"He owns the place?"

She nodded. "He's a silent partner. Felons can't hold a liquor license in New Hampshire. Someone else fronted the place."

"A felon. He was light on jerkys too?"

She smiled. "Nah. He's not a bad guy. He was New Hampshire's top cocaine dealer in the eighties until he got busted moving a kilo of snow in from Hartford—hence the nickname."

"So it wasn't his corncob pipe and his button nose."

She snickered. "Hey, you're funny."

He smiled back. "I try."

She took a sip. "I don't come here unless Satch does. Even if I'm with a bunch of guy friends, I'll look for his bike first. If it's not in its spot, we move on. His dad rode with mine. I've known Satch and his father since I was a little kid."

"Your dad still rides?"

She looked at the ceiling, closed her eyes, and then looked at him. "He passed away."

"I'm sorry." Lutz said, softly.

"It will be a year next week; the third of September. I don't think I'll ever get over it."

Aha! Psychological transference. She's using Torgy as a father-figure to recapture past affections.

"He had a heart attack. My grandfather died young, too. Daddy was only forty-five," she said, her eyes fully moistened. "I figure I got his genes; don't have much time myself. That's why I have to get going, accomplish things."

Rose crept up her neck exposing further beauty and softness.

"My dad wanted me to go to college. But he couldn't afford days, so I went part-time nights. I scored in the top quartile on my SATs for verbal and math...almost a perfect score on Math."

"That's terrific," he said.

She blushed deeper.

"I turned down a scholarship because I had to work.

I got my Associate degree. Figured I'd work a few years to save enough money to get my Bachelor's. After my dad died, Mother went back to New Jersey to be near my aunts. I found a place and a roommate to save on expenses."

"I'm sorry to hear about your dad," he said. "He was special to you." He moved his head up and down for emphasis.

"Very," she replied with a fragile look and continued to sink.

Lutz felt a growing connection with her. She was pretty and soft with a conflicting, attractive roughness—an edginess he could manage, since Torgy could not.

Satch yelled from the bar, "Val, you want a shot of Jaegger? It's on Frosty!" With head down, she hoisted a tiny thumb.

She looked up. "I'm sorry Bob." She sniffed. "I'm having a tough time getting over Daddy. He fussed over me all the time. I miss him so much."

He was pleased that she said his name. Torgy said she was different. The earlier tension had moved to a soliloquy of a young woman's love for her father.

But he had not forgotten his plan.

"Do you like your job?" he said.

Her demeanor changed to serious. "I *love* my job."

"You're obviously very intelligent," he said with a condescending smile. "What in particular do you like about working for Brad?"

She leaned forward and poked the table on each word: "I—make—things—happen."

Lutz always used a basic marketing technique to secure a difficult sale—AIDA: Attention, Interest, Decision and Action. A nice house and tuition for his daughter endorsed the concept. Move a prospect through those elements, and you close the deal.

"Where do you go next?" he said.

"At Torgerson Construction?"

Got her attention.

"No. Could you use your Associate degree to find another opportunity?"

She shrugged. "Like what?"

"What would you like to do?"

She smiled. "I'd like a job that required math."

We now have Interest. Attention and Interest.

He would move to the Decision phase of his plan and deliver Torgerson the finest cake. Prepare the batter tonight; add a teaspoon of pressure and a pinch of threat; wrap it in cash—then bake in the Action.

"That SAT score in math opens up a lot of opportunities," he said, as Satch delivered their drinks and headed off to the dart area.

Her smile broadened.

"Do you get to use math at Torgerson Construction?"

She shook her head. "Not really. I just like working there."

"Tell me more. What do you like about the work?"

She spoke fondly of her fellow employees, smart ladies who postponed careers to raise families, only to re-enter the job market in underemployed positions. Her face lightened when she spoke of her mother who selected books and highlighted passages she wanted her daughter to discover and cherish.

Two more shots of Jaeggermeister appeared. He took a slug of beer to chase the syrupy mixture and the buzz in his head accelerated as alcohol collided with antidepressant.

"I read *Moby Dick* at seven and Vonnegut at eleven," she said. "Then it was Tolstoy, Hunter Thompson, Heller and on and on...all in my teens. Ever read Nelson DeMille?" He had, so they shared the joy of DeMille's prose. He spoke of his favorite writers, those with descriptive genius.

"Try *Geek Love*," he said.

She reached across, took a pen from his shirt pocket and wrote on her wrist.

Over the next hour, they sat in the booth talking about Torgerson Construction and Lutz' years at Allied. He was slurring some of his words and knew he should slow down when another round arrived from the bikers. He tried to advance the marketing plan but couldn't move past Attention and Interest.

He was taking a sip from a fresh bottle of beer when she said, "Want to play with me?"

He coughed into the bottle and a drizzle of suds exited his nose. "Sorry?" He said.

"Darts. I need the practice."

"Oh...ah, geez...I haven't played in years."

"Come." She reached for his hand and led him from the booth. He left his beer on the table.

He squinted at the dartboard before each throw. Satch brought him a coffee after he complained that one more Jaegger would turn the evening into another Woodstock.

After losing fifty or so bucks to her and Satch, he told her that he wanted to spend a few minutes alone with her.

She sat across from him amused by his inability to hit the dartboard.

"Bob, I'm sorry but we can't let you join out dart team," she said, laughing and slapping the table.

He felt so alive. They had connected naturally. They sat. He gazed at her. She looked at him fondly and smiled. He suppressed a sigh.

Suddenly she appeared sad, like she wanted to sob.

He felt pressure in his chest: a nice-heavy kind of rush.

She moved a hand slowly to put it on top of his then stopped and drew it back.

"You look sad," he said. "What is it?"

"Oh, nothing." Her eyes shined with melancholia.

"Talk to me," he whispered.

"Oh, just everything about tonight. You know: my dad, Brad...and now you." She studied him, head tilted, dreamy-eyed. "You're so easy to talk to."

"Likewise," he said, a butterfly finding his chest.

They continued to stare at each other as he fought for control.

"Val, I need to get on the road. I have a proposition. It could be of substantial benefit to a girl like you." He couldn't take his eyes off her, and was suddenly at a loss for the right words.

"What is it?" she said.

"Well, ah... it has to do with your employment and the fact that an intelligent person like you should have an attractive career path and, quite frankly (he cleared his throat), that journey cannot be with the Torgerson Construction Company."

Her jaw dropped. "What?"

"It's time to leave."

She sat back. "My *job?*"

He nodded.

Pink cheeks turned to red. "And why is that?"

He could feel her frenzied heart beating in his own chest and could do nothing but look at her.

She shifted in the booth fighting the force of his

pronouncement until she could speak. "What are you proposing?" She said with forced confidence.

"Val," he said, without looking at her mouth, "How would you like to come work for me?"

HE'S MAKING ME CRAZY!

P at Lutz sobbed on the phone to her sister in California. It was nine o'clock and he still hadn't called. "Bob *never* does this, Estelle. There's something wrong!" She took a pack of Pall Malls from the kitchen counter and lit one. "I told him this morning that I was making tacos. He *loves* tacos. What's *wronnng?*"

"Calm done, Patty. It's still early. He just started a new job. Maybe he got tied up on something and lost track."

"No, no. I called his office a half-dozen times before I called you. I get his voicemail. Nobody answers over there. And his cell phone's turned off." She exhaled into the phone.

"You're not smoking again, honey—are you?"

"I can't help it," Pat said.

"What, after so many years you're on the butts again. What's going on?"

"It's him." She took another drag. "He's making me crazy!" She bolted from the chair and started to pace, the cord bouncing off the oak floor as she retraced her steps. "He's impossible. Talking about how he's going to do this and going to do that. Then he quits his job after interviewing with these people for less than a week." She sat, cradled the phone in her neck, and crunched the butt into a saucer.

Estelle said, "He's depressed. They *all* get depressed. Leo was the same way. It took him five years to get through the change. They brag how they're hunters, but they can only hunt in packs. When Leo retired he didn't know what to do with himself. All he talked about was the start of cocktail hour. He'd rub his hands together at five o'clock. 'Isn't this great, Estelle? Huh, baby, isn't this great?' Then it was noon everyday, then counseling. Is he still seeing the doctor?"

"Yes. Every other Friday."

"Why doesn't he see the doctor more often, Patty? He could certainly use the help."

"Because he's cheap; that's why. Always bitching about the cost." She imitated his grumbling: 'A *hundred bucks for fifty minutes. Jesus Christ.'*"

"Is he taking medication?"

"Yes," Pat said, "he's on an antidepressant."

"And no change?"

"Not for the better." Pat shook her head at the clock. "He's still quick-tempered and impulsive."

"Are you sure he's taking the pills?"

Pat nodded to herself. "I count them every week. I doubt he'd be throwing them away."

"Well, he could be," Estelle said. "You know how he is...how he doesn't like to be told what to do."

"No way." Pat pressed a hand down a bony arm and rubbed at the tension. "He wouldn't buy the pills and throw them away. He just wouldn't get them refilled." She bolted up and pleaded, "Where is he?" and scanned the room for the cigarettes that were on the table, right in front of her.

"Honey, if he's not answering, why don't you drive over to his office and see if he's there? Maybe he's in a meeting."

"I can't." Her jaw tightened. "I *don't* have my car."

"Where is it?"

"He took it after he turned in his company car. Said he was going to get another one this weekend." She was on her feet again—searching for her plastic lighter—tethered to her lifeline in California.

"Is there someone in the neighborhood who can come over and stay with you?"

"No," she said, a palm kneading her forehead. "I don't want anyone to come over. I'm too upset."

"Sweetie, that's why you should have someone come over."

"No, I don't want anyone in the neighborhood to know I smoke."

"Then pour yourself a drink and relax. He'll be along soon."

Pat sat at the table, fumbled with her cigarettes and opened her mouth in a noiseless sob. "I cannn't."

"Why not, honey? It will help you calm down."

She sniffled into the receiver. "He drank it all."

"Huh?" Estelle said.

"He's drinking more than ever. He's not supposed to on the medication. He's got a bag full of those little nips in his toolbox in the garage. He hasn't banged a nail since I've known him and he's always going out to look for his hammer." She looked up at the clock. "Where *is* he?"

"Patty, that's not good."

"I knowwww."

"Have you talked to him about it? Tell him you found the bag and you're concerned for him. It's for his own good."

"Yeah, right," Pat said. "Then he'll blame me. Say that I nagged him into it. You know how he is. He's never wrong. It's always somebody else's fault."

Estelle said, "Honey, I wish so much that I could be there with you—to give you a *great big hug.*"

"I knowww." She stood and started pacing again. "I hate my life, Estelle. I hate what he's doing to me."

"Well you're a big girl, Sweetie; capable of making a big girl decision. You don't have to put up with it."

"Where would I go? I mean, I haven't worked since Janie was born. And I don't meet people all that easy."

"Come out and stay with me. Leo wouldn't mind."

"Oh, I can't do that, Estelle. Bob wouldn't let me."

Estelle gasped. "I can't believe you said that," she said, in a big-sister tone. "You're a fifty year old woman and you need permission from your husband to get on a plane? Listen to yourself. What's happened to you?"

She shook her head in defense of her sister's admonition. "It's easier to just go along with him. It's much more peaceful. Plus, he's too smart with words." She fought another rush of emotion. "I don't know what to do!" She looked up at the wall again.

"Honey, go out in the garage and get the bag. Have a few of those nips. They'll calm you down."

"They're vodka. I don't *like* vodka."

"Force it down. You need to calm down. He'll be home soon. You're getting yourself too worked up. Everything's going to be fine."

Pat rested the phone on the kitchen table, threw the butt in the sink and went to the garage. She returned with the bag, took out a nip, opened it, and took a quick swig. Estelle could hear her gagging in the background. She picked up the phone. "Aaaaagh...I don't know how he drinks that."

"Good," Estelle said.

She wiped her mouth with a sharp knuckle. "Do you think he's seeing someone else?"

"No," Estelle said. "I think he's trying to get off to a good start on his new job and isn't aware of the time."

Pat said, "They say that men get infatuated with younger

women and start acting out. Sarah Welling—you met her last time you were here—her husband got involved with a secretary half his age. He'd pick up his son on weekends in a red Corvette. Bob would look out the window at him and smile." She reached in the bag for another nip.

"Honey, don't let yourself go there."

"I try to do what he likes, but he's not interested anymore." She pulled at her midriff. "He thinks I'm too skinny, that I don't have any boobs."

Another gasp. "He said that?"

"No," Pat said. "I know how men think. I see how they look at younger girls...how Bob would look at Janie's friends when she had them over this summer."

"Patty, come out to California. It will do you both good. You'll appreciate each other after. Come see me, honey."

She was on her feet again and raced across the kitchen to the index card taped above the wall phone. "Do you think he was in an accident? Should I call the police?"

"No. It's too early. They can't be out looking for every guy who's late. There are millions out there. Give him time. He's probably on his way."

Pat said, "I have to hang up. I'm going to call his cell again."

"Okay, honey. Call me back if you hear anything. Love you."

Pat dialed his office, then his cell, and got his recorded voice on both. She sat, looked at the clock, hiccupped, and reached in the bag.

LIKE ROSES NEED RAIN

W*hat?"* Valerie was dumbfounded. "You're offering me a job? Why?"

"Val, it will solve some problems."

"I don't understand," she said, searching his face for dastardly intent.

"You're too smart to work in Collections. I know you do good work for Brad, but you're much more capable."

"Are you saying my work's not important?"

"Not at all. It's just...well...you could do more."

"Like what? What kind of company is it?"

"Internet," he said, adding an extended nod to signal a sure thing. "With your math skills, you'd be a great fit. We're writing software and we need smart people."

She shrugged. "I don't have any software experience. Just one course in school."

He dismissed her concern with a wave. "You'll have on-the-job training," he said, knowing it would be a stretch for her.

She shook her head. "I don't even know you two hours ago and now you're offering me a job. Did Brad put you up to this?"

He nodded through brief eye contact. "He wanted us to meet. And after tonight...well, you're a natural."

"So Brad knew you were going to offer me a job?"

"He was very excited for you," Lutz said, a fingernail finding the label of his beer bottle.

She sat back. "I need time to think about this—talk to the ladies at work. I trust their judgment."

"Take as much time as you'd like."

Valerie looked down and rolled her hands in her lap.

"What are you thinking?" he said. "C'mon, give it a try. I'm sure it will work out."

She looked up and her face lightened as she became engaged in the possibility. "What's the name of your company?"

"iCare *dot* com."

"Everything's dot-com, huh?"

He smiled. "Yes, the Internet is making many people wealthy; if you've got the stomach for speed, risk and long hours."

"Where is it?" She said.

"In Cambridge. A half-hour east of Brad's company."

"I'd have to move. And leave my support systems."

Aw, Satch can't come with you?

"How much do apartments cost in Cambridge? Could I afford my own place?"

He smiled encouragement. "It's more expensive than New Hampshire, but it'll work out if you live outside the city."

"This is too much too fast," she said, taking her bottle and stroking the neck.

"We'll help you find a place. My secretary Lillian just moved into her own apartment in Walpole, thirty minutes from the office. She loves it. I'll have her look start looking for you."

"Whoa, slow down." She set the beer down and wrung her ponytail while stealing glances at him.

He squirmed then turned to scan the bar area. "I suppose that's the men's room on the other side of the DMZ?"

She nodded, "Don't worry. Satch will watch your back." She looked over at Satch, pointed at Lutz, then at the men's room door next to the bar. Satch nodded.

Lutz rose and moved towards the bar past the stools. A skinny, greasy-haired punk, who was leaning against the wall next to the men's room door, saw him approaching and stepped to the bar and put down his drink. He backed against the wall and smiled, formed an O with a thumb and forefinger and poked a finger in and out. "Hey pal," he snickered through blackened teeth, "You gonna whack that?"

Lutz stopped and looked him up and down, wanting to introduce his face to the wall. "Nice," he said. "Real nice. She's my niece."

"Sorry, buddy," the punk said, through a snicker of snot.

While he was in the john, Valerie brought her shot of Jaegger over to Satch. "What a self-obsessed idiot. This is going better than I thought," she said.

"So, you gonna let your boss off to go after him?"

"Yeah, he offered me a job. There's a lot of money in those Internet deals."

Satch high-fived her then flicked his chin at the table. "You'd better get back."

When Lutz came out, Markey's stool blocked his path. Lutz said, "Excuse me," and Markey stood and bumped him. "Hey," Lutz said, "just trying to get by." He looked over at Satch, who was watching, then tried to maneuver around. Markey leaned quickly into his space and filled it with bad breath. "Ever take it up the ass, white-collar man?"

He continued to the table with shoulders tight, half-expecting an object to find his backside. He sat and smiled at Valerie. "There were some interesting tooth-to-tattoo ratios at the bar."

She turned and squinted at Satch, nodding slightly, once.

Satch grinned and went to the board, pulled out a dart, and made a slow pumping action towards the bar.

Lutz watched in terror as the missile approached in a suspended arc, hugging the ceiling on its way. It reached the bar and appeared to drift, sidling and searching—a fluttering, steel beaked hummingbird—divining nectar in the skull of Markey.

"Mercy," Lutz muttered.

The dart hit the crown of Markey's head and dangled. Thinking he had been stung, he slapped it and it ripped at his skull before falling to the floor. A dark circle formed in the bandana and released parallel streams down the back of his neck. He looked down at the object then spun.

Satch puffed his chest, blew a kiss and pulled at his shirt to identify himself as the source of the bulls-eye. Markey turned, grabbed a beer bottle and let it fly as Satch moved in for a collision. The bottle careened off his forearm and headed towards Lutz, who ducked in the booth and raised his legs as it shattered underneath.

"We should leave," Valerie said, calmly.

Lutz moved quickly to the exit and she tagged behind, turning to smile at the melee. He ran to the car, yelling, "It's unlocked!" He was gunning the engine as she entered the passenger side casually. *"Jesus,* hurry! Where to?" She smiled calmly and motioned over her shoulder.

He made a U-turn, the car fishtailing in search of pavement, and headed deeper into New Hampshire, driving the first few miles in silence, deep-breathing, trying to pull himself together.

He grimaced at her, his face twisted. "I can't *believe* he did that."

She smiled at him. "Markey's a punk. It was bound to happen."

"That's a *bad* fucking place. *Don't* go there anymore."

She squinted. "Why? Satch will pulverize him."

He punched the steering wheel with a palm. "We could have gotten killed!"

She shook her head, still grinning. "We weren't in any danger."

"You told him to throw the dart; I saw you."

She turned on the radio. "Satch was totally in charge. The other guys hate Markey. They won't back him. What's your problem?"

He snapped the radio off and shot her a menacing look. They were from different worlds. He used hard work to advance—she a black man to defend: a hundred pounds of beauty moving three hundred of beast.

"Left at the fork," she said.

He continued north fighting the effects of his drink assortment. "How far?"

"Three or four miles; downtown Keene."

He drove the next mile in silence, trying not to replay the exit scene. When the single line dividing the road moved to double, he closed one eye and slowed.

He glanced at her then spoke to the road ahead. "Something doesn't connect."

She looked at him. "Now what?"

"You're smart and attractive; why Brad, a married man?"

She flapped a hand. "I told you why. I just fell for him."

"It doesn't bother you that he's married?"

"Hey, that's something *he* needs to work out."

"Oh? It's not something *you* need to?"

She rolled her eyes at him. "C'mon, it's *his* issue," she said, and slapped his arm playfully with the back of her fingers.

"Did your father ever cheat on your mother?"

"Get out." She turned away to look into the darkness. "He never would have cheated on my mom."

"But, if he did, you would have been okay with it."

"No *way*," she said, turning to face him straight on. "*Why* would you think that?"

"I'm trying to follow your logic. If your relationship with Brad is 'his issue'—your phrase—then wouldn't a tryst by your father be *his* issue."

"Hey, you're all over the road. Want me to drive?"

He tightened his two-handed grip on the wheel.

Minutes later, she peered at him. "Now what are you thinking? You look like a kid who just found an apple in his Trick-or-Treat bag."

"About something that happened many years ago." He glanced at her. "And I'm already paying somebody to listen."

"And?"

"*And,* I'm not interested in sharing it with you."

They rode a few minutes in silence.

"Left at the light," she said, and stared at the radio again then opened the glove compartment and looked inside. "You don't have a CD player?"

"It's my wife's car. I get my new one next week."

She chuckled. "I hope you're not getting another Volvo wagon. Not cool," she said, with a headshake. "Not cool."

After another mile of silence, she spoke to the dashboard: "You really are different, aren't you."

He ignored her.

"One minute you're smart and intense, the next you're funny, then you drift somewhere and come back angry, almost threatening like. You brood then you're funny again. What's with that?"

"It comes with age. You'll discover in time."

"What?"

"How you can't count on people."

She rejected his claim with a headshake. "All of *my* friends are dependable."

"You're young. You'll see. Someday a snowball will scream out of a crisp winter sky and take your fucking ear off. Nasty shit. Trust me."

"You're so intelligent. Why do you swear?"

"Because I was raised by a guy who spoke that way."

She poked him again with the back of her hand. "I like it better when you're funny."

He looked at her. "You said that earlier about Brad."

She studied him. "I don't like it when people put pressure on me. Like he's been doing."

"Ever think that he can't help himself? That he's so smitten with you that he can't live with the thought of you being with someone else."

"But he's a grown man," she said. "Why would he feel that way?"

He snickered. "Honey, there's no such thing."

"What?"

"A grown man."

She turned her head to shake it at the window.

"We're hunters. We'll chase it down if we can drive it, drink it, or fuck it. If something comes on our patch to take it away, we'll kill *that*... *then* fuck it."

"How nice," she said.

He glanced at her. "You don't understand, do you?"

"Not really. I don't think that way at all."

"Care to enlighten me, Miss Quinn?"

She turned towards him and touched his arm. "One day

my dad took me to see the Blue Angels, and when they flew over, I felt I could reach right up and touch them. Dad said, 'look Sweetie, you can see the pilot...see his helmet'. In my mind I could see his face—how it looked from the speed and freedom. When the sonic boom hit, I started crying. Dad thought I was crying because I was scared. I cried because I was so filled with awe."

"Lucky you. You've got one of those Zippidy-Doo-Dah genes."

She sat back and sang, *"My, oh my, what a wonderful day."*

"Too few people have that gene." He smiled at her. "But, you've got it. You don't have the slightest sense of why you feel so damn good. Do you?"

"Why are you dissing me?"

"I'm not. I'm jealous that I can't experience the same optimism. Everything I feel, particularly lately, has a gray tint to it."

"Feeling down is such a waste," she said. "Don't let yourself do it."

He raised his thumb in an A-OK sign. "Ooh, thanks for the tip."

She rolled her eyes and smiled at him.

"I bet you're too young to know this one. Lutz hummed, said *'trouble'* then sang... *"dust yourself off...And start all over again."*

"I know that one, too," she said. "It's cute."

"No it's not," he countered. "It's more meaningful than cute; particularly as you age...I mean the dusting off part."

"Yeah?"

"Yeah," he said. "What happens—to men anyway—if you've been in the trenches too long, you succumb to the pressure and lose your resilience. It's hard to dust off, even harder to start all over again. You get depressed, snappy and immensely resentful."

"About what?"

"About choices, how you might have made some without having been adequately informed. How nobody helped, took you aside to point out options with softer repercussions. Then you wake one day and realize it's too late."

"For what?"

"Just too damn late," he said.

She studied him, her head tilted. "So, you're seeing a shrink."

"I didn't say that."

"It's the way you talk. Everything so heavy. Relax," she said, and poked him again.

Lutz wondered if he would appreciate her intelligence if she were heavier or whiny in disposition. But she was pert, pretty and spontaneous.

"Next right," she said. "First driveway."

He pulled in and imagined the scene that Torgerson had described—his truck racing from the same dirt driveway heading for the solace of jukebox and drink.

He turned off the ignition and they sat. There were no streetlights but the moon was close to full, casting enough light to illuminate her face and glisten her eyes. She was smiling broadly, still entertained by their exit from Frosty's and not at all affected by his moroseness.

She studied him in the moonlight, then threw her head back in laughter and slapped her knee. "Fix your hair. You look like Kramer." She licked her fingertips and leaned across to groom him, gazing in his eyes as she brushed back his hair. "There...better."

"I'm usually not this sloppy," he said. "I figured a little mussing would help me fit in back at the Ritz."

"Oops, there's Funny again."

He smiled at her. "I'm glad you see it. I'm prone to edgier moments."

"But you make *me* smile."

"You're smiling because you're loaded up on cough syrup and beer."

"Cough syrup?"

"That's what that Jaeggermeister tasted like."

She laughed. "It *does*, doesn't it? You are *too* funny."

"Val, if you really got to know me, eventually I wouldn't be able to make you smile."

"Why?"

"It's something that happens to men."

She looked at him and continued to grin.

"You reach a certain age and you replay decisions you've made, cringing at the major fuck-ups, and you try to pinpoint the causes. And you realize that you've placed too much trust in others and they let you down."

She stopped him. "Where's Funny?" She twisted to look into the back seat. "Wasn't he just here? Oh Funny...Mr. Funny! Come out; come out—wherever you are!"

"*Stop*," he said. "I'm serious about this."

"That's why you have to stop thinking about it. It *is* serious."

She rubbed his arm and he smiled at her.

"Bob, did you know that we're made of stardust?"

His jaw fell in mock awe. "*Get* the fuck out!"

She giggled. "Really," and reached for and held his hand. "Read Carl Sagan. Life on earth was created from comets and other heavenly bodies."

"Oooooh...I *love* heavenly bodies." He lunged and tried to tickle her.

"*Don't.* I'm wicked ticklish." She dodged his hand and pushed it away, then reached for and held it again.

"Okay. I won't tickle. I promise. But, can I be serious just one more time?"

"Okay, but don't brood."

"Val, I appreciate you being open with me tonight. I enjoyed our discussion very much."

"Me too. You're awfully easy to talk to." She reached over and tapped his chest. "There's a real man in there. Only a very nice person would do what you did tonight. Brad is very lucky to have you for a friend." She took his hand again and cupped it in her lap. "You're a very special man."

"Thank you," he said.

She gazed in his eyes, tilted her head and moved it side to side in exaggerated wonderment. The corners of her mouth twitched and a smile began then spread to a mischievous grin. "And you're kinda cute."

Aw Val, don't do this to me.

Valerie Quinn put Bob Lutz' fifty-year-old aggravated face in her tiny hands and kissed his Jaeggermeister mouth—a soft little kiss—releasing with a nibble of his bottom lip.

He licked his lips to taste her.

She put her face against his chest and cooed. "Want to come up for a nightcap?"

***

We're dancin, real romantic, when she just stops in the middle of the 'Twelfth of Never' and takes my hand, leads me over to the couch and gives me a little push. My arms are up so I won't spill my beer. Then she kneels down right between my legs and starts fiddle-fuckin with my belt and takes it out. She grabs it Bobby, looks at it...then down she goes.

***

His heart raced at the thought of replaying Torgy's scene— with a new little guy in the leading role.

You're twenty-three. I have a daughter, twenty. I can't do this.
"Got any Johnny Mathis?"

She nodded and squeezed his hand. "My roommate's in bed. You have to be quiet. She gets mad if I wake her."

***

Need you...oh, my darling,
like roses need rain.

G-L-O-R-I-A

Jack Reese was in his suite at the Charles Hotel wearing Pixie's panties—strutting like Mick Jagger—holding a champagne bottle out for balance as he spun, his lips puffed. Mrs. Sullivan would have been so disappointed in Gloria—her sweet little barfly daughter, into her fifth hour of frolic with a total stranger.

He jumped up on a chair and crooned: "G-L-O-R-I-A— Glo-o-ria. G-L-O-*R-I-A*—Glo-o-o-o-ria." Pixie sat on the edge of the bed in her blouse, clutching her skirt—her pantyhose in a balled fist—seething. "Hey," she demanded, "Give me my panties back; you're stretching them."

"I'm gonna shout all night...Glo-o-o-o-ria!" Reese stuck his butt out and started grinding it at her. "Gonna shout it *ev*-eryplace." He jumped down, grabbed a roll from the room service cart and threw it at her. Then he wound up on his imaginary pitcher's mound and whizzed a chocolate covered strawberry that struck the wall above her head.

She threw a pillow at him. "Stop it! You're being an asshole."

He stopped with fire in his eyes. "What did you call me?"

"Nothing," she said. "Come on, give 'em back. I have to get going."

He grabbed the panties, ripped them off, and threw them at her. "*Here*, whore!"

"Why'd you do that?" She bent to the floor to retrieve them. "What the fuck's the matter with you?" When she turned away to step into her skirt, he rushed, grabbed her shoulders and pushed her face into the mattress—a knee pressed into her lower back. She forced her head to the side. "I can't breathe."

"Don't *ever* fucking talk to me like that, you two-bit cunt." He grabbed a handful of bang-puff and yanked, turning her hairline white against the crimson of her forehead. "Do you know who I am?"

"Yes," she said. "I didn't mean anything by it. You're *hurting* me."

"You fucking broads are all the same." He pushed her head into the bed before releasing her and went back for the bottle, took a swig and slammed it against the service cart, breaking it at the neck. "Meals on wheels. Cunts looking for a free dinner."

"What do you mean?" She was on her feet, moving at him, her faced twisted, an arm flailing. "What the hell do you call the last couple of hours over there?"

He lunged, grabbed her throat and slammed her against the wall. "Did I ask you a fucking question?"

She fought his strength, unable to move. "Get away from me you creep—I'll scream!"

He released her and she moved back to the bed for her things. She was putting a toe into a high-heel to turn it upright when he attacked again, using her pantyhose to silence her, stuffing them in her mouth and forcing her wrists into the plastic handcuffs she playfully wore earlier. He pushed her down on the bed, lifted her skirt and mounted her from behind, leaning into her neck to taunt: "You like it this way—don't you, Pixie-bitch?"

She twisted her head to the side and mumbled.

"You like to talk when you're getting it—huh slut?"

He ravaged her for the next minutes, and when finished, leaned into her neck to calm her. "Are you going to be a nice, quiet girl and leave civilly or do you want to lie here for a couple of hours until you settle down?"

She went limp. He waited then released the cuffs. He grabbed her pocketbook and tossed it on the bed. "Don't be a trouble maker over this. Just leave quietly and don't cause a stink. My lawyers can make it pretty difficult for you if you want to go down that road."

She nodded and picked up her pocketbook then her shoes. She chose a defensive path around him, opened the door, then suddenly lunged and attacked—a ruby nail finding the side of his face. His punch knocked her into the hallway.

"*Shit.*" He put a hand to his face, eyed the blood on his fingertips and rushed to the bathroom to view the damage.

Pixie got to her feet pressing her ear. Blood trickled through her fingers—droplets trailing as she moved quickly past the elevator and took the stairs to the lobby. She stopped and hopped on the marble floor to put on each high heel, exited and hurried to a line of Yellow cabs.

SHAME ON THE MOON

It looked like Christmas Eve at the Lutz home when he pulled into the driveway. Every room appeared to be lit. He saw Pat's skinny neck and peanut head zip across the living room to the kitchen. She met him at the door to the garage; a cigarette between her teeth, a puff headed his way in defiance.

She yelled at him as he opened the car door. "Where *were* you!?"

"Out," he said, and moved through the smoke, waving. "*Where?*"

He brushed by her, threw his sport coat at a kitchen chair and moved quickly down the hall to the bathroom.

She staggered after him, caught a chair with her hip and limped with exaggeration to the bathroom door and talked to it, her nose inches away. "Where...? Why didn't you call?"

He didn't answer. She waited. She heard a flush, then water running in the sink. He brushed his teeth while she swayed outside the door.

He bolted out—startling her backwards into the wall— and headed down the hall to the bedroom. "I said I was *out.*"

With her head down, she went after him. "Robert, that's un-assseptable."

He sat on the edge of the bed to remove his pants. "I'm Bob. And please put that out."

"You never do this...stay out late and not call." She stuck

the end of the cigarette in a potted plant. He saw her do it and shook his head. "Why now?" she said, half sitting on the wall for support, hands on pelvic bones.

"Blame it on midnight. Shame on the moon."

"What does that mean?" She straightened and glared at him, swaying in failed equilibrium.

"It's a song by Bob Seger. Listen to the words for a better understanding of man."

"Everysssing's a song to you."

"You can learn much from songs. Feelings are best expressed in lyrics."

"Fucking bastard!"

"Nice," he said, and stood holding his pants, emptying the pockets onto the nightstand.

She eyed a bottle cap and then spotted the folded bills. She slapped her thigh and announced, "Awww, now you're a gambler!"

"Hey, I gamble every day with my career." He waived an arm at a sitting area with custom draperies. "How do you think we afford this?"

"You're not suppoze to drink."

He looked at the bottle cap that was bent into a semi-circle then back at her. "I had one beer."

She tapped up her forearm the first time, closer to her wrist the next. "Til now?" Her finger circled the top of her hand before finding the watch dial.

"I should have called, but I didn't. Let's move on," he said, yanking the covers back violently, scattering a half-dozen odd-sized pillows in the process. Women don't get that whole calling thing, he thought. A pay phone was not an option—bad karma; it would have altered the evening's cadence. She would have picked up on his drinking and given him a psychological setback over the wire. Women don't understand how they can crush a good time from a distance. That's why men don't call.

He looked her up and down. "How much did you drink?"

She swept an arm towards the garage before staggering back. "I finissed your bag."

"My treat," he said, and walked to the closet to hang his pants. He came back unbuttoning his shirt, stealing glances at her.

She ran a hand through her outdated page-boy hairdo, leaned back against the wall and dropped her head in thought, then slowly raised her eyes to look for him. "You're so *meannn*." She wet her bottom lip. "Why did you turn on me?"

"Pat, I haven't turned on you. I said I was out and you won't let it go." He shook his head at her. "You'd better sit before you fall down." He tossed his shirt in the air and rolled onto the bed.

"I called my sister. She wants me to go see her."

"So go," he said, fluffing his pillow.

She pointed at him and squinted through her olive tint for emphasis. "She says you're going through the change."

He smirked. "Wonderful. Free advice from Estelle. I'm already beginning to feel better."

"Don't you say anyssing bad about my sister." She lurched forward, stopped and replanted her feet.

He pumped a thumb towards the bathroom. "If you're going to puke, don't do it on me."

"Where *were* you?"

"Look...I should have called. I fucked up. Let it go." He puffed up his pillow again, punched an indentation, rolled onto his stomach and put his face in it. He waited for a few moments and didn't hear movement. "Go to fucking bed," he moaned, rolled onto an elbow, reached to the nightstand to set the alarm and turned out the light. She got in on the other side of the bed, still wearing her dress. They lay back-to-back. Within minutes, she was breathing deeply.

But he couldn't sleep, and lay there breathing softly into the pillow, eyes open. He couldn't get the song out of his head: *"I just died in her arms tonight."* He sighed and rolled onto his side then tossed to the other. And a little angel kept dancing on his pillow.

A PAYROLL TRANSFER

L utz rose at 5:00 the next morning, shaved and showered quietly to avoid rousing Pat, who he figured—once she got vertical—would be nauseous and nasty. He called on the way to the office to check voicemails. Torgerson left a message at 5:30 demanding a 'report', his nervy attempt to deflect accountability. Lutz shouted at the recording: "You get yourself into a mess and pull me in; now you want a *report!*"

Now, what will he say to him? If Valerie agreed to join iCare, an offer he would not rescind, how will Torgerson react? Lutz offered her a job when he was convinced she was not establishing a base from which she would later extort. He was good at all the elements of the sales cycle and excelled at working out the details later.

It was Valerie's intelligence that prompted him to turn his friend's problem into an opportunity. She wasn't the threat that he had been led to believe and certainly wasn't pressuring Torgerson to end his marriage. He now suspected that Torgerson had constructed a scenario that he secretly wished for: abandon Ellen and sidestep the guilt by transferring blame to Valerie.

His achievement last night was an example of using goal-focused behavior to problem-solve. He executed his objective: sever daily contact between a wonderful young woman and an aging, weak, undisciplined man. He was saving the Torgersons' marriage and the annihilation of their assets. Brad Torgerson would eventually grasp the logic.

Valerie Quinn was a survivor who leveraged opportunities. She was smart and stunning, and used that combination to control an oblivious Torgerson, who was further blinded by oral prompts. Lutz was keen to how a woman can control a man, with the schmo having no sense that he is being directed.

Valerie adapted to survive. She was happy, unashamed of her lifestyle, and didn't lie or embellish. Lutz believed her fondness for Torgerson was genuine, with the sex being part of a natural free-spiritedness. She would not do anything spiteful to injure him. He would talk to Hinckel about having her work on the pricing files for the iCare pilot. She said she would get back to him with a decision.

***

His office phone rang at ten minute intervals. It had to be Torgerson.

At 7:00, Phil appeared in his doorway. "Morning Bob, ready to start?"

"Let's do it," he said, through cobwebs.

Phil studied him. "You don't look so hot. You sick?"

"I put a nasty one on last night," Lutz said, massaging his shoulder.

"Geez, Bob. We've got a big day today. Reese is here. Even I stayed home last night."

"I know, but you don't have a goofball friend who's always in need of rescue."

"You want me to come back?"

"No. Sit. We need to get the presentation done."

Phil used his heels to propel a chair closer. "We should keep it short." He handed over a folder with PowerPoint slides. "The first slide deals with market size and demographics; slide two shows the VNA locations nationwide; the next one highlights the economics of Home Care with projected financials, and the last is Conclusions.

"Nice," Lutz said, scanning the first.

Phil smiled. "That's what I'm not getting paid to do."

Lutz looked up through bloodshot eyes. "As soon as we get the funding, I'll put you on the payroll."

"How about some stock options until then?"

"Consider it done," Lutz said, looking through the slides, then back at Phil with a shrug. "What about the valuation? How much do we say iCare is worth?"

"The real leverage is in a relationship with the VNA," Phil said. "That's our blocking strategy. Competitors would need an alternate nursing service to compete." He grinned. "To build that would take a lot of time and money."

"But, couldn't a corporation with deep pockets do it?"

"A big insurance company or an HMO could." He winked at Lutz. "But it would be cheaper and faster to buy us."

Lutz grinned too quickly and a spray exited from underneath his tongue. "We could be worth millions."

Phil shook his head. "Tens of."

Lutz' eyes bugged. "You think so? So, what valuation do we propose to Reese?"

Phil leaned back in his chair, smiled smugly, and drew a circle in the air. "Nothing."

"Huh?"

He leaned towards Lutz. "We leave it blank and let Reese put a value on it. Let him make the first move. Then we'll have a number to negotiate from."

Lutz stood and shook his head on the way to the window. "But, we should have a number in mind."

Phil turned in the chair. "Trust me, Bob. I checked it out.

A company in California with the same number of employees raised a round at an eighteen million-dollar valuation."

Lutz spun. "What do they do?"

"Distribute digital printing."

He shook his head in ignorance.

Phil said, "You use their system to e-mail a presentation to the city you're flying to and pick up copies professionally prepared when you land."

"That's worth eighteen million?"

Phil rubbed his hands together, briskly. "God bless Internet economics."

"I'll go through the slides," Lutz said. "Let's get together after lunch to rehearse before Reese shows up."

Phil left and Lutz reached for his notebook.

Hours later, Lillian appeared in the doorway. "It's Brad Torgerson for you. He's been calling all morning."

Lutz took a deep breath and picked up. "Torg!"

"Geez, why didn't you call me back? Didn't you get my messages? I've been nervous as hell waitin for you to call."

"HELLO. I have a very important meeting this afternoon. I can't drop everything to take care of you."

"Well, did she take the money?"

"Before I answer, let me ask you something." He picked up a new pencil and moved through the pages in the notebook. "If she did, would you consider the situation resolved?" He was stalling to find an appropriate way to tell him.

"Did she or didn't she?" Torgerson said, with suspicion in his voice.

"You need to control your emotions," Lutz said. "She's not a kook. She cares very much for you." He doodled in the book, outlining a V and drawing another one above it, then penciling them in.

"What did she *say* about me?"

"Listen to me. Keep a distance. Give yourself a chance to cool off."

"I thought you said that you'd figure out how we'd do the distance thing. Did you? What happened last night? Where's my money?"

"I spent time with her. We talked through a lot of things."

"I thought she had to be someplace? How long did she stay?"

"Hours," Lutz said. He printed next to the V: a-l-e-r-i-e and drew a happy face.

"Hours! Why?"

"She's a complex person. I didn't want to move until I got a feel for her. And what a hellhole Frosty's is."

"So, what happened?"

Lutz continued to be evasive. "She knows Nelson DeMille, you know."

Torgerson struck a match. "Who's he?"

"The writer."

He exhaled into the phone. "Where'd she meet *him*?"

Lutz shook his head. "No, she knows his writing. She's well read."

"Bobby, what happened?"

"Did I ever tell you how marketing strategy is like a military campaign?"

"Huh?"

"The plan is always tweaked after the first shot is fired." He shuffled the phone messages Lillian left on his desk. "You adapt your strategy once you get a feel for the terrain. Good marketing people do that."

"Damnit, *what happened?*" Torgerson's angst filled the line.

Lutz sat back in his chair and breathed deeply. "I offered her a job...asked her to come work for me."

"Why'd you do *that*? She didn't make a pass at you, did she? Did you fuck her...huh...*did* you?"

Lutz put the phone down, got up and closed the door. He came back, sat, and through clinched teeth said, "You ingrate! I'm working you out of a jam and you're suspicious of *me*, your best friend. Do you believe I would do that?"

There was a long pause before Torgerson replied. "I'm sorry. I'm thinkin real stupid lately."

Lutz' jaw tightened. "You're having a problem with your own promiscuity and you're projecting that weakness onto me."

"I'm sorry," Torgerson repeated.

"Hey, fuck you! I take a night out of my life to help a friend and I get this for thanks."

"Bobby, I apologize profusely."

"*What?* You can't apologize that way just by saying the word."

Torgerson's pushback brought stronger doubts about the merits of the job offer. "Did she show this morning?"

"Yeah, she was in at her usual time. I saw her goin through her files gettin ready to make calls."

"Did you talk to her?"

"Yeah, I said 'good mornin' and she smiled at me real friendly. That's why I thought everythin worked out and she took the money. She looked tired though. Did she have a lot to drink?"

Lutz thought about it. She sipped at her beer but he didn't remember seeing her drink any shots of the cough syrup. "Not really."

"What if she decides to take the job with you; how are we gonna work it out?"

"Do a payroll transfer."

"What?"

"She'll work for me and be on your payroll. She's off your premises and I keep down my expenses." Lutz looked at his watch. He needed to leave soon for his appointment with Dr. Felton.

Torgerson said, "Aw, I don't know about this. I don't want any problems with the IRS."

"Trust me," Lutz said.

Torgerson's immediate retort: "Why?"

"Because, I'm your friend." A wave of dread moved through Lutz. It came from his stomach, flashed to his chest and settled in his throat. He choked into the phone. "I'm your fucking *friend.*"

"Bobby, what's wrong?"

"I'm under serious pressure. I gotta go."

"Sure, Bobby. Are you gonna be okay?"

"Yeah." He was about to hang up then thought of something. "If Pat calls you, we were at the Elks Club last night playing poker."

"The *Elks?* Bobby, we haven't been there in years."

"Well, we were there last night."

"Sure," Torgerson said. "What time did we leave?"

"You left at ten. I'll work my story from there. I gotta go."

Lutz reached for his handkerchief and wiped his forehead. He sat for a minute, rubbing his palms on his thighs, shaking his head. It took just two weeks for his job, friendship and marriage to all head south. *Fucking people are ruining things for me, again.* There was a knock and Lillian poked her head in. "Are you okay?"

"Oh...yes... I just called my daughter." He blew his nose. "I miss my little girl."

She puffed her lower lip. "Ohhh, how sweet," she said, and closed the door.

I'M NOT A DIRTBAG

Lutz was fidgety when he entered Felton's waiting room, unsure about sharing the previous evening's activities. *Bzzzzzzzzzzz.* He figured that a psychiatrist didn't need to know everything; it was the afflicted's responsibility to sort through relevant behavior and surface significant issues accordingly. A shrink was no more than an interpreter who dispensed—a gatekeeper, as it were; a provider of an empathic pathway through drugs and talk. There were plenty of issues to explore beyond the twenty-three year old ponytail. He sat, picked up 'People' magazine, and studied the cover. *I bet Valerie likes that Ben Affleck guy.*

Dr. Felton appeared minutes later, smiling, and motioned him in. Lutz faked a smile back.

They sat and looked at each other. Lutz looked away to a gold-framed studio portrait of a young woman on the doctor's credenza. She grew prettier with each session.

Felton started. "You were angry last time."

"Very," Lutz said, and brushed at a shirtsleeve.

"Want to talk about it?"

"Not really," Lutz said, his shoe carving a line in the carpet.

Long silence.

"You're increasingly miffed. What's going on?"

"Yeah." He looked up. "Pat thinks so too. I'd like to explain, but she's not approachable." His eyes wandered back to the young woman's picture. "She's not too open to what I have to say. I used Rusty to talk to her through these times, but with the dog gone... well, you know."

"You used your dog to speak to your wife?"

"Yeah, whenever she was mad, I'd say, 'Rusty, I'm going to the dump, wanna go? And ask your mother if she wants us to pick up anything at the store'."

Felton smiled slightly.

"Eventually, Pat would reply to the dog and that's how we'd break the ice. Rusty loved those quiet times—the rides and the extra food."

Felton sat up, his smile expanding.

"If she stayed mad, and I got home late, she'd say, 'your dinner's in the dog'." He forced a grin at Felton. "I've always had a problem apologizing."

"Convenient, having your own Mr. Ed to manage spats. May I ask why she is angry?" Felton was now in full grin, an inappropriate demeanor for the question. Lutz didn't think that the horse metaphor was particularly funny.

"I got home late last night and didn't call."

Felton turned attentive. Lutz put his hands together, cracked his fingers and gazed around the room, stalling, not wanting to get into the previous evening.

"Where were you last night?"

Lutz replied immediately, "You know what pisses me off? Fucking people who don't take the ball and run with it. People who look to others to clean up their messes. People with no courage. Frozen people." He wiped his palms on his knees as he looked away.

Felton started to reach for a folder then stopped when Lutz continued. "We've talked about this before. How I'm always the white knight. People expect me to intervene. What about *my* life?"

"Why do you put yourself in that position? Let people fend for themselves."

Lutz smirked at him. "Because people, in the main, are fundamentally unequipped to solve basic issues." He flicked his chin at the doctor. "You should know that from your line of work."

Felton nodded. "Unfortunately, some have been damaged by their environment and don't have the tools to reason properly."

"Isn't that what I just said?"

"No. You said 'in the main'. Many people—in fact, most—cope quite well."

"And you're here to heal the rest." Lutz smirked again.

"Am I? I'm far from a healer."

Lutz said, "Didn't you take an oath to help others?"

Felton nodded. "But, I decided years ago to focus on those who wanted to help themselves."

"Oh, Doctor Cliché," Lutz said. "Nice to meet you."

Felton was irked by his patient's disrespect but saw it as a smokescreen to avoid discussing the previous night.

"I see things quicker than others. I've never been able to sit by and watch someone on the slippery slope. Things tend to flow more smoothly when I step in."

Felton said, "You believe that?"

"Yeah, but I've about had it." Lutz sat back and looked up, pensive.

Felton reached for Lutz' folder and opened it to his dosage log. "Have you increased the Zoloft to one-hundred milligrams?"

Lutz looked away to answer. "Yes, since you told me last time. I started the next day. But I don't feel any different."

"It may take another week."

Lutz shrugged. "Whatever."

Felton closed the folder. "What reason did you give for not calling?"

Lutz shook his head. "I told her, 'blame it on midnight—shame on the moon'." He shifted in the chair and looked over at the picture then back at the doctor. "It's a song by Bob Seger. It about what's inside a man and that secret place where solitude lurks. And at midnight, that's where we go." He released an exaggerated sigh before adding, "We men are acquainted with the night."

Felton put the folder aside.

Lutz said, "Ever read *The Celestine Prophecy?*"

"No. But I've heard of it."

"It's fascinating fiction about destiny, how people meet for a reason. Relationships don't always happen by chance." He picked at a cuticle. "It's eerie, how you can connect spiritually with another person through some sort of mystical plan."

Felton gave him a nod of encouragement.

"I met someone." He shifted in the chair. "She's got enough oxygen to feed the Fleet Center. I've never met anyone like her. I was intoxicated by her flower child spirit. She blew me (he coughed to clear his throat) away."

A retriever head tilt from Felton.

"That's how I've always wanted to live but didn't realize until last night that I still have choices. She made me ache for all that I've missed." Lutz felt clammy and wiped his forehead. "I don't know what it is about her."

"Where did you meet her?"

Lutz hesitated before responding. "In New Hampshire."

"You were drinking?"

Saying 'intoxicated' was a mistake. Psychiatrists use word association tricks to get at deeper meaning. Lutz knew he had slipped. "I had a couple of beers."

"What's going on?"

"Pressure," Lutz said.

Felton leaned forward. "You shouldn't be drinking at all on antidepressants. We've talked about that, how each drink has an elevated effect when combined with Zoloft."

"I can manage it."

"It's dangerous, Bob. I'm serious about this."

"Yeah, I know. I'll get on it. I'd rather stick to the subject of the girl and how I see myself in her." Lutz smiled. "That didn't sound right, did it?"

Felton didn't react to his patient's cavalier attitude.

"She's not even half my age but has experienced much more freedom. She's unbelievable. Really cute. A hundred pounds soaking wet. A real cute kid."

"Will you see her again?"

Lutz forced an awkward smile. "She may start next week."

Felton's eyes widened. "At iCare?"

Lutz nodded, and found another fingernail to work on.

"And, what was the impetus for you offering her a job?"

Lutz sat up. The doctor could benefit from some background. "I've got this friend. Well, he got himself in a hell of a mess. Seems he was having a fling with a younger woman at work and it caused him problems."

"Couldn't he be fired for that?"

He squinted at the doctor. "Huh? He owns the place."

"Being an owner doesn't make it okay," Felton said, sitting up with a head shake.

Lutz, surprised by the doctor's naiveté, said, "If you're an owner or an executive in a public company, you'd be surprised with what you can get away with." He brushed what looked to be a cat hair from his thigh. "Anyway, he was quite emotional about her. I didn't want to get involved, but I was worried what would happen if his wife found out. So I drove to a bar in New Hampshire to pay the young lady a surprise visit. I didn't want to do it. I'm a busy man."

"Why couldn't your friend take care of it? Couldn't it best be resolved by the two people themselves?"

Lutz shook his head. "He was too strung out. I had to step in to guide the process. He couldn't figure out what to do. He's not too good at putting together a plan and sticking to it."

Felton wanted to hit that last comment straight on but let it pass. "White knight?"

Lutz looked away, sheepishly. "I was concerned that he would sabotage his marriage. I'm very fond of his wife. She's a really nice person."

"What was your plan?"

"To offer her financial support to move to a new career." Lutz looked down. "With up-front money to move it along."

"Hush money," Felton said.

Lutz looked up to correct him. "There's nothing wrong with incentives."

"So, why didn't you follow your plan and help your friend as you had intended?"

Lutz felt warmth in his face. "Because, before I knew it, I was smitten. She had me singing love songs in my head. I got a feeling I haven't had in a long time. It just happened. I offered her a job. Just like that."

"Was that the responsible thing to do?"

"Why not? It was simple, logical thinking. Get them separated until they figure out their relationship. It solves a lot of problems."

"Does it?" Felton said.

Lutz shrugged. "Now my friend is angry because he suspects I'm working something else."

Felton sat up and stared at his patient. Lutz lowered his eyes. He looked up again to meet the doctor's.

"Are you?" Felton said.

Lutz didn't know where he was headed with Valerie.

He had avoided compromising situations at Allied. After he was made a Vice President, a gorgeous marketing rep hit on him one afternoon at a sales conference. Later that evening, she tapped on his hotel door asking for help with a bottle of champagne delivered to her suite by 'mistake'. Lutz talked to the door while ogling her in the peephole. Told her to go away, afraid someone would see her outside his room.

"I don't know what it's all about: why I am so attracted to this woman. She snuck up on me and crept into my head."

Felton reached for the folder, wrote something quickly, and closed it.

"I've always liked young women. I mean, don't all men? But I figured if I ever strayed, it would be with one of those harlot types in detective novels. You know, the grieving widow with platinum hair and legs long enough to trip a marching band." Lutz knew he was rambling and wanted to stop. "Women like younger guys. Boy toys. Who knows what they're thinking? They just don't obsess about it like men do."

Felton sat erect and motionless, listening carefully for a cue.

Lutz continued, "I'm sure this will end up positive all around. My friend keeps his marriage together. The young lady starts a promising career—out of that dangerous environment—and I get additional help for iCare."

"What do you mean, 'dangerous'?"

"The bar. We're talking a freak show. There were two, maybe ten felons in there."

"Why did you go in a place like that?"

"Because *that's* where she hangs out."

"And how long did you stay?"

"Until her friend put a dart in a guy's head."

Felton grimaced. "My *good*ness," he said.

Lutz winced. "I know."

Felton leaned forward. "Are you sure that where you're headed won't prove to be problematic?"

"How so?"

"That you're acting in the moment without reflecting on the consequences. And, there is alcohol involved."

Lutz looked away. "Yeah, whatever."

"I'm serious," Felton said. "Your defenses are down. If you act on these impulses, it could introduce new problems into your milieu. I'm concerned with your fixation on a woman—girl, you called her—that you've met only once."

Lutz furled his brow. "*I'm* fixated?"

"Well what would you call it?"

"I didn't say that word when I talked about her."

"You said 'smitten'," Felton reminded.

"Smitten-schmitten. Where are we going with this?"

"Bob, whatever term you choose will work. It's not the feeling that is important, but the action. And the action you took is not that of a person in control."

Lutz found the carpet again with his toe.

Felton continued, "It's not a mature state, particularly for one in your position, to be reacting to a feeling you had in the moment."

Lutz was indignant. "I'm old enough to make such judgments."

"It's not about age," Felton said. "It's about self-destructive behavior."

Lutz shifted forward to challenge. "Hold *on*. Isn't your fine profession supposed to withhold judgment? I was trying to help a friend. When I tell you about my feelings for her, I get heat. What's *that* all about?"

"It's about your wellness."

"Aren't you supposed to encourage me to share my feelings? Am I supposed to come here each week and have a staring contest with you?"

Felton held his professional ground. His patient's behavior the previous evening was a serious lapse in judgment.

"I'm trying to get at what's making me crazy and you want to give me 'I shall not' assignments. Why don't you put a blackboard in here and I'll write *I won't fuck Valerie* on it a few hundred times and we'll be done with it." Lutz knew he had slipped again.

"Did you engage in inappropriate behavior?"

Lutz looked down. "I don't like your tone. Too parental."

Felton studied him.

"It depends on what the definition of 'inappropriate' is. Some people do things that they feel real good about in the morning."

"And others live to regret their actions," Felton replied at once.

Lutz feigned bewilderment. "Why do you see this episode with the girl as being such a big deal?"

Felton said, "I'm reminded of an Erikson quote: 'The playing child advances forward to new stages of mastery, the playing adult steps aside into another reality'."

"What is that supposed to mean?"

"Just be careful."

"Don't you think I have enough character to do the right thing? I'm not a dirtbag. I was just trying to help out."

"So why didn't you stick to your original plan?"

He palmed his cheeks and looked down. "Because I was afraid."

"Of the people in the bar?"

Lutz wrung his hands and studied the floor before raising his eyes to meet the doctor's. "No," he said, "I was afraid I would never see her again."

THE GRANNYCAM

Lutz got back to the office and reviewed the slides again for the Reese presentation before joining Phil in the lab with Hinckel. He waved an arm to the room as he entered. "Hi guys." The engineers swiveled in their chairs, nodded, and went back to writing code.

Phil said, "Bob, the team has put together some neat stuff." Phil elbowed Hinckel. "Show him the e-mail feature."

Hinckel said, "Sure," and clicked on an icon. "That's the Scheduler Module for our fictitious patient, Granny Smith. He moved the cursor. "See where she's scheduled to receive nurse visits each day at 10:00 AM?"

Lutz nodded at the screen.

"Once the nurse finishes the visit (Hinckel clicked and a page appeared with a menu of services) she logs each service performed. Granny Smith was given her meds, a bath, and her blood pressure was taken. There are fields available for the nurse to free form comments." He typed *Blood pressure 130/80.* "That will go into her medical file." In the other field he entered *Mrs. Smith's blood pressure has stabilized and she is in good spirits.*

Lutz said, "You've got the computer in front of you. Where does the visiting nurse see this information?"

"Many have laptops to get access to patient records," Hinckel said. "If they don't have one, they can call it in on an automated telephone system and update it centrally. In the future, they'll use wireless handhelds that we'll provide."

Phil said, "Show him."

"See that e-mail address at the bottom of the page. That's the sponsor's: her kid, Sonny." Hinckel clicked *Send*.

"Now Sonny just finished a nice dinner at home and wants to see how his mom is doing. He goes into his e-mail." Hinckel clicked on *Sonny's Mailbox* and opened the e-mail from the VNA.

To: Sonny Smith
From: The Visiting Nurse Association
Sj: Mrs. Smith

Mrs. Smith was visited today by Nurse Ratched. She received a bath, medications and her blood pressure was taken. Mrs. Smith's blood pressure has stabilized and she is in good spirits. Her next visit is scheduled for Saturday, August 28, 1999 at 10:00 AM (EDT)

"Wow," Lutz said. "The son gets an update after each visit, is kept informed and feels good about doing something for his mother."

"That's the objective," Hinckel said, and winked at the engineers, who were stealing glances at the demo.

Phil bounced on his toes. "Show him Sonny's other e-mail."

Hinckel opened it: *Mrs. Smith was visited today by Nurse Ratched. She received her medications and her blood pressure was taken. She should have a no-slip rubber mat put in the tub. To order one, please click below.*

Hinckel clicked and the screen showed medical products provided by the iCare Corporation, with prices next to each. "This is not what the final screen will look like. It's a mockup."

"Geez," Lutz said. "It's a whole other revenue stream." He looked at Phil. "But, it would be expensive to warehouse all those products."

Phil smiled. "We'll outsource it to a medical supplier and take a percentage of each sale. Sonny clicks on the rubber mat, orders it for his mom, and it's done. We already have his credit card information, so there's no hassle on either end. The order is routed to the supplier and filled."

Lutz was grinning. "We can build a host of economic models around outsourcing. On Granny's birthday—Sonny gets a reminder. Mother's Day—Sonny gets dinged for chocolates. Valentine's Day— 'Hello, Flower man'. Has the professor seen this?"

Hinckel snickered. "I see the professor once every three weeks. He spends five minutes with me and the rest of the time flirting with Lillian."

Lutz said, "The next time he's here, I want you to show it to him."

Hinckel nodded, and when Lutz playfully poked Phil's shoulder, rolled his eyes.

Lutz was pleased that he had enough background to give to Reese. He looked at his watch. Reese was due to arrive in another half-hour. He was about to leave when he looked up at the monitor at a dog asleep on a couch. He pointed. "What's that?"

"My dog," Hinckel said. "He was in that very same position at 11:30 and hasn't moved since. See how he has his paws? Watch." He typed commands and the video re-set: 11:30. The dog was asleep, his right paw draped over the other. He looked at his watch. "It's just after 2:00, and he's in the same position. I guess I should have taught him to roll over."

"You bought a camera to keep an eye on your dog?"

"No, it's the GrannyCam."

"Huh?" Lutz said.

"It's a camera that broadcasts over the Internet. It's an

early model with low pixels, hence the grainy image. The later version using our software on Fast Ethernet will be much sharper."

"What do you mean, '*our* software'?"

Hinckel said, "Last year, my mother fell and broke her hip. She lay on the floor until my sister went to see why she wasn't answering the phone. I'd like to include the GrannyCam as part of our in-home offering."

Lutz said, "Has the professor seen this?"

"Yeah, he said 'No go! no go!—HIPAA'."

"What's that?" Phil said.

Lutz turned to him. "It's a law that will protect patient information. It will prohibit the use of security cameras in nursing homes and assisted living facilities."

Hinckel said, "It's dumb. They should really allow them. I wish I had one of these in my mom's place." He shook his head. "Poor woman."

Phil said, "Could we install one in a patient's home if she agrees to it?"

"I'm an engineer, not a lawyer," Hinckel said.

"How far along are you with the camera?" Lutz said.

"I've been trying to archive video straight to the hard drive. That would save on storage." Hinckel looked over at a rack of servers. "I have to delete my dog's sleep marathons every morning to free up some space."

Phil said to Hinckel, "How will we store all of those images when we have tens of thousands of GrannyCams installed?" Lutz was thinking the same thing and nodded at Phil.

"We'll use a trip feature that's essentially a motion detector. The camera comes on only when there's something to broadcast so we're not recording air space. That way we're not storing gigabytes of video."

"How close are you to having that?" Lutz said.

"At least a month," Hinckel replied. "I'm also looking at a medication dispenser. If pills are not removed by a certain time each day, a reminder will flash on her television. If there is still no response, we can dispatch an accredited home care specialist to look in on the client."

Phil chuckled. "Maybe we can sell those pill dispensers to Sonny for a hundred bucks."

Hinckel said, "There's another feature I'm thinking about: putting multiple screens on the feed so Sonny can watch Mom move from room to room. But, we're a few years away from having the wireless technology we need."

Lutz shook his head. "This is all Greek to me."

Lillian came into the lab. "Mr. Reese has arrived. I put him in the conference room." The face she made at Phil suggested something was wrong.

Hinckel squinted at Lutz. "You gonna get us the money?"

Bob looked at Phil and said, "Let's hope so."

"I have other features planned for the system but I'll need more engineers to pull it off."

Lutz touched Hinckel's shoulder. "We'll do our best." He turned to the room. "Thanks, guys." A few hands went up in small waves; most stayed typing.

A NO-BULLSHIT GUY

The conference room had a wall of glass facing the lobby. Reese was standing with his back to it looking at a framed photo of old Kendall Square. They entered. "Hello, I'm Bob Lutz. This is Phil Breen, my CFO." Reese turned and they stared at his cheek.

Reese said, "Hello," shook their hands, and answered their reaction to his injury. "A moron kid at the Charles stepped into the elevator with a dozen roses and nicked me." He slouched as his fingertips lightly traced the length of the scratch.

Lutz said. "That looks pretty nasty. Can we get you something for it?"

"Nah, it'll be okay," he said, and straightened his posture.

Lutz waved at the second-hand chairs surrounding the chipped Formica conference table. "We have some exciting things to show you." Reese and Lutz sat while Phil stood next to the overhead projector and began. "Our presentation is short and to the point. Just four slides. Please interrupt if you have any questions."

Reese nodded at Phil then smiled at Lutz.

While Phil put up the first one, Lutz said, "Would you like to start with some introductory comments about your firm?"

"Sure," Reese said. "We're a new firm with significant funds. We move fast. My partner is based in London." He put his hands to his hips and stretched with importance. "Sumner raises cash—I spend it."

Lutz said, "How many investments have you made to date?"

Reese lied. "Three. But I'm not at liberty to tell you names until they announce it on their end." He smiled. "You know how that works."

Lutz nodded. "We understand." He flicked his brows at Phil when Reese looked away.

Reese said, "I don't know much about iCare, just what my partner gleaned from the Goldman guys. You said Goldman is still kicking the tires."

"Yes," Lutz said. "They like the dynamics of the aging population and the potential market size. They believe we can gain first mover advantage." Phil fidgeted with his slide folder in reaction to the lie.

Reese waved a hand at Phil. "Well, show me what you've got."

Phil turned on the projector and put up the first slide. "By 2030, twenty percent of the U.S. population will be over sixty-five, and the supply of nursing homes and assisted living facilities will lag considerably."

Reese was smiling.

Lutz said, "Did Phil say something incorrect?"

"No." Reese slapped the table. "I'm reacting to twenty percent of the population being over sixty-five. That means seventy million people will be driving around at twenty miles an hour."

Lutz and Phil laughed generously.

Lutz said, "Phil, jump to the VNA slide."

Phil put up the slide showing locations in the U.S. "Our strategy is to tie all VNAs into our system at no charge and take a transaction fee."

"How many of those VNAs have you signed to date?" Reese said.

Lutz motioned over his shoulder with confidence. "We're in the process of signing the first one, right down the road in Plymouth."

Phil looked down at the folder and shuffled the slides. *What the fuck is he doing?*

Lutz continued, "They have concerns with confidentiality. Our chief engineer is an expert in the encryption required to safeguard the transactions."

Reese said, "So, how does someone enroll? My understanding is the elderly aren't big Internet users."

Lutz said, "They aren't. But their children are. Ours is a migratory society with more and more families dispersed. Mom's on one coast and her kid's on the other, or Sonny's up north and Mom's in the Sunbelt. Our system allows Sonny to see what nursing services are available in his mom's location. We take payment on a credit card up front—there's a nice float there—and the service is scheduled."

"How do you know where Sonny is so you can market to him?" Reese said.

"Great question," Lutz said. "We're currently working with AARP to get their mailing list to see where the baby boomers are clustered."

"How much will that cost?" Reese said.

Phil said, "I spoke with AARP this week and their ad rates for the AARP magazine are quite reasonable."

Reese said, "Why would the VNA want to do this?"

Lutz smiled. "Money. They need to be more efficient users of nursing resources. Our Scheduler optimizes travel times; they can see more patients per day. We also believe they can charge higher prices."

"Interesting," Reese said.

Lillian entered the room with a tray, set it on a small table next to Reese and bent over to pour. Reese eyed her. Phil saw the ogle and looked at Lutz, who furled his brow. Lillian said to Reese, "Sugar and cream?" Reese smiled at her. "Black." Lillian poured three cups and left. Reese measured her with his eyes as she exited, absently tracing the scratch down his face.

Lutz said, "Next slide, Phil." Phil showed the revenue as each VNA was brought on line. "We plan to establish a virtual economy from our captured audience: from bedpans to candy to flowers...all outsourced."

Reese said, "Have you established any of those outsourcing deals?"

"Yes," Lutz said, promptly. "We are currently under non-disclosure with a flower provider and in discussions with two medical suppliers." Phil glared at him briefly then looked away. "We're unable to tell you more." Lutz said. "You understand."

Reese smiled. "I certainly do."

"There's an Excel spreadsheet to back up the numbers," Lutz said. "Phil can e-mail that to you and you can run some what-if scenarios."

Reese took out a business card and slid it over to Phil. "I'd like to do that."

Lutz was about to prompt Phil to go to the next slide when Reese said, "How much do you need and what's the pre-money valuation?"

Lutz said, "Six to eight million, but our thinking is more six than eight. This opportunity is huge and we don't want to sell too much of the company in this round. We'll sell more of the company when the model is proven." He smiled at Reese. "At a higher valuation, of course."

Reese nodded. "And the valuation for this round?" Phil

held his breath as Lutz fumbled with his pen and sat up to answer.

Lutz said, "We'd prefer not to speculate at this time." Phil exhaled.

Reese said, coyly, "How then do I figure out what percentage of the company I get for my six million?"

Lutz said. "A company in California just got funded at an eighteen million-dollar valuation and they don't have a market nearly as big as iCare's."

Reese pressed. "So your valuation is eighteen million?"

"I didn't say that," Lutz said, his eyes darting to Phil.

Reese turned to Phil. "You're the bean counter. What's it worth?"

Phil looked at Lutz and shrugged.

Reese said to Phil, "What's your current capitalization?"

Phil reached into the folder and put a slide on the Viewgraph machine.

Reese studied it. "Who are Maltbie and Hinckel?"

Lutz said, "Professor Maltbie is the seed investor. That's his million dollars there. Hinckel is the founder. They each owned fifty percent of the company. Then each put ten percent in a pool for employee stock options so their respective ownership is forty percent."

"When did Maltbie put the million dollars in?"

"One year ago," Lutz said.

"So, Maltbie got fifty percent ownership for one million."

"Yes."

Reese sat back, looked at Lutz quizzically then smirked. "You're saying that iCare is now worth eighteen."

Lutz nodded. "Hinckel has hired a dozen engineers. They've written a million lines of code. The Scheduler is almost complete, we have a new CEO—*moi*—and we're talking to the VNA."

"Eighteen million," Reese said. "How much cash do you have?"

"Three-hundred thousand."

"And your run rate?"

"About a hundred-thousand a week, now that I'm on the payroll."

Reese said, "Phil, could you e-mail me the slides so that I can review this with my partner?"

"Sure." Phil reached into the folder. "Once you sign the non-disclosure agreement." He handed a sheet of paper to Reese, who read it, signed, and slid it across the table. Reese looked at Lutz. "Eighteen sounds a bit steep."

Lutz smiled nervously. "Now that you've signed the non-disclosure, I can tell you about an exciting product that further revolutionizes our concept." Phil sensed another misrepresentation and looked away. "The GrannyCam," Lutz said.

Reese grinned. "The what?"

Lutz said, "Hinckel is designing a video system to watch the elderly. Sonny can view Mom from his home or office computer. The motion detection and zoom features are quite remarkable." Phil's face was crimson. "Want to see a demo?"

"Sure," Reese said.

Lutz said to Phil, "Tell Lillian to alert Hinckel that we're going to take Mr. Reese into the lab for a demo. We'll be over shortly."

Phil moved to the door and rushed around the corner to Lillian. "Tell Hinckel that the potential investor wants to see the video of his dead dog."

"Huh?" She said.

"Bob's bringing Mr. Reese into the lab."

"He's a creepy guy, huh?" Lillian said. "How did he get that scratch on his face?"

"I don't know," Phil said, and returned to the conference room to manage Lutz' enthusiasm.

"Phil," Lutz said. "Mr. Reese has a flight at 4:45 and with the Big Dig traffic would like to leave no later than 3:15." Phil said to Reese, "So, what do you think so far?"

"I like it: the market potential, the first mover advantage and the VNA relationship. All positives. Particularly if we can lock up the VNA and block others from competing." Lutz looked at Phil and raised an eyebrow. Reese said 'we'.

Lutz said, "Let's go see the GrannyCam," and stood.

They entered the lab and Hinckel was typing commands to the video camera. The couch was on the monitor, but the dog was gone. "The little shit is sleeping on my bed," Hinckel muttered, as he stood and turned to shake Reese's hand.

Lutz told Reese how the camera innovation could be the hook that differentiates the iCare in-home solution. "The current product is on all the time and it takes too much storage to archive the images. What Hinckel is developing is a motion-detection process that turns on and records only when the client passes into the room."

Hinckel commented, "It's a software challenge, nothing to do with the camera. I need to assess the size of the mass moving in front of the camera before triggering activation. As people age, they tend to shrink; women shrink and tilt forward."

"Osteo," Lutz said, and Reese nodded.

Hinckel continued, "If, for example, the client's dog comes into the kitchen, we don't want the camera to go on. A big dog with an erect tail structure will map to an elderly female." He smiled at Reese. "Particularly, if the dog's a wagger."

"You don't want the camera recording indiscriminately and jamming your equipment," Reese volunteered, looking over at the bank of servers.

Hinckel nodded.

"How close are you to solving it?" Reese said.

"Anywhere from one to two months. I need more code writers to free me up to work on it full-time."

Reese said, "Couldn't you have the client wear something that triggers the camera?"

Hinckel shook his head. "Trying to get the elderly regimented is not realistic. They have difficulty following basic instructions. Wearing a digital activator would be too difficult for them to manage. They'd forget to wear the device, the camera wouldn't activate, and we'd be constantly sending people over to check on them."

Reese pointed at the monitor. "What's that?"

Hinckel smiled. "The couch in my apartment. I've been using my dog as a test but he doesn't move more than a couple of times a day. Right now he's sleeping on my bed."

Reese said, "How do you know?"

"Because he sleeps in eight hour shifts. I have a one bedroom apartment. He can't be anywhere else."

Lutz said, "Another application of this technology will be a photo attachment to the e-mail. Sonny can download the image of his mother and forward it to siblings." He grinned. "We'll charge for that feature, of course."

Reese said, "Do you have any real subjects for this video system other than the dog?"

"Yes," Lutz said. Hinckel squinted at him and Phil grimaced behind Reese. "We are ready to go live next week with our first beta site. The elderly woman and her son were quite excited when we scheduled the installation." Phil turned and looked over at the servers.

Reese nodded. "Impressive, I'd like to see it in operation the next time I visit." He looked at his watch then offered his hand to Hinckel. "Thank you...nice work." He smiled at Lutz. "I need to get going."

Lutz said, "I'll walk you outside."

They started to the lobby and Reese stopped. "Just a second." He walked over to Lutz' office. "Lillian, how nice it was to meet you. I hope to see you again." She hesitated slightly before taking his hand. "It was nice to meet you, too, Mr. Reese." He turned and left the building with Lutz.

The limo driver saw them approach and got out and opened the door for Reese.

"Thanks again for coming," Lutz said, and offered his hand.

Reese put a hand on Lutz' shoulder. "If we become partners, you'll discover in short order that I'm a no-bullshit guy. If we can agree on a realistic valuation, Broadline is prepared to invest. I can have a term sheet prepared for your review next week."

Lutz squeezed Reese's hand and pumped. "Then I will have a valuation number for you on Monday."

Reese got into the limo and went off towards the Big Dig traffic.

Lutz went back into the building and walked briskly to his office. Phil was waiting for him, pacing. Lutz punched the air as he entered. "He's ready to invest!"

Phil hurried to the door and closed it. He turned with a taut jaw and flushed face. "*Why* did you tell him those things?"

"What?"

"You said we had a relationship with the VNA—we don't. You said we have partnerships with suppliers—we don't. You said we have the AARP's mailing list—we don't... *and*, we never fucking will. They can't give us their mailing list. It's confidential for Christ's sake! You said we have a beta site for the GrannyCam—we can't."

"Why can't we?" Lutz said.

"Because it's illegal, that's why." Phil's color continued to brighten. "We just can't put a camera in a client's home. We need to understand all of the HIPAA requirements before we do such a thing. We'll never be able to sort through all of the legal issues by next week. Then we need to find a customer who will agree to it."

"We already have one."

"Get out," Phil said.

Lutz said, "Eloise."

"Eloise who?"

"Eloise Lutz," he said, delighted with his degree of cleverness. "My mother."

THAT RED ONE THERE

Saturday morning, he woke to the smell of coffee and went to the kitchen in his robe and met a pouting Pat, who was making unnecessary noise emptying the dishwasher. She saw him glance at the coffee pot but made no effort to pour him a cup. He sat at the table, reached for the paper and scanned the sections.

"Are we going to talk?" she said from the corner of the kitchen, elbows on the counter—a determined prize-fighter resting on the ropes.

"About what?" He found the *Sports* section and studied the scores.

"About you showing up after 11:00 Thursday night."

"I was playing poker," he said from inside the newspaper. "I need a night out once in a while. Can't you understand that?"

"You were playing *po*ker," she said with heavy sarcasm. "Is *that* the best you can do?"

He put down the *Sports* section and reached for *Autos.* "Yes," he said matter-of-factly. "I was at the Elks with Brad."

She put her coffee on the counter. "Why didn't you say that when you came home? Why were you so evasive?"

He looked up and met her eyes. "Because of the way you came at me. The only mistake I made was not calling. You attacked from the start and didn't give me an opportunity to apologize. Plus, you had way too much to drink...were combative." He could deflect any planned offense on her part by quickly putting her on the defensive. It had taken just a year of marriage to perfect his form of crystal blue persuasion.

"They don't have a phone at the Elks?" She lit a cigarette knowing she would struggle with his volleys. "And why was your cell turned off all night?"

"Jesus," he said, with an exaggerated headshake. "Guys can't get calls when they're playing cards. We'd get laughed at. Plus I was up nineteen hundred bucks. I couldn't leave. I had to give the guy a chance to get his money back."

"I almost called your doctor and left a message."

"*What?*" He swung his head to glare at her. "Why would you do such a thing?"

"Because he should know what's going on."

"Like what?"

"How you've been lately. How you're impulsive." She sat, then moved her chair away from the table, not trusting his mood. "Why did you quit your job so suddenly? Why would you throw away a twenty-year career and go to a little company after meeting with them for just a week?"

"I don't want you *ever* to call him. Do you understand?" His clenched jaw pumped a neck muscle. "He's my doctor and what goes on between me and him is my business."

"My sister says that he should know what's going on."

He stood and moved to the coffee pot. "Oh, fucking Estelle is now Doctor Joyce Brothers?"

She pointed at him. "Don't you say anything mean about my sister. She's a smart woman. She's done a lot with her life. She's well-read."

Well-read. He saw himself on the couch, a beer in one hand, the ponytail of another 'well-read' in the other. He smiled.

"What's so funny?" She said.

"I find it humorous that a woman who's never made a contribution outside the kitchen is now your sage."

"You're an asshole," she said, and rushed from the room.

Minutes later, he heard her talking on the phone. He stepped out of his slippers and tip-toed down the hall to listen in. "So, he *was* there. What time did he get home?" She was talking to Ellen Torgerson, checking out his alibi. He walked softly back to the kitchen and stepped back into his slippers before starting on the newspaper again.

She came back. "What time did Brad leave?"

He looked up. "I have no idea." He shrugged. "Was it an hour before I did?" He lobbed it back as a question, trying to trip up her inquisition.

"You're lying to me," she said.

He shook his head with confidence. "I have no idea why you would say that." He looked down at the different Chevrolet models and snickered at the come-on arithmetic in car ads.

"I just talked to Ellen and she said Brad got home at eight o'clock."

He looked up. "Perhaps Ellen's confused. I've never lied to you and am not about to start."

She lit a cigarette and watched him flip through the ads. "And when are you going to get your own car?"

He stood and approached her. She backed up defensively. He took the cigarette from her mouth and threw it in the sink. "Today." He put his hands on her hips. "Come with me to pick one out and we'll have lunch after." She looked down, pouting. "Hey," he said. "I was with Brad." She looked up at him, wanting to believe. "Honest. That's where I was."

"I want you to promise me that you will never make a major family decision again without first discussing it with me and getting my agreement."

His sincerity found pleading eyes. "I promise."

***

The automobile is a statement of personality and accomplishment—a projection of one's hopes for the future; an extension of how Lutz saw the world and his placement therein. They drove past dealerships on the Autoroute and stopped at Chevrolet. He got out and walked over to a row of Tahoes, looked at the sticker prices and waved Pat out of the car. She joined him momentarily until a salesman approached. "I hate this," she said. "I'll wait in the car."

"Good Morning," the salesman said, extending a hand.

Lutz refused the handshake. "I just put an offer on a Ford across the street," he said, motioning over his shoulder. "But first I wanted to see what you've got for deals. I'm buying a car today. Let's make it easy on each other, Mac. No fucking the duck."

"Sure," the salesman said. "We're the top Chevy dealership in New England. You'll always get the best deal here." He patted a Tahoe tail light. "Want to take her for a test drive?"

Lutz was looking over the salesman's head at the Corvette displayed in the front of the showroom. "Nah," he said, and pointed. "I want that red one there."

***

A half-hour later, he re-joined Pat and started the car. "So, how about Benny's for lunch?"

"That was quick," she said. "Did you drive it? I didn't see you drive out of the lot. I wanted to go with you."

He smiled. "I pick it up Monday."

She was pleased to be getting her car back and rummaged in her purse for a congratulatory butt then stopped, not wanting to light up in her own car. "Which one did you get?"

"The red one," he said, rubbing his hands together.

"I didn't see a red Tahoe on the lot."

He winked at her. "Neither did I."

***

Later on in the afternoon, Dr. Felton was in a luxury box at Saratoga with his head in his hands, rocking. "I can't believe she stumbled coming out of the gate. She was a sure thing. I know the trainer."

Felton's companion, Bee Bee Fontenay, a refined woman of forty-five, stroked his arm. "Don't be so upset, Laurence. It was only the third race. You'll pick the next one."

"There's not going to be a next one," Felton said, and stood.

She held out the racing form to him. "There's another six races."

"Not today, Beeb," he said, ripping it from her hand. "I had fifty thousand on that nag."

I CAN'T WAIT TO GET INVOLVED

The following Wednesday, Phil appeared in Lutz' doorway, shaking his head. Hinckel stood behind him shifting nervously, tugging at his lower lip. Two guys with *Up-Time Leasing* patches on their shirt pockets stood in the background. "Shit-storm time," Phil said, and entered shaking a fistful of paperwork. He glanced over his shoulder while thrusting the papers at Lutz. "Those guys are here to take away our computers. Seems we don't own any of our equipment; we lease it."

"So," Lutz said, leafing through the invoices.

"Well, we haven't made a payment in over six months." Phil turned to Hinckel with a sneer. "Our head engineer has been sticking the invoices in his desk."

Hinckel stepped around Phil. "The guy before you told me to hold them until we got financing. Said he talked to the owner of the leasing company and it wouldn't be a problem."

"Shit," Lutz said, scanning the billing amount on each document. "How much do we owe them?"

"A hundred-thousand." Phil said, while glaring at Hinckel. "They've been dunning us for ninety days, and he's been ignoring those, too."

Lutz said to Hinckel, "Are there any other outstanding invoices we should know about?"

Hinckel looked down and kicked at his shoe. "About forty grand for telephones and high-speed lines."

Phil said, "We lose the computers or the lines—we're

out of business—and the last man standing can turn out the lights."

Lutz stretched in his chair to look out at the guys from the leasing company. "Pay them," he said. "And throw ten thousand at the phone bill."

Phil grimaced. "After this week's payroll, we're broke. No more oxygen. Have you heard from Reese?"

"No," Lutz said, picking at his fingers. "I called him twice on Monday, and again yesterday. He hasn't gotten back to me." Hinckel turned away with a groan.

"Reese is playing with us," Phil said. "He wants to run our cash to zero to negotiate a better deal. We panic and he gets a bigger percentage of ownership for his six million. We should have been talking to other VCs; we needed another option to use as leverage."

Professor Maltbie had made the same point to Lutz and had urged him to look for alternative funding. Lutz figured it was unnecessary work. He took Reese at his word in the parking lot when he agreed to fund iCare. *Why isn't he returning my calls?*

Phil said to Hinckel, "Tell them I'll be out in a few minutes to give them a check." Hinckel shuffled out with faltered shoulders and Phil closed the door behind him. He turned to Lutz. "You know, it's not a problem for me if we go belly-up. I'll find something. But you? Didn't you check out this deal before you agreed to join?"

"I-ah...I didn't know about the unpaid bills. I suspect the professor didn't know either. Hinckel's an engineer, not an accountant. It's not what he thinks about. He's a creative type."

"Well he just created a huge fucking hole for us to dig out

of," Phil said. "If we don't get Reese to fund us and wire money in the next week, we'll have to pull the plug."

Lutz sat up. "Why?"

"Because, you and I, as officers of the company, are responsible for employee wages if the company can't make payroll."

"No way!" Lutz said.

"Way!" Phil said. "It's state law. And I'm not putting my financial ass on the line based on a handshake in a parking lot. If we don't get the money soon, I'm resigning."

"Phil, you're over-reacting. Reese was sincere. He wants to do the deal. I'll call him again." He grimaced at the phone.

Phil said, "He's fucking with you," and left.

***

Lutz dialed Reese's number.

"Broadline Ventures, Mr. Reese's office."

"Yes. It's Mr. Lutz again from iCare. May I speak to Mr. Reese?"

"I'm sorry, Mr. Lutz, but he is in London. I have given him your messages. I'm sure he will be contacting you shortly." She winked at Reese who stood in his office doorway bouncing a ball.

Lutz hung up and walked to the window and looked out at the new Corvette parked diagonally across two spaces. He smiled, feeling surprisingly calm, and admired the candy-apple finish. There was over two-hundred thousand dollars in his retirement account that he could access if the funding didn't get to iCare in time. He will withdraw the money—Pat didn't need to know—loan it to the company, then put it back after Reese wired the funds. There was no way that he'd pull the plug on his future. No way that a guy with no job would be seen driving around town in a new Corvette.

Lillian appeared in the doorway. "There's a Valerie Quinn on the line."

"Oh." He moved to his desk as Lillian closed the door. It was two days since he heard her voice. He called her twice on Monday at Torgerson Construction and hung up when she answered.

"Hi," he said, with a measured tone of executive bass.

"Well, hello there," she said, prompting his pulse to accelerate. "Long time, no see." Her voice was confident and sexily melodic.

"How have you been?"

"*Wonnn*-derful," she said.

He opened his notebook to a dedicated section and began to doodle, absently starting with a large V.

"Brad said I can go once I hand off my accounts to one of the other ladies."

"Great," he said. "How's Brad doing with all this?"

"He's been super. He's throwing a going-away party for me tonight after work. Want to come?"

Ooooh...Do I want to come.

"You should spend the time with your associates, Val. I'm sure they're going to miss you." He had already planned to take her out for congratulatory cocktails once she started at iCare.

"So, how about I start tomorrow?"

Yes! He surrounded the V with happy faces. "Perfect, any time between eight-thirty and nine. My assistant, Lillian, will greet you and show you around."

"How exciting," she said. "I can't wait to get involved."

"Yeah," he said, pinching the pant material in his lap. "Me too."

"Hey, boss," she said softly, "I gotta go." She giggled and hung up.

***

He dialed Fidelity Investments. "Premium Account Representative Paul Valent speaking."

"Yes. This is Robert Lutz. I have an IRA with Fidelity and would like to look into withdrawing some funds."

"Your account number, Mr. Lutz?"

"Fucked if I know," he said, and gave the rep his social security and pin numbers. "And I'd like to pick up the check in person. Don't send it to my home."

"Certainly, Mr. Lutz."

Lutz reached for a pencil. "How much is in the account?"

He heard keystrokes on the other end. "Just over two-hundred and seventy thousand."

Lutz smiled and wrote down the figure. "The investments have done well."

"Yes, sir. Your technology holdings continue to outperform."

"I'd like to take out two-hundred and fifty thousand."

"Certainly." There were more keystrokes. "Mr. Lutz, I'm looking at your account profile. You are aware that this represents an early withdrawal and a penalty will apply?"

"Shit," Lutz muttered. "So send me two-hundred and twenty-five. Again, call me when the check is ready and I'll come and pick it up."

"Yes sir. I'll see to it personally. Thank you for calling Fidelity."

THE BALL'S ROLLING

B zzzzzzzzzzz.
This time, Lutz was anxious to start the session. He wanted the doctor's opinion on Reese's failure to communicate—why he didn't find the time to call from overseas.

"Hello, Bob," Felton said, and motioned him in.

Lutz spoke as he got seated. "Things aren't going well on the work front. Everything I touch lately is for shit. I had the meeting with the VC two weeks ago—right after I left here—and thought it went well, but the guy hasn't gotten back to me." He looked at Felton for comfort. "What do you think that's all about?"

"Did he say specifically when he'd get back to you?"

"Yeah," Lutz said. "I was to call him the following Monday with proposed terms and we would agree on a valuation and he'd take it from there." He picked at a finger. "My CFO thinks he's stalling so we'll run out of money."

"He just might well be," Felton said. "How much money does the company have?"

"We're broke." Lutz' face wore the reality of bankruptcy.

Felton nodded. "He knows that?"

"I told him we had three weeks of cash, but we discovered some problems with the accounting; now we're down to chump change."

"So what are you going to do?"

Lutz shifted. "I was hoping you'd give me some ideas."

"Me?" Felton was dismayed. "Why would you think I could act as your counsel on such a matter?"

"Forget it," Lutz said, feigning nonchalance. "If I don't get a solid commitment by next Monday, I have two options. Shut it down—and everybody gets laid off. *Or* (his toe found the carpet), I get the money from somewhere else."

"Do you have the time to seek another source of funding?"

"Hey," Lutz said, setting his jaw, "I'm not letting Valerie go; she just started yesterday. Plus, we made offers to three engineers to start next week. The ball's rolling."

Felton sat up. "You moved forward on the young lady's job offer?"

"I don't go back on my word. Plus, she had already resigned her former position; it wouldn't be ethical."

"But didn't you have time to rescind the offer after we spoke about it? Why didn't you call your friend and put the problem back to him. Certainly, he would have understood you were having second thoughts."

Lutz couldn't get Valerie out of his mind. Not only did he make hang-up calls to her, but one early evening he drove his new car over to Torgerson Construction to watch her leave work. She came out with a good-looking guy in his twenties and was flirting with him—poking at his stomach and pinching his butt. He wanted to strangle the guy.

"I've got a quarter of a million in my IRA. I'm going to withdraw it and loan it to the company. I can close Reese in the next couple of weeks."

"And, if you don't?"

"I will," Lutz said, looking down.

"You could lose it all," Felton said. "Will you inform your wife?"

He looked up, irritated and firm. "It's *my* retirement money."

"Well, wouldn't it be her retirement as well? If you lose it all, it certainly will impact her later years." Felton leaned forward. "You should really think this through. You're going down a path that could add to your dilemma. You do have an option less painful than that."

Lutz stared at the doctor, hopeful.

"Shut it down, walk away, and look for another job."

"I'm not a quitter," Lutz said.

Felton said, "This could—no, it *is*—developing into a circumstance that is dangerous to your emotional and financial well-being. You could lose your savings and your marriage. Losing the first is not a show-stopper; exercising both certainly is. I strongly urge you to re-consider your plan."

Lutz reddened at Felton's charge. "I thought you guys are supposed to be impartial. Why are you telling me what to do?"

Felton shook his head. "My job is to help you to think more clearly—to get you to a point where reasoning precedes action. In my mind, you have not given proper weight to the possible repercussions. I would be negligent if I didn't point that out to you, and do so with adamancy."

"You sound like a fucking priest."

"That, I am not. But I am your physician, and with that comes the responsibility for candor."

"Well, it's too late," Lutz said.

"Why?"

"I already did the transaction. I pick up the check next Tuesday."

"Can't you reverse the withdrawal and put it back into your account?"

"Yeah, then I'm back to square one." He gritted at the doctor. "Can't you see that I'm boxed in?"

"You're not," Felton said. "Consider my suggestion and look for another job."

Lutz glared at him. "I can see that you're not going to be of any help on this."

Felton reached for Lutz' folder and began to open it when Lutz stopped him. "*Don't* open that fucking thing. You're not increasing my dosage. You'll turn me into a zombie."

Felton put the folder down. "I was going to review the notes from our last session, not increase your medication."

"This is a real-life arithmetic problem," Lutz insisted. "The solution is not in those notes. I need so much money. I got so much money. Do the math."

"Bob, you were put in a quandary by an organization that misrepresented its financing and poorly managed its accounting. Why do you feel compelled to keep your end of the bargain? Now you are willing to risk your own personal finances—possibly your marriage—to keep the company afloat. Why?"

"Because I know what the upside is. This is a tremendous opportunity. Someone's going to jump on this and make a fortune." He fanned his chest with his thumbs. "That someone is me."

"It is worth taking a risk where you can suffer debilitating losses?"

Lutz nodded, assured. "Who's going to hire me—a fifty year-old sales guy with one month of experience as a CEO of a bankrupted company? Huh? Who?"

"You can find something that matches your skills. You're still young."

"I can see that I'm not going to get any further support

from this discussion." Lutz stood and moved to the door. He turned. "You need to reassess your methods. I've been paying you big money every other week for over six months. There's been little progress."

Felton immediately countered. "Perhaps you should consider coming weekly."

Lutz dismissed his suggestion with a flick of a hand and left.

***

Felton was at his desk scanning his next patient's folder when the phone rang. He looked at the caller I.D., and would deal with it now. "Dr. Felton."

"I assume there's no crackpot in the office with you, so you can talk," the caller said. "You'll save me from chasing you down at home tonight."

Felton knew the voice all too well.

"My boss says your check was missing a significant digit."

"I received fewer payments than anticipated," Felton said, opting for a firm tone. "My accountant assures me that there will be cash available by mid week."

"How much?" The caller said.

"Twenty-five is the best I can do."

"That puts you almost a dozen payments behind."

"I know," Felton said. "If you would let me in on some action, I'm sure I can make it up."

The caller mocked him with a snicker. "Yeah, want to bet on another nag at Saratoga? You can have a look at the last one in your next squirt of *Elmer's* glue."

"She would have won if she hadn't stumbled," Felton said. "Let me in on some action this weekend and keep my gains."

"Listen. Where we're at, is serious shit. My boss chewed on a substantial chunk of my ass. He wants this cleared up or else."

Felton challenged. "Or else what?"

"Remember that pretty Hollywood actress who got her face carved up by a maniac years ago?"

"What does that mean?" Felton said, straightening in the chair.

"We have similar psychos on our payroll. And your daughter's a might pretty girl. My boss wants his fucking money— *asshole.*"

Felton fought to contain his terror. "I told you, I'll have twenty-five by next Wednesday."

"Fifty," the caller said. *Click.*

***

Felton paced then went to the file cabinet for the latest statement and studied the receivables to see which patients were late with payments. He could scrape up twenty-five thousand, but the insurance companies had to reimburse heavily for him to come up with more. He had already sent the bookie the money he got from his ex-wife and the sale of two paintings from his home collection. He looked at the two on the wall and shook his head, then at the picture of his daughter. He picked it up, traced her image with his fingertips, moved to his desk and put it face down in a drawer.

DESPICABLE HUMAN BEING

When Phil walked into Lutz' office the following Monday, Valerie was leaning over the desk wearing a long, black, cotton skirt that hugged her figure down to her bare feet. Phil eyed her curves and the absence of a panty line, and an involuntary guttural noise escaped. She was showing an employee insurance form to Lutz. "So, I should go with Blue Cross," she said. Lutz heard Phil's grunt but didn't react. She turned to leave. "*Hi*, Phil." She brushed her hip against the thigh of the titillated CFO as she slipped by. Phil knew the contact was intentional, as did Lutz.

"Come here," Lutz demanded.

"What?" Phil turned, looked behind, then back at Lutz. "Why?"

"Come here," he repeated, and thrust an arm to the floor.

Phil moved in defensively and Lutz lunged for his elbow and squeezed. "You moan one more fucking time in this office and I'll throw you through the window."

Phil shook free. "Hey, what the fuck!"

"I'm serious. Hands off."

"Hey, I didn't do anything."

Lutz bared his teeth. "Well, *don't*."

Phil rubbed his elbow. "You need to say something to her."

"About what?"

"How she dresses. She's been here less than a week and she's got the engineers gnawing on their wrists. It's not right, Bob. We need to get that code out."

Lutz shook his head in refusal. "I'm not going to talk to her. A woman should talk about those things with other women. It's not men's work."

"Then have Lillian say something to her. She's dresses nice. She's mature."

"Oh, Valerie's not mature?" Lutz said, tapping his pencil on the notebook.

"Hey, that's not what I meant; if it came from a female who was with it. You know—what's appropriate dress and what's not. Lillian could do it. Why is she always in your office, anyway?"

"She's not always in here," Lutz said with little command in his voice. He leafed through his notebook. "She needed advice on which insurance plan to choose."

"Well she's pissing off Hinckel. 'Bob said this, Bob said that.'" Phil's limp-wrist imitation of Valerie was poorly done. "He's already asked me if you two have got something going."

"Nonsense," Lutz said. "Our illustrious head engineer would be better off focusing on the GrannyCam, not his boss's love life." He looked up with furled brows. "Which doesn't exist, by the way."

Lutz was hurt by Valerie's refusal to acknowledge their initial meeting, yet she flirted with him constantly. He wanted to see her again, even told Pat that he might have to go on the road to see customers so he could plan a sleepover with his new employee. But Valerie didn't bite at his cues and politely declined his invitation for a new-job congratulatory drink after work.

Lillian appeared. "It's Brad Torgerson." Phil left.

Torgerson called a dozen times since Valerie joined iCare to see how she was doing. His withdrawal pangs were unmanageable.

"Torg, what's up?"

Torgerson choked with emotion. "Bobby, my father had a stroke. He's in a hospital in West Palm. Ellen and I are leavin first thing."

"Aw, Torg… I'm sorry. Is he going to be okay?"

He sighed into the line. "It's too soon to tell. They said he's not gonna die, but he'll have to do therapy. I gotta help out my mom."

"How long will you be gone?"

"I don't know. Ellen doesn't want to stay down there by herself. She and my mother will get into it. So I'll have to stay."

"You take care of yourself, pal. Let me know what I can do to help."

"Okay, Bobby. And take care of Valerie." Torgerson coughed into the phone. "Well, I don't want you to take care of her take care of her. You know, just take care of her."

Lutz let the comment go. "She's off to a good start. Don't worry about her."

***

An hour later, he was still in his office, alternately pacing then sitting, doodling and staring at the phone. He had received a call from Reese's secretary first thing that morning saying to expect a call. Reese had returned from London the previous evening and would connect today at noon. He didn't tell his CFO. He was prepared to make concessions to Reese and didn't want Phil screwing up the negotiations. It was half past twelve when it rang.

"Bob, it's Jack Reese."

His pulse raced as he reached for the notebook. "Jack, you made it back."

"Yeah. Sorry for the delay, but my partner and I had to kick a few opportunities around across the pond."

"Things are popping for you guys, huh." He began to sweat.

"Yeah. Hey, I spoke to my partner about the particulars of this deal. He says it's too rich."

Lutz sank. "What does that mean?"

"You value your company too high. He thinks we can do better elsewhere."

The tip of Lutz' pencil snapped on a doodle. "You told me that you were ready to invest...now you're not?"

"I told you we'd invest, but we never agreed on a value. Don't get pissed."

Lutz wanted to scream at him but lacked the negotiating power to push back. "So, you'll still invest six million."

"No," Reese said. "And you'll have to take a haircut."

"How much?"

"We'll put in four. And the valuation will be ten million, not eighteen. That's the best we can do. Plus."

"Plus what?"

"We want some other rights."

Lutz sat back and grimaced. "Yes?"

"First, I become your paid consultant and you give me an office there so I can keep an eye on my investment."

"What else?"

"We want two board seats and a third if you don't meet some metrics we'll put together around iCare's performance."

"When will we get the money?"

Reese looked over at the speakerphone on a table in his

office and smiled. "Oh, I'd say within five business days if we can get a term sheet signed off quickly."

Lutz stood to pace. "Can you fax it to me?"

"Sure. Our lawyers are working on it now. By the end of the day?"

"Yes. I'll look for it and FedEx it back first thing in the morning."

"Okay." Reese hung up and roared at Shanes who was conferenced in on the call from his office in London. "Do you believe that wimp, buckling like that?"

Shanes echoed his partner's howl. "And he's a former *sales* guy?"

"I told you we'd get him with a delay. Once he told us he was running out of money, we had him." Reese picked up the document his lawyers had finalized the previous week. "Wait'll you see the other nuggets our shysters put in. We'll get it signed off quick."

"Beautiful," Shanes said. "Let me know when it's finalized. I've already started shopping the company over here."

Lutz called Reese's office each hour beginning at six o'clock and got his voicemail. He waited until nine o'clock for the fax from Reese but it didn't arrive.

***

He entered the darkened house and fumbled for the light switch. Pat's car was in the garage but she wasn't home. He went to the fridge for a beer and saw the envelope on the kitchen table: ROBERT. He opened it and took out a drawing with surrounding notations.

This is me— an arrow pointed to a stick figure in a triangle dress.

These are my walking shoes—an arrow to clown feet.

Oooh...this must be my boarding pass—another arrow to a hand holding a ticket.

The figure's other hand was upraised, with the middle finger extended.

A kid from Fidelity called today. He needed to talk to you but didn't have your work number. He said your money (OUR MONEY!!!) won't be ready until Wednesday. HOW COULD YOU?

"Shit," Lutz muttered, and read on:

And when your daughter calls. YOU can tell her that her mother has decided she can no longer live with a self-serving LIAR and that she can reach me at her Auntie Estelle's. You are a despicable human being!!!

P.S. That is a stupid red car. A fifty year-old man driving his dink around— DISGUSTING

Lutz moaned, "Jesus *Christ*, here we go again. Why does an established firm like Fidelity have to put a six-buck an hour jerk-off on my account? *Why?*" This was, yet, another example of someone dropping the ball. Someone not thinking ahead. Someone not heeding specific instructions to hold a check for personal pickup. How difficult an instruction was that? "Jesus H.!" He threw down the note, gulped his beer and went into the den for the single-malt scotch he had hidden for pressing occasions.

He poured and swallowed. *Fucking people. A planet of shitbums, lacking the slightest penchant for speedy follow through. Hordes of malaise-infested lollygaggers settling goods into bags in slo-mo, without the slightest sense that a body needs to be elsewhere. And, if they end up getting fired because some new store manager wants them to anticipate, pick up the pace—they mumble 'Fuck You' behind their pimply-faced smiles and go work for Fidelity.*

But, as the barrel-aged nectar found his senses, a silver

lining emerged from his rag of a day: his friend was on the way to Florida; his wife in the air to California; and, landing just last week, in his very office, was the most beautiful creature he had ever known. He moved to his desk for a cigar, bit off the end and touched the tip into another pour. *Shit works out.*

WEEKS LATER: REESE MOVES IN

DADDY

Daddy,

*I am wicked pissed at you!!! I spoke to Mummy at Auntie
Estelle's every day last week. Why don't you call? She's been
there two weeks and she said you called only once. I remember
times when you two got along normal but lately the thought
of you two together under the same roof gives me the creeps.
What's wrong? Mummy said that you are having problems
paying attention. Like everything is going wrong on your new
job and things are messy because the people lied to you when
you went there. Then <u>why</u> did you take the stupid thing???
She wouldn't tell me anything but Auntie Estelle kept nosing
in the background telling her to tell me what you did. Are you
guys getting divorced? You promised me that I could go here for
four years. If you get divorced, you better keep your <u>PROMISE</u>.
Why do things always happen to me? Everyone here has money
and they go to neat places on the weekend. Why can't you send
me more of an allowance so I can keep up? Auntie said she
wasn't eating much and had to see a doctor. Everybodys parents
here are divorced and most of the girls hate their fathers. Do <u>not</u>
force me into that situation! Call her!*

Janie

Lutz put the letter down on the table and looked up at the clock. He got up and looked for the number on the index card next to the phone, dialed and moved to the refrigerator for a beer.

Estelle answered: "Hello." He smiled at her matronly rasp, enjoying the image of his last in-person experience of her: how hormones had bathed her cords in bass on the way to planting whiskers on her chin.

"Estelle, it's Bob."

"Bob who?"

"Let's not get smart," he said, looking in a drawer for an opener. "Can I talk to her?"

"Some husband," Estelle said. "She's been moping here for weeks. You can't fucking call to see how she's doing?"

He took a swallow. "I called the first week but she wouldn't talk to me. I figured she needed more time to herself, to calm down."

"Maybe that's something you should consider."

"Estelle, I didn't call to get in a pissing contest with you. Please put her on."

He heard Estelle's muffled voice in the background, and from the tone, could tell she was coaching Pat to be strong.

"Hello," Pat said in a voice sated with defeat.

"How are you?"

She didn't reply.

"Janie wrote me a letter."

"I know," Pat said. "She told me she was going to."

He took another gulp. "She wants you to come home."

"*She* wants me to come home?"

He didn't answer.

"Robert, why did you do that with our money?"

"You didn't let me explain—how it was only a loan. There's no way we can lose it. They'll pay me back."

"When?"

"They're doing the paperwork now. We should get it back in a couple of weeks."

"Are you telling me the truth?"

"Yes," he said, without hesitation. "It got us through a cash crunch. We got the funding since. They're paying me back."

He heard more prodding in the background before she continued. "I'm not coming back unless you promise me something."

He took another swallow. "What?"

"I want you to go to your psychiatrist every week."

"Why? You think I'm nuts?"

This time, she didn't answer.

INSECTS AND THEIR HABITAT

Lycosa tarantula, of S Europe, whose
bite was supposed to cause tarantism,
a condition caused by hysteria.
-Columbia Encyclopedia
Sixth Edition

I can't fucking believe you did that." Phil, his face crimson, and with spittle in the corners of his mouth, waved the Broadline document at Lutz. "They get forty percent of the company for four million, two board seats, *and* another seat if we screw up? How could you?"

"Where'd you get that?"

"Lillian took it from Reese's briefcase and made me a copy."

"Calm down, Phil, it's not as bad as you think."

"Wait." Phil raised a palm to Lutz as he read aloud: *'Should iCare not sign a minimum of twenty VNAs by November 1, 1999, Broadline shall be entitled to an additional board seat with full voting rights'.* He slapped the document on his knee. "They'll have control."

"No they won't," Lutz countered. "If that ever happened, it would be a tie. We'll have me, the professor and Hinckel to match up against their three votes."

Phil shook his head with certainty. "No way; their seats are solid. They could swing Hinckel's vote; offer him something and put their guy in to run the place. You know how goofy he is...they'll get him to flip." He put his head in his hands and exhaled frustration before looking up. "Have you called on any of the VNAs yet? November 1 is five weeks away. When are you going to close them?"

"Stop it! Lutz demanded. "The last time I looked at my business card, it said 'CEO.' When did I start working for you?"

"Open your eyes, boss. Reese has been on the premises over two weeks now. Don't you see what he's doing?"

"What?"

"He's in the lab constantly, looking over Hinckel's shoulder, asking all kinds of stupid questions: 'When are you going to launch the GrannyCam? How many lines of code have you written? What about this? Who's doing that?' Hinckel's ready to walk. *And*, he's on our payroll at twenty thousand a month. Did you agree to that?"

Lutz shrugged. "What could I do? It was one of the terms."

"And he ordered fifteen thousand bucks worth of furniture for his office, another ten to spruce up the conference room *and* moved into an apartment...all on our tab."

Lutz said, "Well, you're the CFO. Cancel the furniture."

"He can't stay in a hotel? Why's he here every day, anyway?"

"You'll have to ask *him* that."

Phil shook the document at Lutz. "You promised not to do anything without my review. This is the most important aspect of a start-up. It's about control. They can march in here, piss off the other investors, get you to quit—or fire you—and flip the company."

"What do you mean?"

"They'll sell at the first opportunity; take their money and run."

"Give it to me." Lutz moved around his desk and snatched the agreement from him. "It's not your copy. Lillian shouldn't have gone into his personal effects."

Phil stood and started to leave. "You've got problems in River City. He's on Hinckel, big time. You gotta talk to him. Tell him to back off."

Lutz put the document face down on his desk, sat, put his head on his arms and moaned. He sat up abruptly, slapped the desk, opened his notebook and started on a plan for the VNA. Lillian walked into his office softly, almost on tiptoes, and closed the door. "Can I talk to you?"

"Sure." Lutz looked up and leaned back in the chair.

"It's about your mother," she said.

His grip tightened on the pencil. "Is something wrong?"

She scratched under her watchband and looked towards the window. "Hinckel has a problem and he came to me. He feels kind of funny talking to you."

"Yes?"

She glanced back at him then returned to gaze absently outside. "Your mother is drinking."

The pencil dropped into his lap. "Booze!?"

She nodded at his shoulder. "Vodka. Hinckel says she starts every day with some. She puts it in her milk."

Lutz spread his arms. "Why didn't he say something to me directly?"

"Like I said." She brushed her pleated skirt and ironed a wrinkle with a thumb. "He feels kind of funny telling you this."

"Thank you for letting me know," he said, and reached for the phone.

Lillian started to leave and turned. "She keeps it under the kitchen sink." She backed through the door and closed it, her eyes to the floor.

***

His brother answered on the first ring. "Pete Lutz."

"Pete, meet me at Ma's in half an hour. She's flavoring her milk in the morning and it ain't Bosco."

"*Shit,* I knew something was up. She's been strange lately; accusing me of weird stuff."

"She keeps it under the kitchen sink. I'll keep her busy and you dump it."

"Okay," Pete said. "I'll see you there."

***

Lutz turned onto his mother's street and saw his skinny brother leaning against his beat-up Volkswagen. He parked, got out and walked to him. "Jesus, Pete, look at you."

"What?" Pete looked down and tucked in his shirt.

"Are you still running every day and living on energy bars?"

"Yeah." He slapped his hard stomach with pride. "Six miles every day—ten on the weekends."

"I feel sorry for you," Bob said, and brushed by him. He turned. "Some day, many years from now, you'll be lying in a hospital bed, dying of nothing." Then he poked Pete's shoulder. "Thanks for coming. She freaks when I come alone."

"When did that start?" Pete said, hurrying ahead of his older brother.

"July. She saw a snake in the cellar and said I put it there."

Pete said, over his shoulder, "You know, she still won't go in your room."

Bob stopped him with a hand to an elbow. "You're kidding me."

Pete nodded and bounced up the step, knocked, and opened the door. "Ma, it's Petey. Bobby's here too."

Eloise came from the kitchen wearing an apron over her nightgown. Though it close to noon, she hadn't passed a brush through her hair, and a sparse, doll-head arrangement of white roots exposed her pink scalp. "What are you boys doing here? Don't you have to work?"

Bob scanned her on his way to the kitchen, saw a purplish coiled vein puffing atop each kneecap and suppressed a gag. "Ma, you wore that yesterday."

"How do you know?" she said, shuffling after him in slippers Pete had bought her thirty years ago.

She saw him glance at the GrannyCam on top of the refrigerator. "When are you taking that thing out?" She stuck her tongue out at the fridge. "It stares at me."

"Soon Ma," Bob said, looking over at the dishes piled high in the sink.

Eloise said, "I need to talk to you." He looked down at a swollen-knuckled hand covered with ugly brown spots as it pushed him to the pantry. She leaned in and perfumed his space with peppermint and alcohol. "If your father was alive he'd kick his ass."

He stepped back to look at her. "Who?"

She motioned her head to the kitchen. "Petey."

"Why, Ma?"

She gritted through rows of worn, yellow-grey teeth. "He's having sex with a Puerto Rican."

"Pete is?"

She swayed her hips awkwardly, staggered, and grabbed his arm for support. "He had her over here yesterday. They were doing it."

"Pete?"

"Yeah. And if it doesn't stop, I'm going to call Denise. I never thought my boy would do such a thing. You? For sure. But, not my baby."

"Ma, Pete was here yesterday when the visiting nurse arrived. I saw you all on the monitor. That lady is a nurse. She's Filipino."

"Oh," she said, straightening the apron at the expense of her balance. "You want something to eat?"

"Nah," he said. "I just wanted to come by and say hello. See how you were doing." He sniffed her again while Pete looked under the sink for the jug.

"Pete says you still haven't been in my room. I told you I took my collection out of there and sold it when I went away to college."

"Bullcrap," she said with a scowl. "I saw a snake down the cellar and two frogs in the yard."

"Ma, they're natural things that live in the world. They're not mine."

Pete found the near-empty jug, poured it down the sink then took it back to the same level with water from the tap.

He took her hand. "Come with me into my room and I'll show you it's safe."

"Oh no," she said, breaking away into a slight stagger, her eyes pink saucers. "I'll make some egg salad."

Pete waved at Bob and put up a thumb.

Bob looked at the door to his room, thought for a few seconds, then walked to it and went in. It was much smaller than he remembered. The twin bed in the corner still had an original Boston Patriots bedspread that he bought in grade school. At the head, a tarantula poster hung—a remaining tack pinching a corner to a knotty-pine wall—while his favorite poster, the Tungara frog, hung faded on an adjacent wall. He studied it and a flashback stood the hairs on his arms: the argument; his father and Eloise going at it, then his drunken father reeling in his room.

He sat on the edge of the bed, then stood and ran his fingers across the poster. *Tiny.*

They started drinking in late afternoon; he sipping at his water glass of Canadian Club, she on vodka. Ballads from a scratched Perry Como album filled the house. They always started out nice, he pouring and pinching her at delivery, she calling him Victor. Then it would escalate to name-calling and insult, with his insistent demand for respect. "Godamnit, Eloise, I'm a Class-Three Fire Suppression Specialist. Don't talk to me like that." And she would goad and push. Get on him and push. "You don't know shit about nothin. Vick the prick, the fireman dick."

He walked to the desk with the built-in bookcase; everything as neat as he had left it. A photo of Torgy and him with their prom dates was on the center shelf. Next to it was a picture of his father at his retirement party, hoisting a drink with other firefighters, all likely dead, too. The third was of him with Pete, each holding an end of a string of perch. *Perca flavescens.* Pete was smiling proudly with the same easy grin that he'd worn throughout his life.

He scanned the books on the shelf: *Water Life of the Amazon, The Genus of Amphibians* and *The Exotic Creatures of South America,* then stopped at his favorite: *Insects and Their Habitat.* He took the book down and leafed through it. Almost every page contained neat printing in the margins. He read his notes next to the photograph of the Tarantula. *'The male tarantula will rub the back of the female during copulation to mesmerize and relax her. Should he lose focus, he will become her next meal.'* He smiled at the naiveté in the printing of a young adolescent. He turned the page to more of his notes: *'Spiders (mostly deadly ones) will lay their eggs in bouffant hairstyles, under human scabs, or in bubble gum (they like Dubble-Bubble)'.*

He took the book back to the kitchen and continued through it while his brother rinsed out a pan for Eloise. He stopped and looked up at his mother. The sassy, post-war firebrand, who as a young woman would move their Norge refrigerator to clean behind, stood dazed and crooked, fighting to recognize the boy washing the pan. She looked down at the eggs on the counter then at her elder son. Her face came alive with recognition. "Bobby, Janet Allison died. I need to make some egg salad sandwiches for Mr. Allison. You can bring them over."

"Ma," he said, now back into his notes, "Mrs. Allison died twenty years ago. Mr. Allison's dead, too."

BOMB TIBET

Crab louse, *plural* crab lice: a sucking louse
of the genus *Pthirus (P. pubis)* infesting
the pubic region of the human body.
-Merriam-Webster Medical Dictionary

Reese charged into Lutz' office the next morning, slamming the door behind. "You some kind of fucking punk?" Engorged veins in his neck pumped rage as he moved in with menace, coiled to launch across the desk.

Lutz bolted up, toppling the chair. "What's wrong?"

"You're a fucking wise-guy, eh?" He moved in with a raised fist.

"Whoa, whoa," Lutz said, his hands up in defense. "What *is* it?"

Reese struggled in his back pocket to produce a piece of laminated paper, unfolded it, and held it up for Lutz to read: BOMB TIBET. "You fucking jack-off." He tore it into pieces.

"What's that?"

Reese pumped his grip into the edge of the desk. "Did you put that on my bumper?"

Lutz gasped, immediately connecting Hinckel or an engineer with it. "No...no. Why would I do such a thing?"

"Who did it?" Reese lunged for his shirt.

"I don't know!" Lutz scrambled backwards as a button launched and bounced off the wall. "Jack, please!"

"I've been driving around this bleeding-heart liberal town with that thing for days. I couldn't figure out why everyone was honking at me and shooting the bird. Who did it!?"

"I don't know, Jack. *Really.*" He up-righted the chair, felt light-headed but was afraid to sit.

"It's somebody in this office. Find out. *Fire* his ass!"

"Jack, calm down. Please." He pointed at the window. "It could be anyone out there—a prankster. M.I.T.'s just up the road."

"Listen, dickwad, you and I aren't exactly synchronized swimmers. Stay out of my fucking way." Reese started to the door then turned to kick at the remnants of the bumper sticker before leaving.

Lutz sat down, took out his handkerchief and wiped his forehead.

Lillian came in on tip-toes. "Are you okay?"

"Yeah."

"What was that all about?"

"Get Hinckel," he said. "Tell him 'right now'!"

"Sure."

"Fucking jerk," he muttered, and reached for his notebook.

Minutes later, Lillian delivered Hinckel and closed the door.

Lutz glared at him. "What do you know about a bumper sticker?"

"Huh?" The engineer said with mock innocence.

Lutz gripped the chair. "You heard me."

Hinckel looked down and tapped a shoe on an ankle. "Our engineers are pretty good at desktop publishing."

Lutz pressed. "Who *did* it?"

Hinckel shook his head at the floor.

He stood and came around the desk and Hinckel took a step back. He was pleased that Hinckel had the gumption to push back at the bully. "Awesome," he said, extending his hand and grinning broadly. "But, knock it off for a while." Hinckel took his hand, pumped it once, snickered and left.

Lutz closed the door and went to his desk, opened his briefcase for a little black book hidden inside a zippered pocket, found the number and dialed.

"Madame Rochefort's Massage."

"Hello," he said. "May I speak to Madame?"

"May I say who is calling?" Cooed a syrupy Asian voice.

"No. Please tell her that it is very important and I must speak to her directly. I am a very old friend."

"But, of course. One moment, please." She put the phone down and he heard music in the background. He looked at his watch. It wasn't yet nine o'clock and they were playing *C'est ci Bon.* Such a global enterprise, he thought: a French love song backing up Asian girls working in the Greek section of Peabody, Massachusetts.

He opened his notebook to the scripted plan and looked under PROCUREMENT. Two options were considered; the first he had researched and deemed not feasible.

1. collect gym samples and cultivate at home
2. call Madame

***

"Hello, this is Madame."

He sat up immediately. "Madame, this is Mr. Lutz. How *nice* to hear your voice." (He pronounced nice as nee-say, in an effort to sound Cosmopolitan.)

"*Merci beaucoup.* We don't see to you, *Monsieur.* We have made the disappointment?"

"Not at all, Madame. I've taken a new job and haven't been entertaining clients as before."

"*Tres bien*. But we could bring the *joie* to *you, Monsieur.* Miss Lilac can give to you happy ending."

"You are so kind, Madame." He underlined the opening sentence of the script he would read. "I will certainly make a point to visit you shortly, but I do need some help with a matter and would be willing to pay in accordance with my appreciation and need."

"*Monsieur, sil vous plait*, I assure to bring my best to help your every wish."

He cleared his throat. "Madame, I hope that my request does not surprise nor offend you."

"*Monsieur*, my girls and I will not be for surprise. It is—how do you say—a meaning of our *plaisir?*" He heard her muffled voice sing '*au revoir*' to a client followed by '*Come* again, *Monsieur*', sweetened in double-entendre.

He coughed, and with a measured amount of professional bass, began: "Madame, I am now leading a company that is doing very important research for those in need. As you know, there are many young children—and we are helping many little ones in France, as well—who suffer from disease carried by insects."

She gasped. "*Très, très mal, Monsieur.* I watch to them on T.V. "*Les enfant…c'est terrible.*"

"Yes. Very much so, Madame."

"Do you call Madame for money, *Monsieur?* I am please to help."

"No, Madame. I am in urgent need of specimens for our doctors in the laboratory." He cleared his throat. "Madame, do you have any girls down there *avec* the *lee-say?*"

"*Quoi?*"

"*Les femme avec* the *lee-say.* Down there."

"*Ou, Monsieur?*"

His finger curled in his lap. "Down there."

"*Monsieur,* I have not the *comprende.*"

Unique requests were normal in Madame's line of work. He knew she fully understood the gist of this one and was being coy; he pressed: "*Madame, les* girls *avec* the scratchy-scratchy."

"*Ooh-la-la. C'est ne pas possible, Monsieur.*"

"*Madame,* it is for *les enfant.* They need your help."

"*Mais, oui.*"

***

While Lutz was on the phone with Madame further explaining the lab experiments—and making a formal commitment to conduct clinical trials in France—Reese was at his desk reading through the *Personals* section in the Phoenix looking for an SWF with dominatrix tendencies. Lillian poked her head in. "Mr. Shanes for you. Line three."

He winked at Lillian before picking up. "Sumner, what's up?"

"Are you in your office?" Shanes said, lacking little control over his excitement.

"Yeah."

"Is the door closed?"

"Wait." Reese went to close it, came back and sat.

Shanes said, "Guess who just called me?"

"Hey," Reese said, "Get to the fucking point."

"Goldman's M&A guy called to see how iCare was progressing on its home-care software. There's a big medical outfit here in Europe that is shopping for an Internet solution for its U. S. operations."

Reese sat up. "Who?"

"He wouldn't tell me. Just that they wanted to move fast and would we be interested in pursuing discussions."

Reese jumped up and pumped his fist. "Are you shitting me?"

"No. He wants a non-disclosure agreement signed before they go forward. Is Lutz there to receive a fax?"

"He's here, but he won't receive it," Reese said. "Send it to me. I'll sign for iCare."

"But he's the CEO. He should sign."

"And I'm a director. I can sign. Keep him out of it for now."

"Why?"

"Remember the clause you put in the term sheet?"

Shanes chuckled. "Which one? We've got this deal tied up on all ends."

"The one where he has to sign so many VNAs before November 1 or we change the liquidity preference."

"Yeah. Why he agreed to that I'll never understand."

"Well, today's September 22nd; he's got five weeks to accomplish it. If we keep him out of the loop on this until the last minute, he won't have time to reach the goal; we sell the company, recover our four million dollar investment, keep the next eight million and forty percent of the rest."

Shanes chuckled. "We get first dibs on everything up to the first twelve."

Reese said, "An eight million dollar profit on a four mill investment, in a couple of months. Not bad, my friend."

"What's your fax number?"

Reese stood and went to the door, opened it and called to Lillian. "What's our fax number?"

Lillian came in and handed Reese a slip of paper—

keeping her eyes down to avoid another wink—and closed the door. Reese read the number to Shanes. "Couldn't they e-mail it to me so no one sees it here?"

"They already sent me the non-disclosure via fax," Shanes said.

"Alright, send it."

"Okay. Don't go anywhere. It'll be there in minutes."

Reese was up and pacing. "This is out-fucking-standing, Sum. I want to get out of this dump anyway and move onto the next deal."

"Isn't capitalism great, Jack? These Internet deals are like shooting fish in a barrel. *Ciao.*"

Reese pecked on his calculator, running different sale price scenarios to see how much money he would personally make. Shanes' experience negotiating term sheets was paying off in just months of operation. The potential financial gain stimulated him and he felt himself growing inside his silk panties. He rubbed at his fly before leaving his office for the fax machine. It was idle, so he decided to chance it and walked briskly to the men's room. Lillian passed by him in the opposite direction, consciously looking off to the side. She walked by the fax, and when it started to transmit, she stopped, glanced around for Reese and began to read.

PUPPY BREATH

Lutz was at his desk writing when he looked up and saw Maltbie standing in the doorway, fattened and bronzed from his trip. He stood and swept a hand at the academic. "Professor, you're back. Look at you. How was the cruise?"

Maltbie entered in an agitated state and closed the door. He held a document and slapped it with the back of his fingers. "You signed this?"

"Yes; if that's the term sheet. You gave me your signatory authority."

He shook it at Lutz, the tension in his face trumping the glow of the tan. "Why did you agree to this?"

"What's wrong with it?"

"Did you consult with our attorneys?" The professor fought to contain his ire.

"Yes. I had them check the legalese."

"And?"

"They said it was okay."

Maltbie leafed through the pages, and with a short, fat, shaky finger pointed at a paragraph. "This little group of words here says that a change in the liquidity preference will kick in if we don't perform. Did you know that?"

"Yes," Lutz said. "It shouldn't be an issue. You need to understand that we were in a tight spot after you left on your trip. We found some unpaid invoices and were flat out of money." He shrugged away any semblance of blame. "I had no choice. If I didn't agree to all their terms, we would have had to shut it down."

"And their board seats. You agreed to that also?"

"Yes."

He flipped to the next page. "And they've got a guy on the premises as a consultant?"

Lutz nodded and exhaled his annoyance with the grilling.

"Is he here today?"

"Yes—Jack Reese. Why?"

The professor leaned out the doorway and spoke to Lillian. "Ask Mr. Reese to join us." He turned back to Lutz. "We pay our law firm good money to advise on these matters. I find it incomprehensible that they would counsel you to grant these rights."

"Well, they did say that Broadline's demands were somewhat unorthodox, but I explained our situation to them... you know, we would have to shut down to avoid bankruptcy." Lutz wiped his forehead. "Hinckel was sitting on some invoices. They would have taken our computers and shut us down." He felt a rush of anger. "Professor, those expenses were incurred before I joined the company. Did you know about them?"

Maltbie was indignant. "I knew nothing about any such bills. How dare you?"

"Well, you need to understand what I was up against." Lutz turned to sit, wanting to say, I had no access to you on the *Love Boat*. What was I supposed to do?

Reese walked in and Lillian closed the door behind him. "You must be the professor." He offered his hand. Maltbie refused it.

"Mr. Reese, our CEO and I were just going through the

term sheet. You might say that I am less than pleased with the favorable terms you were able to extract in my absence."

"What do you mean, 'in your absence'?" Reese smirked at Maltbie. "Then why didn't you stick around and see to it yourself?"

Maltbie shook the document at Reese. "The liquidity preference change is one of the oldest VC tricks. It puts your firm in a position of limited risk...the antithesis of your role in the funding chain."

He looked Maltbie up and down. "Come on, Pops. You've been around long enough to understand risk. Why wouldn't my firm try to protect itself on the downside? Do you think we're in this business to gather friends?" He snickered at Lutz. "If we didn't come in at the last minute, your boy here would be greeting friendly shoppers down at the Wal-Mart. You sow and you reap. You've got to make sure you're protected if you drop a seed on arid soil."

Maltbie twitched in anger. "Thou shalt not reap from another man's hectare."

Reese rolled his eyes. "If we all pitch in and make this work, that clause doesn't kick in. Don't get your panties in a ball."

The professor put the document in his coat pocket while scowling at his new adversary, then said, "The essence of capitalism is in the saying: 'There's no such thing as a free lunch'. However, with the advent of investors such as yourself—a new breed of vagabonds—it's been rationalized to: 'Where I stand is a function of where I sit'. And Mr. Reese, you and your firm are sitting on a potential gain that was negotiated from the duress of others." He headed for the door and turned. "And, in due time, we shall see whose briefs end in a ball." Maltbie left this time with neither cackle nor song.

Reese smiled at Lutz. "Grandpa sure has a bug up his ass."

"Show some respect, Jack. He's got a million of his own money in this thing. He's got a right to be testy."

"Bullshit," Reese said, waving him off. "And I've got four mill in this. You want testy; I'll show you fucking testy." He glared at Lutz with a macho look heavy with threat before leaving, grabbing his genitals on the way.

Lutz slouched forward at his desk, his face in his arms. The disrespect that Reese had shown to the professor was uncalled for. He had had enough of Reese and was determined to act on his plan. He reached down for his briefcase and brought it up on the desk, opened it and looked at the black lace panties in the baggie. *Merci, Madame.*

***

A half-hour later he appeared in the doorway of Reese's office. "Jack, Lillian's going out to run some errands and asked if you have any dry-cleaning she could pick up for you."

Reese jerked a shoulder in surprise, grinned, stood, then reached into his pocket and handed Lutz a twenty. "It's at Sunrise Cleaners: a suit and a couple of shirts." He rubbed his hands together. "It's nice to see she's finally warming up to me. Nothing sends me to Tingle Town faster than a dink-toed redhead."

"Huh?" Lutz said.

"When she wears that yellow dress that clings to her V, you can see the outline of her yo-yo." He moaned. "I'm gonna have a piece of that one day." Reese inhaled deeply through his nose. "Sweet Jesus, there's nothing better than a face full of auburn snatch."

Reese must stay focused on Lillian, Lutz thought, and nodded with enthusiasm. "I think she likes you. But, you know how they are at that age: they're moody." He was certain that Reese would eventually acquire an office conquest and had conjured in his mind a scenario where Lillian would become secretly attracted to the bully, thus saving Valerie's bosom for him.

Reese smiled. "Yeahhh, I *do* know how they are at that age. They've got puppy breath."

Lutz squinted at him, not understanding the comment.

"Young chicks—you know, get 'em heated up and they pant on your neck like a puppy." He slapped Lutz on the shoulder.

"Yeah...right," Lutz said, and returned to his office to pace. He waited a few minutes, spread papers on his desk, sat, and called in Lillian. "Could you go out and get me a sandwich?"

"Sure," she said, "Tuna on a baguette?"

"Yeah." He stood to hand her money. "Get something for yourself...my treat. Oh." He reached back into his pocket. "And pick up Reese's dry-cleaning. It's the one across the street from the sandwich shop."

She stepped back. "Why should I do anything for that creep?"

"Hey, Lill, help me to keep the peace." She looked into pleading eyes. "Do it for me." He handed her Reese's twenty. "He's got a suit and a couple of shirts. Bring them back and hang them in here. I'll give them to him so you don't have to."

"Yeah, okay," she said, and headed out, a stiffened arm waving at the floor.

***

She returned a half-hour later and hung the dry-cleaning

over Lutz' door and put a bag and Reese's change on the desk. He motioned to the chair across from him. "Why don't you join me so we can talk?" She looked at him suspiciously, put her sandwich and Coke down, and sat.

He unwrapped his sub and said, "Did you know that you can slit somebody's throat with a day-old baguette?"

She looked up at him and frowned.

"Really," he said, entirely serious. "Not here; in France." He took a bite and spoke while chewing. "The French don't put preservatives in their breads like we do." He snapped the roll with a finger. "The crust gets so hard; after a day they're like shards of glass. The French choke on them all the time."

"I didn't know that," she said, on the way to her first bite. She chewed, took a drink and said, "The professor didn't flirt with me today. I've never seen him mad like that before."

"Nor have I."

"What's going on?" She studied him as he wiped mayonnaise from the corner of his mouth. "It's Reese, huh?"

"Yeah. The professor isn't taking too well to our new investor."

Lillian put her sandwich down. "I don't know if I should tell you this." She hesitated, looked towards the window then back at him. "The first week Reese was here, he kept getting calls from a lawyer. I gave him the messages, but he would never call back."

He sat up. "What did the lawyer want?"

"He told me that if Reese didn't call him back, his client would take it to the next step."

"What does that mean?"

"Well, Reese didn't return that call because the lawyer called the next day and said to tell him that a Miss Gloria Sullivan would be filing charges. I called the number back, got a law firm in Belmont and hung up."

"Who's Gloria Sullivan?"

She shook her head. "I don't know; but he sounded like she meant business."

"Well, it's Reese's problem; keep it to yourself."

She nodded assent into another bite, chewed and avoided his eyes.

He said, "You haven't told anyone, have you?"

Her immediate instinct was to lie. She hesitated then said, "I might have said something to Valerie. But she's cool."

"How are you two doing?"

Lillian lit up, chewed quickly, and swallowed. "She is *so* much fun; I've gone out with her in the evening a couple of times. She's not afraid to do anything."

That last comment made him sit up. He often fantasized about that first night. But any effort he made to repeat that evening with Valerie was quickly rejected by her and the subject changed. "Is she seeing anybody?" He said.

She thought the question was inappropriate, and looked at him strangely. "Not really; she doesn't want to get tied down. When we go out, she dances with everyone."

He saw Valerie out on the floor, twirling her arms and swaying like a hippie-chick in the mud. He believed that how freely a woman danced was an indication of her performance in bed.

She put her sandwich down and started to wrap it. "Can I ask you something?"

"Sure."

"Where did Reese get all his money?"

"I have no idea. You'd have to ask him." She was doing an inadequate job of acting naïve so he probed. "Why do you ask?"

"Phil said he checked him out with his stockbroker buddy

in Pittsburgh and *he* said Reese is a high-roller. Phil's buddy has a stripper friend who works in a club on the outskirts of the city. She said Reese is in there weekends all the time. He thinks nothing of dropping thousands in a night on champagne and lap dances."

"You're kidding." He put down his sandwich.

"Really. She said they love to see him come in."

"Wow," he said, sitting back.

Lillian leaned in discreetly, though they were the only two present. "She said he's got a favorite there who he goes in a back room with."

His eyes involuntarily flashed that he wanted to know more. "Is that legal in Pennsylvania? It's not in this state."

"You're asking me?" She brushed her skirt, stood, and took her sandwich. "I gotta get some work done for Phil." She left.

He waited a moment, then brought the briefcase up again, opened it, and took out a pair of latex gloves. He put them on with the efficiency of a surgeon then took the panties from the baggie, turned them inside-out, walked to the doorway—his hands behind him—and peeked around the corner. He took the dry-cleaning from the top of the door, closed it, and placed it on the top of his desk, lifted up the plastic wrap on Reese's suit pants and rubbed the panties along the inside of the fly and leg seams, muttering in self entertainment: "Avec the lee-say...avec the lee-say."

When the transfer was completed, he put the panties and gloves into the baggie, put it into his briefcase then opened his notebook, anxious to record his progress. He put a checkmark against PHASE 1.

SHE'S ON, HOUSTON!

Blowfly: of the genus *Calliphora* and related
genera that lay their eggs in rotting meat, dung,
carrion and open wounds. (family *Calliphoriae*)
-The Collins English Dictionary

The following week, the GrannyCam successfully triggered for the first time when Eloise entered the kitchen. She moved to a cabinet and bent over for a pan then shuffled to the refrigerator and took out a carton of milk and an egg, placed them on the counter, then went to the sink and found a glass and rinsed it. She filled it half-way with milk, scratched her behind then reached under the sink, brought up the jug and topped off the glass. Hinckel looked up from his keyboard, saw the broadcast on his monitor and shouted, "She's on, Houston!"

An engineer exploded from his chair to get Lutz while everyone crowded around the monitor, murmuring with excitement.

Eloise ran water into the pan then stopped and brought it to her face. She sniffed, then poured it out and turned the pan upside down on the counter.

"It must be dirty," a female engineer said.

She went back to the pots-and-pans cabinet just as Lutz entered the lab with Lillian. He scanned the room quickly for Valerie and eyed her bending over a printer working patiently on a paper jam, turned away, then stole a second look before turning to the monitor.

He slapped Hinckel on the back and sat, admiring the quality of the video. "Pixels look great." He studied his mother's image. "Beautiful," he said. "How's she doing?"

Eloise was in the same shrunken nightgown that crossed above her knees. Lutz shook his head and—loud enough for Valerie to hear—said, "I bought her two nightgowns and a housecoat for her birthday."

Hinckel rubbed his hands together then held them out like a concert pianist ready to perform. "We loaded the new zoom release last night. This is our first live test." He typed commands and the camera moved in for a close-up as Eloise bent over to get another pan. A collective groan filled the room. She wore no underpants. The portal that introduced her son to the world fifty years earlier now filled Hinckel's screen.

Lutz yelled, "Jesus Christ, turn it off!" Hinckel jerked in the chair and punched at the keys but the video continued. "Turn the fucking thing off!" Lutz lunged and slapped at the keyboard but the image remained on the screen. "Turn it off!" Lillian moved calmly between the two of them, pressed the 'Power' button on the monitor, and the screen went black.

"*Jesus.*" Lutz glared at the head engineer. "Why didn't you shut it off?"

"I tried, Bob." His nostrils spread and he coughed. "I tried." Hinckel coughed again to disguise hysteria and caught snot in his palm. Half the engineers in the room coughed also and bolted for the door.

"Come," Lillian said to Lutz. She looped her arm firmly through his and jerked, prompting him to rise. They walked out of the lab directly to his office, locked together, and she deposited him in his chair.

She pulled a chair to his side of the desk to face him, sat, and jabbed a finger at him. "Calm down," she said. "You're out of control."

"*Excuse* me," he said.

"You're self-centered, abusive and moody."

He looked at her, then down, defeated.

"Who the hell do you think you are? You've put us through two months of agony. Your people work hard and you don't give them the time of day." She looked him up and down with disapproval.

He looked up. "Young lady, I work hard, too. I'm here—late—every night."

"Do you ever think to stop in the lab on your way out to say 'good night'? They'd certainly appreciate that. Hinckel hasn't had a day off in over a year. Wise up."

He sulked. "You don't understand."

"Give me a *break*," she said. "You come in here from a huge corporation where you managed thousands of people and you can't lead a handful of renegades? Spare me." She looked away, annoyed.

He looked down with a sigh.

She bolted up, started pacing, turned and flailed an arm. "And what are you going to do about Reese?"

I hate that bastard, he thought. "What do you mean?"

She had her hands on her hips, a toe tapping. "He's running roughshod over the engineers. Hinckel's going to walk if you don't get that jerk away from him."

"What's he doing?"

She raised a balled fist. "He's on Hinckel every day. Wants to know when the new release will go live."

He spread his arms to her. "He's an investor. He has a right to ask those questions."

"Well he's been hounding the women, too."

Lutz sat up. "Who?"

"He's been hitting on a woman engineer since he got here. Now he's eying Valerie."

A jolt of jealousy found his stomach. "What do you mean?"

"He's a pig, Bob. Always making weird remarks. Thinks he's funny."

"Like what?"

"I dropped something at the copy machine the other day while he was walking by. He says, 'You're a bad little girl. I may need to give you a spanking.' That's weird."

He waved her off. "All guys flirt like that. It's a guy thing."

"Uh-uh," she insisted. "He's got a look. He's weird." Her eyes grew. "Then he told Rosemarie that if she and a girlfriend came over to his place for a pillow fight, he'd give them each a hundred bucks."

"Get out!"

She poked her finger in her mouth, Valley-girl style. "He wants them to dress up like cheerleaders." She studied Lutz for a reaction but got none. "He's a creep. Rosemarie could get him in serious trouble."

"What would you like me to do?" His tone was more of a plea than a call to action.

"Keep an eye on him."

"Okay," he said, and lowered his eyes.

"Hey."

He looked up. She was gauging him, her jaw firm.

"Lead," She said.

"What?"

"Step up and lead."

"I'm trying to do that," he said, with a pout that bordered on effeminate.

"Well it's not evident to the people in the lab. They never see you. At least Phil goes in there every day and works with them; brings them pizza in the evening." Lillian started to leave, stopped, and pointed at him. "I'm serious about this. You keep that tomcat away from us or we'll take his eyes out."

He nodded, stewing in the news that Reese was preparing to move on Valerie.

She started to leave again and turned, suddenly uneasy with the confrontation. "Are you going to be okay?"

"Yes," he said. "Please close the door behind you."

She mouthed 'lead' again and began to back through the door, hesitated in thought, stopped and re-entered. "By the way, do you mind if Valerie moves in with me?"

"Huh? Why would I mind?"

"She can't find an apartment within her budget and has been commuting from New Hampshire." Lillian smiled. "I like her a lot. I've got a two-bedroom; we can share expenses. I won't tell her what goes on in here."

Lutz wrinkled his forehead. "What does that mean?"

Lillian began to blush. "You know, I won't tell her stuff about the business."

"Yeah, sure." Lutz said, anxious for her to leave.

He spun in his chair and started dialing.

His brother answered, "Pete Lutz."

"Pete, I want you to buy some underpants and bring them over to Ma."

"Why?"

"You want everyone to see where you and I came from?"

"What are you talking about?"

"Go to Marshall's and get the biggest ones they've got. I don't want them too snug."

"Huh?"

"Just do it." He slammed down the phone.

Fucking Reese. Hitting on my Valerie. He reached down for his briefcase and brought it up on the desk, opened it and took out the book he retrieved from his mother's house. He flipped through and found the photograph of the blowfly and read the notes he had written almost four decades earlier.

The blowfly will deposit its eggs on rotting flesh and open wounds. It has also been known to lay eggs into the nostril of a sleeping human with the hatched larvae using capillaries in the nose to enter the bloodstream. The adult maggot will later travel under the skin in search of an orifice. If unable to find one, it will break through the surface in search of oxygen.

"I'll lead." He leaned back with hands clasped behind his head and stared determinedly at the ceiling. *I'll lead that shitbum into madness.*

He spun in his chair, grabbed the mouse and clicked on a search engine to look for insect stores in Massachusetts. Two hits came up. He clicked on the first and went into their on-line catalogue. There it was; just what he needed: the 'Life in a Rotting-Log' insect farm. He opened his notebook to a fresh page, wrote the address of Willy's Wild Things at the top, underlined it, and began to outline an expanded plan of attack.

THE TUNGARA FROG

Tungara frog (Physalaemus pustulosus)-also
called Central American mud-puddle frog:
terrestrial, toadlike frog common in moist,
lowland sites from Mexico to northern S America.
-Encyclopedia Britannica

They spent the first half of the session discussing Pat's behavior. She returned from California but was still upset. She was wearing Estelle's thumbprint, for she was challenging him on all fronts—raising issues from years before and blaming him for discouraging her career early on. He promised to get home from work earlier but was unable to. Though she tended to her appearance more, she still mistrusted her husband, communicated little and continued to smoke— often chewing Nicorette gum as she lit. Felton suggested tools Lutz could use to reach her. He was inattentive to the doctor and would nod at each idea, his mind elsewhere. They sat in silence for minutes before Lutz continued.

"I visited my mother last week and went into my room. I hadn't been inside there for years." Lutz shook his head. "And she hasn't been in it since I went away to college...says there's frogs and snakes in there."

"Why would she think that?"

"I was crazy about insects and amphibians as a kid. I mowed lawns to get the money to collect them. The more exotic, the better."

Felton nodded approval of Lutz' early avocation.

"Ever hear of the tungara frog?"

Felton signaled early amusement. "No, I can't say that I have."

"I had one; named him Tiny." He put a thumb and forefinger an inch apart. "Full grown, he was this big. I thought I was saving that little guy from a calamitous existence. Paid twelve dollars for him. My old man was pissed."

Felton saw tightness in his patient's jaw.

Lutz continued, "As you know, most species call to attract the opposite sex. And that advertising leaves many males vulnerable to a predator's prey-detection system."

Felton nodded through a smile. "Nature finds intriguing ways to work the odds."

Lutz said, "The male tungara advertises for a mate using complex calls...a series of chucks and whines. If there isn't competition around, the male will use a simple whine only. Do you know why?"

Felton shook his head with interest.

"Because fringe-lipped bats prefer tungaras that chuck."

Felton's smile broadened. "I see a dilemma."

Lutz leaned forward to expound. "Particularly when other males are vying for the females. The male has no choice but to gamble and out-chuck competitors. It will start with a slight whine followed by a series of chucks, like a kid imitating a dive bomber. The females hop towards the chuck like groupies to Aerosmith. But the bats tune into the sound also and swoop in to grab the male. So, the more often the tungara has sex, the higher the probability he'll be eaten by a fringe-lip."

Felton said, "There's a moral there."

Lutz nodded firmly. "The more chucking I do about the weakness of others, the more likely I'll be eaten by the system."

Felton perked up, sensing the importance of what was about to happen.

Lutz looked up at the ceiling and cringed at the memory. "Know what happened to Tiny?"

Felton shook his head in support.

Lutz gritted his teeth. "My dad killed him. I had him for about a year...in a tank in my room. Seems the little guy was getting more and more frantic about never getting laid. Every night, the chucks and whines would go on for hours. I would close my eyes and imagine the skies of my room filled with dog-fighting toy airplanes." He sat back—his face taut—his jaw determined. "Tiny's nightly agonizing bugged my old man. He'd yell from his bedroom, 'Goddamnit, Bobby, shut that fuckin frog!' One night he came into my room—drunk, of course—after a fight with my mother. He was rambling; bragging about how much he knew about firefighting. 'You got your accelerants, Bobby, and you got your drafts. Your draft can be your enemy or your friend. You gotta know where to punch the hole in the roof...you gotta know your release points. Your mother couldn't put out a fire in a fuckin waste basket.' Then he reached in the tank. 'So, this is the little fucker makin all that noise.' Tiny hopped onto his finger, like I had trained him, and it spooked my old man. He lurched from the tank, reeled and dropped the frog. Said, 'Oops,' and stepped on him. 'Oops', he says. Breaks my fucking heart and all he says is 'Oops'."

"Did he apologize?"

"No. He said, 'I'll buy you a new one.'"

"Did he?"

"I didn't want another one. I wanted Tiny."

Felton saw his patient as that child and eyed him with sympathy.

"The cruel irony is that I bought Tiny to protect him from predator bats and he succumbs to the foot of a bumbling drunk." He gazed at Felton with eyes wide for effect. "Do you fucking believe that? That's why I never trust anyone to look after important things. Why I see to it myself."

"That's a powerful insight," Felton said.

Lutz swallowed hard. "I didn't realize what effect that little frog had on my behavior."

"It must have been tremendously traumatic for you."

Lutz rubbed his hands on his thighs and nodded at the floor.

Felton continued, "Many times trauma becomes hard-wired in our neurology. It's an insidious form of torment— much like the replaying of horrific scenes that bedevils the combat soldier. That frog could be the underlying cause of your anxiety when you are forced to trust something important to somebody else." He leaned forward for emphasis. "But, your father wasn't entrusted with your frog. He took it."

No shit," Lutz said. "He had no right sticking his hand in there. I couldn't have stopped him." He picked at a fingernail and gazed around the room. "I could never count on the old bastard."

"Perhaps he wasn't capable. We live in a different world. How old were you?"

"Eleven," Lutz said, full of self-pity.

"So, 1960. Parents raised in the Depression, back-to-back wars and bomb shelters in the back yard. Your father lived in a darker time. And his occupation didn't provide additional sunlight. You said he saw some pretty disturbing things."

Lutz nodded.

Lutz saw forced sincerity when Felton continued, "Perhaps it is time for you to forgive him."

He gave Felton a *'you're kidding me'* look and said, "Aren't you compelled by law to say that at some point in the therapy? Forgive him, forgive her... forgive the fucking dog. It's bullshit." He glared at the doctor. "He never apologized." Lutz put his elbows on his knees and squeezed his cheeks for a moment then looked up with mischief. "But I got even. I fucked with him real good: put a snake in his shoe; a spider in his bed; a creepy here, a crawly there—freaked him whenever I could. Eventually, he wouldn't come home. He'd stay down at the firehouse; wanted my mother to sell the house. Said it was infested. My mother said I was mean—that I put the snake in his shoe—but I never owned up to it."

"Should you, now?"

"Why?" Lutz said.

"Closure."

"Oh, come on." Lutz waived him off and shifted away.

"Perhaps your mother carries some resentment from having her husband ousted from their home."

Lutz stiffened with anger. "People need to be held responsible for their actions. He did something awful to me. I just can't let it go."

"Bob, it was forty years ago."

Lutz said, "Nah. I worked hard on that collection. I had it just where it needed to be: a contained eco-system; all catalogued and cross referenced; all future purchases scheduled and costed out. That prick." He sat back and exhaled. "I don't want to talk about it anymore."

Felton was summarizing in his mind the rat-tat-tat flow of insight, a most beautiful cadence of psychiatry. There was anger, but he recognized it as the important cathartic type, not the grumbling he was accustomed to hearing from Lutz.

Lutz said, "Do you know that the first time I got laid, I asked her to marry me?"

"Well I'm sure that there was something special about that moment with Pat."

"I'm not talking about her. I mean the first time I had sex with anyone." He gazed around the room and came back to the doctor. "I was so overwhelmed, that at climax I'd say 'Marry Me'. Pat said, 'yes'—I scared the others away."

"How is it going with Valerie?" Felton said, pouncing on the cue.

"Huh?"

"Have you been seeing her outside of work?"

"Nah, she doesn't have her own place. And now she moved in with my secretary. She's been stand-offish lately. She'll start seeing someone once she's settled. Brad's out of the picture and all of her hoodlum friends will be up in New Hampshire. She's not one to sit at home."

"So, you've abandoned any plans to see her again?"

Lutz said, "I don't know." He studied the room then came back. "Women can really fuck up a guy's head. One minute she's in my office acting sexy-like, then I don't see her for days unless I go into the lab. She's been playing hard-to-get since Reese showed up."

"Why would she do that?"

Lutz squinted at the doctor. "You're married, aren't you? You know how they are."

Felton shook his head. "Was."

"They'll make you sit in the corner and lick your dick until you're fetched. It's some sort of fucking game they find fascinating. I'll bet that's what they talk about when they go to ladies rooms in packs."

"Do you really believe that?" Felton said, surprised at the depth of Lutz' resentment.

"Listen." Lutz sat up. "So, I'm pissed all the time, but I'm really trying to get at what makes me act the way I do. I can't tell you how many hours I spend outside this office trying to understand events in my past that could have caused this; why somebody would do this to me." He shook his head and bit at a nail. "I know I'm gruff, but inside I feel exactly the same way I did when I was nineteen. I have genuinely warm feelings for people, but they'd never know." He looked over at the paintings for a moment, pensive, and returned to the doctor. "Yeah, the frog is an insight; but there's more."

Felton wanted to urge him on but elected not to probe.

Lutz continued, "You know, I love my daughter. I love that little girl so much." His eyes took on a fresh shine. "Yet, I can't pick up the phone to call her. I feel such anxiety about the thing I'm working on that I can't let go. I do the same thing to Pat. She's talking to me and I'm out ahead of her, thinking about something else."

"Have you always had a problem maintaining attention?"

Lutz shrugged. "Not when I was working on my collection. I was incredibly focused. I used to fantasize about having the biggest in the world. People would come by in buses to see it. They'd pay me fifty cents to enter and a dollar to hold Tiny. My dad could sell shots of Canadian Club for twenty-five cents, so he'd let me do it."

"When were you not?"

Lutz threw up his hands. "Every *other* time. There's always been a reason for me not completing things: in my twenties, I didn't have the money; in my thirties I didn't have the time; my forties—no inclination." He squinted to confirm his next statement as factual. "After that, you realize that most of it is small stuff. If it's not worth doing, it's not worth doing well."

Felton glanced quickly at the clock on the table next to Lutz. They were nearing the end of the session. "What if Valerie becomes more receptive to you? What will you do?"

"I don't know," Lutz said, looking away.

"Perhaps we should plan a course of action so you don't succumb?" He nodded the importance at his patient.

Lutz flipped a hand at him to dismiss his urgency. "Jesus, don't be so dramatic. I'm going to succumb? Succumb to what?"

Felton leaned forward. "Remember your use of the word 'smitten'. *And,* you did follow through on the job offer. You should be prepared if she makes an advance."

Lutz made a face. "I told you she's been stand-offish. Why would she do that?"

"You are still in her hold. We should plan your reaction if it should come to that."

Lutz thought about it momentarily. "Well, what should I do?"

Felton said, "First, do not meet with her outside of the office. There is no reason why you should see her elsewhere."

Bzzzzzzzzzzz.

Lutz looked at his watch. "Yeah, what else?"

"No alcohol."

"Is that it?"

"No," Felton said. "If she comes into your office, call somebody else in."

"Who?"

"Anyone. Don't allow yourself to be alone with her."

Lutz sat up. "That's pretty drastic, isn't it?"

"No," Felton said. "I want you to promise that you'll follow those rules."

Lutz thought about it briefly. "Okay, I promise you."

Felton rejected Lutz' pledge with a headshake. "Don't promise me; promise yourself."

"Yeah, sure," Lutz said, and began to rise.

Felton stood ahead of him and went to his desk and returned with an envelope. He handed it to Lutz. "For the last three sessions including this one."

Lutz took it. "Don't you normally send the bill to my house?"

"My accountant's system has hit a snag, so I'll be doing it this way for now." He smiled at Lutz. "Oh (he wiggled a finger over the envelope), I put next month's billing in there as well. If you pay that in advance, you can knock off ten percent."

REESE'S PIECES

Reese awoke Sunday morning in his Arlington apartment and turned over to look at the prostitute. He pulled the covers back and slapped her on a buttock that was still red from the previous night.

She bolted up, twisting to her side, briskly rubbing her cheek. "Hey! That hurt."

"Time to get up, Lovey. I gotta go to Mass."

"Yeah, *sure*," she said. "Got any coffee?"

"Yeah," Reese said, rose, and moved to the closet.

"Good," she said, and stretched an arm over the side of the bed and tapped along the carpet.

He came back, tying his robe. "Why's that good?"

"I'd love some." She started to move by him, twirling her thong on a finger. "I have to pee."

He grabbed her arm. "Get the fuck out!"

"Hey!" she said, pulling free. "What's with you?"

"Now!" He bolted from the room, came back with her bra and nylons, and threw them at her.

"Give me my fucking money," she said, stepping into her dress. She put her underthings into her purse and headed from the bedroom.

Reese went to the nightstand, got some bills and rushed after her. He stuffed them into her cleavage, grabbed her arm again and pushed her out the door.

***

"Fucking sluts," he muttered, as he straightened his tie in the mirror. He looked at his watch, opened the medicine cabinet, popped open the vial of Viagra and took two. Though it a fall morning, he would go without a coat so that prospective playmates could see how he took care of himself. He left the apartment, exited the building and walked the hundred yards to the entrance to the T and went down.

***

Father O'Malley had noticed him at last week's services. Reese had attended three Masses beginning at nine o'clock, receiving Communion at each. He sat in the front pew this week, as he had the last, and after receiving the Holy Sacrament, walked down the aisle, his head swinging left to right searching for someone. He knelt in the last pew—head bowed, lips moving, eyes peering upward.

He was looking for the tall, full-figured blond from last week, who after the eleven o'clock Mass had disappeared into a rush of people. He finished praying and stood momentarily to canvas the congregation and spotted her. She was wearing a black cocktail dress with spaghetti straps; sufficiently formal to suggest she was headed elsewhere after the service. He studied her shape a dozen pews ahead and guessed her to be a size fourteen. When the congregation stood for the sign of peace, he watched her offer a smile and a confident handshake to those around her. He gauged her to be in her mid-twenties; broad shouldered, but not too heavy.

"Go, the Mass has ended," Father said, and Reese watched her exit towards him carrying her coat. "Perfect," he muttered then stepped out and bumped her slightly as she passed. "Excuse me," he said, and put his hands around her waist to steady her. "I'm so sorry," he added with feigned embarrassment.

"No problem," she said, and displayed a smile showing attractive, white teeth—a smile likely wired in adolescence for such an occasion.

They stood outside and he took her coat and held it out to her. "A lovely day," he said.

"Thank you." She clutched a silk scarf in her hand and put it into the arm of the coat. He noticed the fullness of her breasts and moved in for a quick scent of rose. "There aren't many gentlemen around these days," she said with a Southern accent, a dash of color finding her cheeks.

Reese said, "The Lord attracts gentlemen to His house."

"How sweet," she said, smiling broader, her eyes scanning his physique.

"Where are you from?" he said, and glanced quickly at her feet. She wore high heels, short of stiletto, with a half-moon of satin on each toe. The size of her feet matched her stature. He shook from an involuntary chill.

"Now or then?" The belle replied.

"I know your accent," Reese said, and gently clasped her fingertips. "South Carolina. Can't be too far from Charleston."

"Why, that would be right where Daddy bounced me on his knee. Rutledge Street," she said, and squeezed in response.

"Well, beautiful lady, you are presently holding the hand of a Bulldog." He found her eyes and tightened his grip. "Class of '79."

"Maah, maaah," she said, the drawl thickened. "A Citadel man." She wagged a finger at him. "Daddy always said to stay away from Citadel men 'til they've been out for at least fahve years."

Reese leaned in to smell her hair. "Now, why would your daddy tell you such a thing?"

She stepped back and admired him. "Seems with all that

discipline, they spend years after graduation sowing oats and reapin trouble."

"I *do* love discipline," he said, with suggestive eyes.

"Maah, you sure are a randy ole Bulldog." She lifted her sleeve to check her watch. "And I *do* have time for that cup of coffee."

"I wasn't aware that I had asked," Reese said, an arm now around her waist. "It's too late for coffee, but just the right time for champagne." He stepped back holding her hands and took her in: from the string of pearls tight on her neck, to the thin, gold bracelet lightly imbedded in an ankle. "Look at you," he said, his own drawl now surfacing. "Praise the Lord."

ISABELLA ALREADY KNEW

Triatoma protracta, Kissing-bug; family of
Reduviidae. Will take a blood meal from the lips
or eyelids while the person sleeps and will defecate
in or near the wound while feeding. Can cause
Chagas disease, a rare form of sleeping sickness.
-www.everythingabout.net

When Phil saw Lillian standing in the doorway peering into the darkened lounge, he stood, called to her and waved her in. She walked over smiling, put her pocketbook on the table and kissed him. "Sorry I'm late." She removed her coat and draped it over a chair. "He wanted me to type up some things he had written in his notebook."

Phil's jaw dropped. "He *gave* you the notebook?"

"No," she said, as she pulled out a chair. "He tore out the pages he wanted me to type." She sat and squinted at his drink. "What's that?"

"A braincracker," he said. "Want me to get you one?"

She shot him a disapproving look as she fanned at imaginary nausea. "You know I can't drink martinis." She picked up a drink card, scanned it, made another face then put it down. "I'll pass." He reached for it, his eyes expanding— wanting her to have a beverage to loosen up—and pointed at a picture of a pink cocktail with a tiny umbrella tilted to the rim of the glass. "Get a foo-foo drink."

She shook her head. "They make me sick, too."

He put down the drink card as he sat. "Did you bring a copy of the fax?"

She shook her head. "When Reese was in the lab, I went in his office to look for it but his briefcase was locked."

He moved his chair in. "So, tell me again what it said."

Lillian was irritated by his insistence to know every detail. "Like I already told you, it was from Broadline's London office. It was on their letterhead. His partner wrote on the cover sheet: 'What we talked about. Please sign and fax back directly to the party's banker at the number below'. That's all it said. The next page was a nondisclosure agreement that didn't say what company in Europe the banker represented, but it did mention iCare."

Phil was convinced of Broadline's intentions. "They want to sell us. And you still believe that Bob knows nothing about this?"

She said with assuredness, "My bet: he doesn't have a clue."

"Has he been doing anything different the past few days: any meetings scheduled or calls from banker types?"

She replied holding a puzzled expression. "No, but he's been preoccupied with something. Every time I walk into his office, he stops writing in his notebook and closes it." She moved a hand over her wrist quickly to mimic Lutz. "Like he's working on something secret that he doesn't want me to see. Then I hear him laughing in his office. He's not on the phone or anything; he's all by himself and he's laughing. And when he leaves the office for anything, he puts the notebook away. He doesn't leave it out on his desk like he used to." She furled her nose at Phil, who was staring off in deep thought. "Was he like this when you worked with him at the last place?"

He turned to her and grimaced, unable to hide his disappointment with Lutz. "Bob changed for the worse months before he quit. Some of the guys were complaining about his lack of follow through. He was tuned out to discussions, had new strategies every week and didn't implement any of them." He reached over and squeezed her hand. "You looked cute today, hon."

She batted her eyes. "You're trying to seduce me; I know your type." She leaned in and kissed him on the cheek. "I wish Valerie hadn't moved in. We could go to my place."

"Let's get a room," Phil said, "I have a problem hearing you. I hear much better lying down."

She slapped his hand. "You are *so* fresh."

His face wore a sudden innocence.

She continued, "Something happened last week that was really weird. He asked me about Valerie: whether she's seeing anybody. It was just the way he asked; like he cared about her or something. When I said 'no', he acted pleased that she wasn't."

Phil, using no hands, went down to slurp at the surface of his cocktail then looked up. "Is she?"

She tilted her head and measured him with suspicion. "What?"

"Seeing someone?"

Lillian slapped at him again. "Why are you so interested?"

He leaned in. "Hinckel thinks they're an item. He doesn't understand why he hired her. She really doesn't have any software skills and the engineers have to spend time tutoring her." He sat back and fanned his face. "And the way she dresses. Can't you help her pick out something in the morning that's looser fitting?"

"Then don't look at her," Lillian said, and stuck out her tongue.

"Do you think they've got something going on?"

"No way," Lillian said with a flap of her hand. "I think she's got a boyfriend in New Hampshire. Last weekend she headed up there."

"Does she ever talk about Bob outside of work?"

"No, never." Then she thought for a moment. "She did ask me early on whether he was rich. When he bought his new Corvette; she wanted to know what that was all about and whether I thought that maybe he was leaving his wife. Other than that, she never mentions him."

"Something's going on," Phil said. "Why would Bob hire someone from an hour north—with no relevant experience—when our office is in Cambridge, where there's a software geek on every corner?"

Lillian defended her. "Well, she *is* extremely bright; *and* she's very perceptive of people."

Phil wedged an olive between two fingers and was maneuvering it up the inside of the glass. When he looked up to say, "What does that mean?" the olive escaped to the bottom.

She continued, "One night I was talking about Reese—y'know, how creepy he was. She said something that really surprised me. She said she likes a certain kind of man with a mean streak. She said that she thought he was kinda cute; that he didn't scare *her*—that she could handle him. Then she said that most men are lugs anyway; that they think with their you-know-whats."

"That's pre*posterous*," Phil protested, with an exaggerated pant; his tongue protruding from the side of his mouth.

"Stop, silly," she said, giggling at him. "Then she says,

'what Columbus started out to discover, Isabella already knew.'"

"What is that supposed to mean?" he said, while making another two-fingered attempt at the olive.

She squinted with feigned support of Valerie's claim. "You heard me; she thinks *all* guys are lugs."

Phil acted hurt and looked at her innocently. "Me, too?"

She reached for his fingertips. "You are *too* cute when you do that, Phil Breen. You look like a sixteen year-old." She pushed her chair back and stood. "Come on; let's go to your place. We need to get that wax out of your ears."

"Huh?" He said—a hand cupped to his ear—and stood, put three fingers into the glass this time, popped the olive in his mouth and grabbed their coats.

***

While Phil and Lillian were striving for auricular betterment, Lutz was engaged in an uplifting discussion with the proprietor of Willy's Wild Things just to the west of them in Belmont.

"Jesus," Lutz said, holding up and rotating the 'Life in a Rotting-Log' insect kit, I wish they had these when I was a kid. I had to bring in debris from the woods and use manure to jump-start it. It'd stink up my room and my old man would get the red-ass." He held it up to the light and checked underneath. "How much you want for it?"

The owner, a middle-aged, dumpy looking bearded guy in a button-down, beige, moth-eaten sweater, pointed to the sticker on the side of the kit. "They've been $29.95 since I bought this place—and that's going on three years."

"It's too big," Lutz said. "I need something that would fit—say—inside a plant. You know, I want it disguised." He squinted across the counter. "It's for my kid... his mother has a thing about bugs so we need to put it somewhere where she won't find it."

The owner put his hand on a product he had shown Lutz earlier and had put to the side. "Then you can't go with the Praying Mantis Nursery either. That would be too big, also."

Lutz eyed the dimensions of the box. "Yeah, we gotta stay smaller."

The owner then reached underneath the counter and brought up a green, plastic cylinder about five inches high and three inches in diameter. "Try the Bug House. We can customize a solution for your boy by combining a few features from the Rotting-Log and the Mantis Nursery and fitting them into the Bug House."

Lutz was pleased with the owner's accommodative spirit and shook his head enthusiastically. "That would work," he said.

The owner continued, "You'll need some mantis clusters, some egg-laying dishes, a dozen or so cotton swabs—your boy will have to wet them occasionally to provide a source of water—and a fruit fly culture kit." He reached underneath again and brought up a baggie of fruit flies and pushed it towards Lutz. "...to feed the baby mantises once they hatch. These are the wingless ones."

Lutz nodded, impressed. "How many mantids could I expect from each cluster?"

"Twenty-five to thirty," the owner said, holding a cluster in his palm and poking it gently with a fingertip. "But once the mantids hatch, he'll have to move each to its own vial, or they'll eat one another."

Lutz shook his head. "Geez, look where we've come. I had to get food to my guys by leaving a banana in my room and picking the fruit flies off one by one and feeding them individually." He smiled in admiration, sweeping his hand at the products on the counter. "This stuff is terrific."

The owner said, "Well, let me put this all together for you," and turned to leave.

"Wait," Lutz said. "Do you know where I can get some kissing-bugs?"

"Huh?" The bug merchant, looking for signs of a leg-pull, started to smile then saw that Lutz was serious. *"Triatoma protracta?"* He said, with a look and tone of full disapproval. "You don't want your boy raising the Assassin Bug, do you?"

"No, no," Lutz said, picking up the Bug House to admire it. "I run a health care company and we're doing research on anti-venom serums for Chagas disease." He put it down, took an iCare business card from his wallet and handed it across. "I can't use the larval stage. I need a couple of three year-olds that can bite now. We'll have them feed on lab mice in phase one of our research and go from there."

He studied the business card. "Mr. Lutz, you'll have to call a big supplier that handles the labs." He smiled, intrigued by such research. "I can't get those blood sucking cone noses."

"Do you know who can?"

He measured Lutz with increasing confidence. "You might call the Entomology Departments of universities in the southwest."

Lutz shrugged at him. "I haven't a clue where to start."

He went into the back room and came back moments later with a slip of paper, handed it to Lutz and pointed at the top entry. "Try them first; they're a wholesale supplier out of San Diego. If they can't help you, call the next guy; he's a former classmate of mine who teaches at Iowa State."

"Thank you so much," Lutz said, genuinely pleased with his cooperative new friend.

"You're quite welcome, Mr. Lutz," the owner said, happy to see insects in a position to contribute to medical science. "Well, let me put the kit together for your boy. It will be just a few minutes." He turned with the Bug House to re-enter the back room.

"Oh," Lutz said, waving and raising on his toes to call after him. "Could you throw in some bed-bug eggs?"

YOU'RE NO GOOD, BOBBY

Monday morning, Eloise entered the kitchen and triggered the GrannyCam. She moved to the refrigerator for milk then to the sink, rinsed a glass and filled it half-way. She reached under and took up the jug and topped off the glass, started to drink then stopped and put her nose in it. She looked up at the camera, muttered something, set it down and left the kitchen.

Hinckel was typing and said to the room, "Mrs. Lutz is on."

"Should I go get Mr. Lutz?" An engineer said.

Hinckel smiled at the monitor. "Let's not," he said.

Eloise returned carrying a wooden stool and put it down in front of the refrigerator. She put her hands on the seat and moved a foot onto the bottom rung. Her face, twisted with anger, filled Hinckel's screen.

He chuckled. "She's talking to us."

An engineer came over to look. "Wow, she's pissed."

She began a two-handed reach for the camera when suddenly her face disappeared from the screen. *"Shit."* Hinckel worked the keyboard to scan the room. She was on the floor, motionless, a leg twisted underneath. "Call 9-1-1!"

***

Eloise Lutz lay in the hospital bed. Pete and his wife Denise were at her side while Pat sat at the end of the bed stroking the old lady's foot through the sheet. Bob walked in and threw his coat at a chair as Pat sprang to her feet. "Where have you been? She had x-rays over three hours ago." Then she mouthed, "She-broke-her-hip."

"I got hung up," he said, and went over and kissed his mother. "How are you doing, Ma? Did they give you something for it?"

Eloise suddenly appeared upset. She raised a hand and flicked an arthritic finger at Pete. "You," she rasped.

Pat looked at the nurse quizzically and whispered, "What does she want?"

The nurse said, "She wants him to leave."

Then Eloise rasped, "yous" and pointed at the ladies, then curled the crooked finger at Bob. The nurse flicked her chin at Bob. "She wants you all to leave so that she can speak to him."

The three of them went over to Eloise and kissed her and moved from the room followed by the nurse. Pete, backing out, said, "I'll be back tomorrow, Ma."

The old lady stared at him for a full minute before he shifted uncomfortably and looked away. "Come here," she said.

Bob approached and put his face down next to hers.

"Remember when your father died? It was right here in this wing."

He nodded.

"He wanted to see you, but you didn't come."

He shook his head with sadness.

"He always wanted to get close to you. How come you never spent more time with him? He saw so many bad things. He loved his boys. But you were always too busy for him. Busy in your room with those bugs and snakes. You should have spent time, Bobby."

He straightened and backed away. "Yeah, Ma."

"And when you let those things loose in the house. Why did you do that?"

"Ma, they needed to expand their environment. I got most of them back."

"You did it to get back at him because of the frog."

He spread his hands. "Ma, I remember; I got them all back."

"Maybe you did," Eloise said. "You had Petey tell him that you were missing a snake. He told me." The old lady sneered at her son. "You know how those things gave your father the willies."

"I'm sorry, Ma. I didn't mean any harm."

"That's why he spent so many nights down at the station. And when he did come home, he slept with his shoes on."

He puffed his cheeks and forced a stream of air.

"Petey said it was a garter from outside."

His head shook with denial. "Ma, it was a long time ago. I don't remember anything about a garter snake."

"You put it in his shoe, Bobby." She measured his face with disgust. "I know you did."

He took another step back, anxious to retreat. "It was a long time ago, Ma, I don't remember too much from that time."

"I used to tell him that young people are selfish—that you'd grow out of it—but I was wrong. You're no good, Bobby." She flicked the finger again. "Get out."

He left his mother's side, grabbed his coat and went in the pocket for his cell phone. He listened to the first message: *"Hello there. I just called to see how your mother is. We're all worried about her. If you get this message, maybe you could meet me at the 'Steak and Ale' for a drink."* He smiled, pumped his fist, and left.

Pete and the ladies saw him grinning as he approached the waiting area and they walked to him.

Pat said, "What did she want?"

Bob put an arm around her and the other around Denise. He sniffed. "Just to say that she loved me."

"Ohhh, how sweet," the ladies chimed in unison.

Pete came over and put an arm around his older brother and kissed his cheek. They entered the elevator as a family: three sniffling, one beaming.

"Hey," Pete said, "Let's go get something to eat—my treat—and we can talk about Ma's care when she gets out."

Bob looked at his watch as the ladies nodded at the idea. "I've got to get back to the office to finish up a few things." Pat looked down and shook her head.

***

He entered the 'Steak and Ale' and spotted her in a booth, her back to him. She was wearing a string of costume jewelry around her nape. He wanted to approach quietly and nuzzle his face into her neck, caress her ponytail—smell her. She would say, *'Oh hi, Sweetie'* and twist away, tickled. *'I missed you.'*

"Hey," he said, and swung in across from her.

She crinkled her face with concern, reached over and put a hand on his. "How is she?"

"She'll be okay." He looked at the angel face that offered comfort; "hip," he said.

Valerie gasped. "She broke it?"

"They all do eventually," he said, eyeing her beer then craning at the bar for a waitress.

She shook her head. "They say that old people die soon after they break a hip." She put her fingers to her lips. "I'm sorry, that was insensitive."

"No problem," he said, stretching up to look at the bar again. "She's a feisty old broad." He smiled at her and took her in. He missed her; hadn't seen her in days. "How's the job?"

Her face lit. "I love it, love it, *love* it."

He lied to her through a smile. "Hinckel seems real pleased."

She sat back, surprised. "I didn't think he cared much for me."

"Why do you think that?"

"I caught him making a face behind my back." She stuck out her tongue at him to ape the head engineer and he looked for the little hole that anchored the pearl.

"He's a nerd," he said, with a knowledgeable air. "They don't communicate very well." The waitress came to the table. Lutz looked at Valerie's nearly finished beer. She shook her head at the waitress, declining another. "I'll have a Bud and a shot of Irish whiskey," he said.

The waitress said, "I can only serve you one drink at a time," as she scanned the room for customers. "It's the law," she added.

He reached over for Valerie's beer, chugged the remaining foam, and put the bottle on the tray. "Bring *her* the shot."

"Yeah, sure." She snapped her gum, crammed her order pad into the back of her pants and left.

He sat back and took Valerie in, studying her features— the ones he saw each night in his darkened bedroom. "You look nice."

She looked down, momentarily embarrassed, then up at him. "I guess you don't want to talk about your mother. Can we talk about something else?"

"Sure," he said, "whatever you'd like."

She sat up. "Why is Reese on Hinckel all the time about lines of code?"

"What do you mean?"

"He asks him in the morning and again when he leaves for the day: 'How many?' and writes it down."

Lutz said, with the polished air of a CEO, "Software start-ups, if they don't have revenue—and most of them don't—use completed lines of code as a measure of value. Another is the number of engineers employed in the company. VCs believe that core technology is the real value when you don't have any customers." The waitress came back with the beer and the shot. He took both off the tray, swallowed the whiskey, and put the empty glass back. "She'll have another," he said. The waitress raised her brows, blew a bubble, popped it, and left.

Valerie squinted at him. "What do you mean we don't have any customers? I thought we were doing this for the VNA?"

"Kinda," Lutz said. "But we need to get enough of a working demo together that I can show to them. I can't call on them if I don't have anything to sell. Plus, if we show them the GrannyCam, they might get spooked about patient confidentiality. I'm holding the GrannyCam as a trump card to show after I get a feel for the personalities involved."

Valerie said, "How have the people been so far?"

"What people?"

"At the VNA," she said, with the look a parent wears when using a child's own logic to box him in.

He swallowed more beer. "Well, ah, I haven't met with any of them yet." He was peeling the label from the bottle, wanting the discussion to move on.

"Bob, how do we make money if we don't have any customers?"

He sat back and spread his arms to her. "It's not about profit with start-ups; it's about first mover advantage. We design a total in-home care solution and block the competition. One of those competitors sees our solution as their entry, buys us and markets our software under their brand. It's all about time-to-market."

Valerie said, "So, you're selling the company?"

He noticed that a guy was looking their way and leaned in to whisper, "I didn't say that."

She studied him for the truth. "The engineers think you are."

He sat up. "Why would they think that?"

"Because of how Reese is acting. He wants a demo up and running by next week. He said to drop development on the camera so "they" (she made quotation marks in the air) could see a live demo of the scheduling system."

"Who are—'they'?" Lutz said, and took another swig.

"Hinckel doesn't know—he figures you do, and are keeping him out of the loop."

"I'll look into it," he said. "Can we talk about something else?" The alcohol provided him with the courage to change the subject. "How come you're not as friendly to me lately?"

She sat back at his directness. "Huh?"

"When you first joined, you came into my office two or three times a day to say hello or ask a question. You don't anymore. Why are you avoiding me?"

She shrugged. "I'm busy. Plus, Phil told me that Hinckel was having a problem with me being in there. So I decided to cool it."

"Am I going to see you again?"

"Do you think that's a good idea?" The waitress came back with the shot. He downed it, jerking his head back on the belt, and placed it on the tray. Valerie said to her, "I think I'll have that beer now." He guzzled the rest of his beer and put the bottle next to the shot glass. "Bring us two."

"What do *you* think?" Lutz said, putting the query back to her.

She made direct eye contact and held it. "I don't think it would be a good idea."

He looked down, jolted by her declaration, but kept his composure. "Why?" He said, careful to not make it a plea.

"I met somebody; I've been seeing him most nights."

He sank as he looked over at the waitress, who was sauntering around tables with an empty tray, popping bubbles of acknowledgement at waving customers.

She continued, "That night at my place was a beautiful thing that happens between two people. But, it's not meant to be. You know, you being married and all." Her insincere smile was intended to comfort him.

He said with irritation, "Don't you remember what you said to me that night?"

She looked at him strangely.

"Run away with me."

She sat back. "I did?"

"Up in your apartment. That's what you said to me."

"Well…if I did…I said it only once."

A kick in the stomach. He stared at her, unable to speak. "Bob, you're married!"

"What do you mean?" His hurt moved quickly to sarcasm. "Brad is married; you didn't have a problem doing him."

"*Doing* him," she muttered, and looked away, shaking her head with disapproval.

He looked at his watch. "Shit, I'm late." He rose, reached in his pocket, slapped a bill on the table and left.

***

Pat was in the kitchen and didn't greet him when he came in. The smell of fresh coffee fought a spousal chill. "I'd like a cup," he said, and went to the bathroom and opened the medicine cabinet, grabbed his prescription, took out a pill and swallowed it. Then he broke one in half and swallowed that, too. He came back to the kitchen and sat. "Come here," he said.

She turned to him holding two cups. "What?"

He nodded at the chair next to his. "You need to know what's going on." She padded over to him in her slippers and sat.

He reached over and took her hand. "The doctor keeps increasing my prescription. He's got me up to a hundred milligrams. He said my behavior these past months is not my fault."

She studied him, her face blank, unsure of what was coming.

"Well, I never took the increased dosage."

She sat up. "Why?"

He saw Valerie's deep, blue eyes looking up at him. "I didn't want to become dependent on it. But, now I think I need to follow his advice." He jerked his head towards the bathroom. "I just took an additional twenty-five and will take seventy-five from now on and see if it makes a difference."

She said, "Shouldn't you take a hundred milligrams like he prescribed?"

"I don't know," he said. "I think you're not supposed to take it up that quickly. I'll wait to see how this change affects me." He looked at her and squinted with sincerity. "You know, none of this has been my fault. The doctor says I'm depressed."

She put her hand on top of his and gazed at him with sympathy. "Well, I could have *told* you that."

"I'm sorry I've been so mean to you. Honey, I couldn't *help* it." His thumb made circles on the top of her hand. "It wasn't my fault."

"I know, I know," she said, putting her own thumb into action. "You're going to get better."

SNOWBALLING

The next day, at mid-morning, Lillian came into Lutz' office looking flustered, wearing an extra blotch of red in her cheeks. "Hinckel wants to talk to you."

He put down the pencil. "Why do you always act as his go-between? Tell him he should just come in."

"He wants me to talk to you about it. I said, 'no way!'" She rushed to the door and spoke over her shoulder. "Want me to get him?" She disappeared before he could reply.

Hinckel entered minutes later and kicked at his shoe before starting. "We've got a problem with Valerie talking too much in the lab. It's getting disruptive to a couple of engineers, one in particular."

"Who?" Lutz said.

Hinckel pumped a thumb. "The new kid from Boston University. He's not too worldly and, y'know, Valerie's been having some fun with him. But it's gone too far."

Lutz showed no outward reaction though he felt a pang of jealousy from the words 'Valerie' and 'fun'. "What's the problem?"

"She's teasing him; telling him stories and he doesn't know how to handle it. The kid is beside himself. You gotta tell her to stop." Hinckel looked down in thought, then back at Lutz, not wanting to explain further.

Lutz, with a roll of a finger, signaled him to continue.

"She—She said this morning that she likes snowballing. You know what that is, right?"

Lutz thought for a moment. "Yeah, we did it in high school."

Hinckel reacted with surprise. "You did?"

Lutz nodded. "We did it for the benefit of the shy kids— you know, in an effort to get them more involved—so they would feel part of the group."

"Wow," Hinckel said. "Maybe I've spent too much time writing code because it's new to me." He studied Lutz then said, "Are we talking about the same thing?"

Lutz nodded with assurance. "Well, at a high school dance, a couple would start, and when the music stopped, each would choose a new partner and it would go from there. You know, it would snowball into a total participation sort of thing."

Hinckel shook his head at the floor, then looked away to collect his thoughts before returning to Lutz. "Seems there's a new form that's been introduced since your time—where the girl, ah...you know, goes down on a guy and, ah...well, he does his thing, and she, ah." Hinckel studied his shoes for a moment and looked up. "She gives it back to him."

"Aw...Jesus." Lutz jerked back in the chair and threw up his hands. "I've got a daughter, twenty. Don't be telling me this."

Hinckel said, with eyes expanding, "Young girls think nothing of doing it. It's not a big deal."

Lutz buried his head in his hands and moaned.

"She keeps taunting the kid—flicking her tongue at him while the engineers hoot in the background. You gotta talk to her."

"Hey—no way. She works for you. You tell her to stop."

Hinckel, suddenly brazen after working for Lutz for a couple of months, said, "What's she doing here, anyway? She's slowing us down. I can't let my guys stop writing code to give her help. Every time she's got a question, half my engineers stop to help. They're all fawning over her."

He jabbed a finger at Hinckel. "You're the boss. Tell them to fawn over their code or you'll show them the door. Your job is more than technical." Lutz couldn't find the right words of inspiration. His mind fought the image of a snowball*er* moving into position over a snowball*ee*. "Show some leadership for God's sake. Step up and run with the ball."

Hinckel's voice cracked. "And Reese, he's in the lab bugging me all the time. I'm a patient man, but I'm running out. He's up to something. Are you in on it?"

"In on what?" Lutz pointed towards Reese's office. "You're a board member. You've got a stake in this. Ask him yourself."

Hinckel headed for the door and bumped into Phil, who was headed in. "What's with him?" Phil stood like a hitchhiker, thumb towards the door—shaking his head.

"Employee problems," Lutz said. "What do you want?"

"You're not going to believe this. Reese wants to take me for a ride in his new Maserati."

"Why's he being friendly to you?"

Phil raised his eyebrows. "I don't know, but it can't be on the up and up."

"So, don't go," Lutz said, just as Reese appeared in the doorway dangling his car keys.

"You ready, sport? This is going to be a thrill of a lifetime; zero to sixty in four-point-five seconds. You'll need a neck brace after this." Reese slapped Phil's shoulder. "Let's go, Sparky." Phil shrugged at Lutz and followed after Reese.

***

Reese's new car was parked directly in front of the

building, parallel to the curb so that it took up two spaces, one of which was a handicapped spot. He pointed the key at the yellow piece of automotive art and the headlights blinked. "Jump in, my friend, for a thrill of a lifetime." Reese started the engine, and while Phil was putting on the seatbelt—his door still open—peeled out and headed for the exit to the main road, tires smoking.

"Jesus Christ! Stop!" Phil screamed and grabbed for the door.

Reese roared with laughter and stopped while Phil, now strapped in, put his hands on the dash to brace for the next explosion forward. "You okay, Sally?" Phil nodded and swallowed. Reese gunned the engine, popped the clutch and they squealed off.

***

Phil burst into Lutz' office an hour later feigning anger though a slight smirk suggested recent entertainment. "He's a freaking lunatic. We're speeding through Kendall Square and he point blank asks me if I'd be interested in making a substantial bonus. I ask for what, and he says 'all you gotta do is put a little lipstick on the chicken'. Do you believe that?"

Lutz' jaw dropped. "What does he want you to do?"

"I told him: 'We don't have any revenue. How can I make anything look better?' He says to make up some fake invoices to a couple of VNAs to show that we're doing transactions. I say, 'No way!' Then he's driving like A. J. Foyt over by the Fenway…" Phil thrust out an arm to shift an imaginary race car. "He sees this black chick on the corner, pulls to the curb, leans across the seat and says to her, 'Darlin, fuck me for the car?' She stands back, hand on a hip—doing that black-chick move with her head—and checks out his Maserati." Phil tried awkwardly to imitate the move. "You know, when a sister's talking to a sister—how she'll do her head to make a point." He aped the head move again with little improvement.

"Yeah, I know what you mean," Lutz said. "And?"

"Well, she leans through my window to poke Reese and says, 'Fuck you for the car? Honey, I'd fuck you for a *ride* in it.' He slaps me on the arm and says, 'Out'. She hops in and I take a cab back here."

Lutz shook his head with disgust. "He doesn't care about anything, does he?"

"*And.*" Phil tugged at his crotch. "The guy's shifting with one hand and scratching his nuts with the other." His eyes grew. "Like he's raising a family in there."

Lutz broke out in a broad grin. "*Really?* That's terrific."

Phil said, "Huh? Why's that terrific?"

"Nothing." Lutz waved a hand at him, turned away delighted, and spoke into his notebook. "If he has a plan to sell the company, why would he jeopardize that by cooking the books?" He looked up, grinning.

Phil was perplexed by Lutz' demeanor. "Why do you find this so amusing? This is serious stuff. We could get busted for fraud."

Lutz giggled. "It's your impersonation of the black girl. You've got too much white in your neck."

Phil figured he'd use Lutz' good mood to interrogate him. "What's going on, Bob? Has he said anything to you about a possible sale?"

Lutz shrugged and shook his head. "He hasn't said a word to me. Lillian thinks he's up to something, too. But if he's got a deal cooking, why wouldn't he just come in my office and say so? Why's he being secretive?"

"Well, I've got a theory and you're not gonna like it."

"What's that?" Lutz said, moderating his interest to camouflage dread.

"He wanted to sell us from the get-go. He and his buddy over in Europe already had a prospective buyer on the hook before they invested in us. When they knew we were running out of cash, they got a big percentage of us cheap then put those preference changes in if we missed some milestones." He squinted at Lutz. "Reese wanted to know how you were doing with the VNAs, *and* he smiled when he asked."

"So?" Lutz fanned the pages.

"So, how *are* you doing?"

Lutz made brief eye contact. "Not good," he said. "The head woman in Plymouth won't return my calls. What the hell can I do?"

"Bob, how did you let it get to this? I mean, why weren't you working on this sooner?"

He glared. "Hey, don't start. I got distracted with funding. I had planned to work on account generation from day one. By the end of that day, I'm working on raising money...per the professor's directive I might add."

Phil said, "Let me play out the scenario for you. A company wants to buy us. They're likely in the medical space; they're big and they have financial resources. Why would they want to buy a little company with no revenue and less than twenty employees?"

"Simple," Lutz replied. "Time to market. They don't have the competence or the time to develop a solution themselves, so they'll buy it."

Phil nodded. "Even if we don't have the relationship with the VNA."

Lutz said, "I don't follow. Are you saying that Reese put the VNA signings requirement in the document even though it wasn't critical to a sale of the company?" He put his head into his hands and rubbed both temples. He looked back at Phil. "Reese put that clause into the term sheet to get full ownership quickly so he could flip the company, take the full sale value and go off to the next deal."

Phil shook his head with a scowl. "No, he's too stupid to think that far ahead. But, his partner's not."

"So, Shanes has been the brains behind this all along."

"We're fucked, Bob." Phil looked at his watch. "You've got two weeks to sign the VNAs or they'll get to keep the first twelve million of the sale. I don't see the company going for much more than that."

Lutz waived him out of the room. "Let me get on this to see what I can do."

He opened his notebook, found the phone number and dialed.

"Hello, may I speak with Mrs. Blaine."

"That's Mrs. Blarne; may I ask who is calling?"

He erased the incorrect spelling and re-wrote his entry. "Yes, it's Mr. Lutz from iCare. Is she available?"

"And the subject is...."

"Well, I'm trying to set up an appointment to see her to discuss how my company can help the VNA automate some of your procedures. I called Monday and again yesterday, but she hasn't called me back."

"I'm sure Mrs. Blarne will return the call as soon as she is available. Her calendar is quite full this week and she's been running behind. I'll give her your message."

"Thank you," He said, and extended a middle finger to the receiver as he hung up.

He had called VNAs in Massachusetts, Connecticut and Rhode Island and had not received a return call from any. He was now thinking that perhaps he should show up at the VNA in Plymouth—it was just an hour ride from Cambridge—and sit in the lobby until the head of the association agreed to see him. That's what he did when he was a young salesman and got paid on new accounts. *I'll close the Plymouth account and reference Blarne's name to get into the other VNA operations. Yeah, that's what I'll do. Then the whole thing will snowball.* (He cringed at the last thought and the image that followed.)

He had just a week left to sign the required VNAs per the funding agreement with Broadline or the new covenants would kick in and Reese's firm would be in the catbird seat. He turned to a new page and wrote PLYMOUTH at the top and began to document a plan.

BABUSHKAS AND GROSSMUTTERS

Early Thursday morning, Valerie cradled a phone in her neck as she slipped into her skirt. "Where did it happen?"

"At the Charles Hotel. He roughed her up pretty good. Did the same to a woman in Pittsburgh."

"And you're sure that this one settled?"

"Yeah," Satch replied. "That's all my source knew. He didn't know for how much."

"See what else you can find out."

"I told you Val, it's not public information. That's all I got." He was irritated with her insistent demands. "Why Reese? Why aren't you working on Lutz like we had planned?"

"I am."

"Oh, you are?" Satch replied with sarcasm. "What are you doing?"

"Nothing," she said.

"Nothing," he echoed.

"Yeah...and it's driving him crazy."

"Well, I can't spend any more fucking time on this. I gotta jump on something else for a client."

"You'd have plenty of time if you stopped watching those *stu*pid cartoons. Call me later after you dig some more—on my cell." She hung up, checked her watch, threw on a blouse and rushed out to work.

***

Reese had already been in the office for two hours, on a conference call with the prospective buyer in Munich and with Shanes and Broadline's attorneys in London. He listened closely for any tonal hints and wrote down key questions to follow up on with Hinckel.

Shanes said, "Mr. Frye, understand that our solution is English-based in this version, but can be easily expanded for multi-language capability in future upgrades."

Frye, the head of the German company, said with intent to criticize, "Our initial focus will be on the U.S. market. Unlike the United States, most European countries have won stability in health costs. Let's just say that we put a premium on caring for our elderly and have legislated the behavior of our providers accordingly." Reese heard a snicker and assumed that it was one of Frye's underlings. Frye continued, "However, with the aging population and the advent of new technologies, we believe that those costs will begin to rise unless we introduce technologies to counterbalance those structural changes. Our plan would be to introduce your technology to your nation as a whole, work out any process deficiencies and import it back here for translations."

Shanes said, "So, you'll want to keep our software engineers to do further work on the product?"

"But, of course," Frye replied. "We are a distributor of medical products, not a software company. We would require your head engineer to stay on for a predetermined period and sign an agreement to that effect. The other engineers would be given incentives to stay also."

Reese was anxious to jump in with an insightful question or pithy comment but had no idea what the German was talking about. All he could gather from that winded declaration was that they wanted to buy iCare's engineers, not just the software.

Frye said, "Wilhelm is our Information Systems man and he has spent the last days navigating your system. He has a request to go to the next phase of our due diligence."

Wilhelm said, "First of all, thank you Mr. Reese for giving me access to your system."

Reese sat up and smiled into the speakerphone. "You're quite welcome. I hope you found it easy to navigate. We do have another feature called the GrannyCam that you and your people will see in operation upon your visit with us."

There was another snicker from overseas.

Reese said, "I said something funny?"

A new voice said, "We have *babushkas* and *grossmutters* over here, but no grannies." The line filled with hearty laughter.

Shanes said, "So how should we proceed?"

Wilhelm spoke. "I have prepared a list of technical questions that I would like a formal response to before I recommend to Mr. Frye that we go to the next step and visit with the iCare engineering team. Who shall I send it to?"

Reese said, "E-mail it to me. I'll sit down with my head engineer to go through it." Reese recited his e-mail address then Shanes spoke, "We look forward to the opportunity to work with such a distinguished firm as yours, Mr. Frye. Will there be anything else?"

"I believe we have accomplished much," Frye said. "Thank you for your consideration. Good day." The conference line beeped signaling the end of the German connection. Reese said, "Are you still on, Sumner?"

"Yes."

"Could you call me when you're done with our attorneys there so that we can summarize the action items?"

"Sure. It will be just a few minutes. *Ciao.*"

Reese hung up, raced across the floor and pumped his

fists. He walked to the door, opened it and called to Lillian. "My partner will be calling soon from London; patch him through right away."

She looked up from her keyboard and nodded at him.

Minutes later, the call came in and she buzzed Reese in his office. "Mr. Shanes for you." She put a hand over her mouthpiece as Reese spoke. "Sumner, do you fucking *believe* that?"

***

Lillian was pressing her hand so tight against the receiver that moisture was forming on her palm. She had heard enough and wanted to hang up, but was afraid that they would hear her disconnect.

"Sounds like those fucking Jerries are serious."

"Very," Shanes replied. "And, we need to think of a way to ensure that Lutz doesn't queer the deal. The silver bullet in this transaction is Hinckel. If he walks, it doesn't go down."

"I doubt that Hinckel knows that we get the first twelve million of the purchase price. If Lutz tells him; that could force a lack of cooperation."

"So, offer him something."

Reese said, "Hinckel?"

"No, Lutz."

"Like what?" Reese replied.

"Well, under the current arrangement, if we sell it for twelve million, Lutz gets nothing. How much of his own money did he put in?"

"Two hundred thousand, plus."

Shanes said, "Offer him a side deal. Tell him we'll give him that amount as a success award if he cooperates and stays away from Hinckel."

"Do you think he'll go for it?"

"What do you think?" Shanes replied.

Reese stood and smiled into the phone. "He's a spineless motherfucker. That's what I think. I'll work on him after I go through the list with Hinckel."

"Okay," Shanes said. "Do you believe this? This big a gain in only two months. Call me if you run into any snags. *Ciao.*"

Reese hung up and Lillian put down her receiver and started to run to Phil's office, stopped, then headed outside to pace in the parking lot.

WHAT A SICKO!

It was seven in the evening when Phil walked into Lutz' office. "Hey, you must need a break. Come on, I'll buy you a drink."

Lutz put his pencil down. "Sure." He rubbed at the weariness in his eyes, yawned and held an exaggerated stretch in the chair. He fanned the pages of the notebook for Phil's benefit and nodded with mock pleasure, wanting to project further progress with the VNA. He stood and went for his coat. "Where to?"

"Let's try Maxwell's," Phil said. "They pour a nice drink and it's quiet there." Lutz took his keys from the pocket before putting on his coat. "Why don't we go together in my car and I'll drop you off back here?" Phil insisted.

"Fine." Lutz moved towards the door holding his briefcase. "I'll stick this in my car so I don't have to come back in."

"Leave it," Phil said. "I want to spend a few minutes with you later to go over a couple of things."

Lutz turned and put it on his desk. "Is Reese still here?"

"No," Phil said. "He left about an hour ago."

"Is he still getting calls from Europe?"

Phil nodded. "Lillian told me he got two today. He was on one for over an hour."

"Was it from Shanes?"

"No. She didn't think so, but thought Shanes might have been conferenced in."

Lutz shook his head, stopped, waved Phil ahead of him and closed the door.

Lillian peered through a crack in the ladies room door and watched them exit the building. She rushed out, moved quickly to his office to the briefcase, got the notebook and scooted back. She went into a stall, locked it, sat, and started reading.

***

"How about tonight?" Reese said.

Valerie laughed, reached back for her ponytail and pulled it over her shoulder to play with it. "You never give it a rest, do you?"

"Come on, I'll get us a suite; order some champagne and strawberries."

She released her hair. "I don't do it in hotels," she said, wetting her lips.

He pressed. "So, when?"

"I'm close to getting my own place. We can't do it with Lillian around." She did a swayback stretch intended as a taunt. "I tend to make a lot of noise," she said, and went down on her straw, her mouth poised to sip seconds too soon.

"Blow me," he said.

"What!?"

Reese dropped his eyes, then shot them back at her, grinned, and tapped the table. "There's a crawlin kingsnake under there."

"I'm *not* going to go down on you in here." She was back at her ponytail then flipped it over her shoulder and played with his fingertips. "My apartment. Period. *And...*"

"Yuh?" Reese shifted and smiled, hoping she was about to describe a new treat.

"Why are you always scratching yourself?"

"Me?"

"Yeah." She made a face. "You're always tugging down there."

He frowned through a grin. "Jock itch," he said. "I work out a lot."

"Well, have it checked out—or we don't do anything."

"Yeah," he said, a smile exploding across his face.

***

They entered Maxwell's upscale lounge. Lutz eyed two lovelies occupying adjoining stools at the bar and moved to them with Phil trailing. "You come here often, little girl?"

A blond inebriate, who was well into sloppy—her hair headed north and her attitude south—slurred her response: "Fuck off old man."

"You're a bit disrespectful, Miss. I fought in Viet Nam."

"Who?"

Lutz smirked. "*Where* would be the correct response."

She poked her girlfriend. "Ginny, who's this fuckin guy?"

Lutz leaned in. "Sweetheart, I would love to engage you in repartee, but I'm afraid it would go nowhere, nor be remembered."

"Huh?"

"Exactly," he said.

Phil grabbed his elbow and led him away to a table where they sat—both looking at drink cards—before Phil said, "I didn't know you served in Viet Nam?"

"I didn't," Lutz replied with a smirk before turning to look back at the tipsy-ette at the bar. The waitress came over and Phil ordered a Beefeater martini, dry. Lutz looked up after a substantial delay and said, "Bring me a non-alcoholic beer and a Miller Lite."

"I can only serve you one drink at a time," she said.

Lutz squinted at her, not in the mood for an argument. "You will," he said. "One's not a drink."

"They're both beers," she insisted.

He glared at her. "If I ordered a beer and a glass of water, would you bring those?"

"Yeah."

"So, what's the fucking difference?"

She peered away. "Hey, buddy. I don't make the rules."

Phil smiled at her, trying to lighten the air. "Bob, why don't you just get a lite beer? What are you trying to accomplish?"

"I'm trying to cut down. I mix them together and I can have more."

Phil shrugged at the waitress.

"Bring me a Heineken," Lutz said.

The waitress, working off Phil's lead, did her best to accommodate Lutz. "If you wanted a lite beer, get Amstel; that's Heineken's equivalent of lite."

He dismissed her with a wave. "No. I'll take the Heineken and it's your fault."

She rolled her eyes at Phil before she left.

***

Lillian shook as she scanned the pages to get a sense of its organization. There were three distinct sections, each chronologically ordered within. Out of what seemed to be about a hundred-plus pages of entries, less than a fourth was dedicated to the iCare business and a work plan for the VNA. Much space, however, was given to insect breeding habits and development. Lutz must have been surfing the Internet for there were scores of insect websites catalogued with asterisks next to two: creepers.org and deathbug.com. She gasped on two occasions at his descriptions of insect-borne maladies. It read like the diary of an amateur spy with scripts written under a number of aliases: he was the head of a company doing research on diseases in France; a researcher of a cure for Chagas disease; a senator's son was dying of a rare sickness and he needed leeches to include in 'a remedial concoction—a groundbreaking advance recently discovered by iCare scientists.' He had two full pages dedicated to a memo that he had e-mailed to a professor at Iowa State attempting to convince him of 'iCare's control processes to manage the containment of the assassin bug'.

Another section was dedicated to dreams and appeared to have been started in the past week. For each workday there was an entry first thing with the time of the writing neatly inscribed above the interpretation. He described 'the myriad of colors' writing joyfully of mustard, bright pinks and yellows, raspberry and mauve. She moved quickly through those pages and back to the business section looking for specific information on the possible purchase of iCare. She found none and continued reading.

***

The waitress returned with Phil's martini and the Heineken for Lutz.

Lutz said, "And could I have a glass of water, please?"

She looked to the ceiling, puffed her cheeks and released a stream of air. "Now you're seriously fucking with me."

He smirked at her. "Nope. Just bring it when you have a chance."

She left as Lutz snickered and took a sip. Phil said, "Cheers," and raised his martini. He started to drink and stopped. He peered over Lutz' shoulder and spotted Reese in a far corner booth, laughing and playing with the fingertips of a female sitting across from him. She was overly animated—demonstrably flirtatious—and her ponytail brushed half-way down her bare back as she gyrated. "Holy shit!" Phil said.

"What?" Lutz began turning to see what had gotten Phil's attention.

Phil said, "Don't. It's Reese."

Lutz turned anyway. "Valerie," he muttered.

"*Fuck* me," Phil said, his face frozen. "That *is* Valerie."

Lutz jerked and elbowed his drink, toppling it.

"Let's go," Phil said, as he took out a bill and grabbed his coat. He began to leave, and after a step, came back to hoist his martini, spilling half of it as he gulped. He wiped his chin as he rushed out followed by Lutz, who turned—his heart pounding—and craned for a last look at Valerie, who released a peg from her ponytail and swooshed her hair like a pole dancer in a strip joint. He stumbled over a chair, straightened it, and then trotted after Phil.

They got outside into a light rain, both moving briskly. Lutz was hyperventilating. *That bastard. That whore.* He didn't know who to be more angered with. *How could she be interested in such a bum?* Phil headed straight to the car while Lutz, confused, was in a circular path, covering a lot of ground but no distance. Phil went to him and guided him to the car. They got in. Phil said, "I don't believe it. Did you see how she was acting towards him? And what was with that dress? At first I didn't think she had anything on."

"Take me back to the office," Lutz said, refusing to discuss what they had just seen. "I need to get my briefcase."

"Un-fucking-believable!" Phil was shaking his head. "The guy's a little old for her; wouldn't you think?"

"Shut up!" Lutz said, and glared at him, his chest heaving.

He drove another hundred yards. "And what was that thing in her hair. You could shish-kebab for four on that."

"*Shut* the fuck up!"

Phil crept along, worried that they'd get back to the office before Lillian finished with the notebook.

Lutz barked, "Why are you going so fucking *slow*? Let's go. *Move* it!"

He sped up another ten miles per hour, drove a few minutes and turned in the wrong direction.

Lutz squealed, "What are you *doing*? You should have turned left."

"Shit," Phil said, and made a U-turn.

***

Then she found a section that was particularly disturbing; it was dedicated to Valerie. He printed her name using different styles and penciled the letters in. She got through the first three pages then came to the notation at the top of the fourth: VALERIE LUTZ. She gasped and slammed it closed, her heart pounding, left the stall, opened the outer door slightly and peered out. Then she ran to his office and put the notebook back.

***

They drove into the parking lot and Phil stopped the car in the direction of Lutz' office. He flicked the lights before shutting it down—a warning to Lillian. Then he hit the horn. "Oops," he said to Lutz. "Sorry." Lutz bolted from the car and headed inside. Phil trotted after him. Lutz entered his office and went to the briefcase, opened it and looked at the key he had copied from the original in Lillian's desk. Phil breathed with relief when he saw the notebook. Lutz closed it, picked up the briefcase and left.

***

He pulled into the garage and left the car running, entered the kitchen and rushed past Pat to the cellar door. He came back up the stairs with a package wrapped in a white towel.

"What's that? Where are you going?" She said.

"I gotta get back. They're waiting for me at the office."

He drove to a municipal parking lot next to a stop on the transit line, parked, took the key from his briefcase, put the package under his arm and exited the car. He walked briskly for a block and a half through a raw, bone-chilling mist, then went down a stairway and entered the T.

Three stops later, he exited to the top of the stairway, stopped and studied the building. He walked to the front door, put the key in, entered the lobby and took the stairs to the second floor, then moved quickly down the corridor to apartment 204, inserted the key and stepped in, closing the door quietly behind.

He had rehearsed this repeatedly in his basement, with a best time of eight minutes. He turned the lights on and moved to the kitchen and put the package on the table, then went to look for the plant he had picked out for Lillian to send. It was in the living room—not his first choice. After he brought the plant into the kitchen, he removed the towel from around the kit, checked his watch and started in.

He left the center stalk intact—the most prominent of the six—and removed a growth next to it, dug out more of the depression and inserted the Bug Farm cylinder. Then he took out a syringe and moistened the mantis cups with sufficient fluid to last for a week or so, depending on how warm Reese kept the apartment. He covered the top of the cylinder with a thin layer of dirt and spooned the excess into a baggie, looked at his watch and was suddenly overcome. *Fucking bastard. Fucking whore.* He hated the two of them.

He finished with the plant and returned it to the living room. He stepped back to study it then moved back to the kitchen for the blowfly larvae, put on rubber gloves, walked to Reese's bedroom, turned on the light and entered the bathroom.

Moments later, he was back in the kitchen for the *piece de resistance.* He took both assassin bugs out and placed them carefully on the table followed quickly by a plastic cup over each. He slid the first cup to the edge of the table and dropped one into his gloved hand—stroking its head gently—then turned and moved to the den. Back to the kitchen, he repeated the process then headed to the bedroom to plant it in a predetermined spot.

Back at the kitchen table, he started the clean-up process, putting the cups into the towel and using the side of his hand to move spilled dirt to the baggie. He used a non-fragrant cleaner to spray the table, wrapped everything neatly and prepared to leave. He checked his watch, started to the door then stopped, turned, and eyed the bedroom. *Why not have a look around?*

He found an envelope under a paperback novel in the nightstand, opened it and viewed the top photograph in the stack. "Holy shit!" He flipped to the next one and slapped his forehead. "What a *sicko*!"

I'M A DIRTBAG

The next morning, Lillian paced the living room in pink flannel pajamas that were covered with frolicking kittens. She stopped to sip her tea, cradling the cup in two hands to counter the chill of the subject matter. "I don't get it. He wrote *talk to the doctor about this one* at least three times in the dream section." She turned to Valerie, her eyes cutting and darting, searching for an answer. "What doctor?"

"Has he ever received a call from one at work?"

"Never," Lillian said, back to pacing. She stopped, furled her brow in thought, and spun. "He goes out every other Friday at the same time. He told me he's got a back problem and sees a therapist for it. But he never complains of back pain." She bugged her eyes at Valerie. "Do you think he's seeing another kind of therapist?"

Valerie jumped up. "That's it! The first time I met him." She caught herself and hesitated. "You know, when he interviewed me the first time, he was talking goofy-like. I even asked him if he was seeing a shrink."

"You asked him that in an *interview?*"

"Oh." Valerie was good on her feet. "We were talking about medical benefits and stuff and it just came up. I think he might have said something about how the insurance covered therapy. I don't remember exactly. It wasn't as weird as you think; you had to *be* there."

"Well, what did he say?"

Valerie spread her hands and shrugged away the need to respond.

"Do you think we should find out who the doctor is and go talk to him?"

"We?" Valerie said, with a firm shake of refusal. "I'm not getting involved in any of that."

"Maybe Phil will go with me."

"No way. If he is seeing a psychiatrist, you can't just go and talk to them. Hinckel says there are all kinds of laws about patient confidentiality. They can't just talk to anyone about a patient of theirs. Especially shrinks."

"What if we say that Bob is in danger? That he could hurt himself."

Valerie said, "You really think that he would?"

"I don't know." Lillian put the cup down and sat, rubbing a finger into each temple. She looked up. "What if he's planning to hurt somebody else?"

"Who?"

Lillian shook from an involuntary spasm. "He had all kinds of creepy stuff in the notebook about bugs: how different ones can get inside a person and crawl through the skin and come out of different holes and stuff."

"Get out!"

"I'm not kidding, Val. He totally weirded me out. He even had some pictures that he printed off the Internet. Icky stuff: worms and maggots—yuck." She swallowed hard and clutched at the neck of her pajama top.

"Have you talked to Phil about this?"

"I couldn't. I left the office before they got back and I was too upset to talk to him last night." Lillian was particularly spooked about the section dedicated to Valerie; *that*, she was not going to tell her roommate about. It was too unthinkable a thing for an older man to do. *What would he do next? Stalk her?* Her mind saw the inscription: VALERIE LUTZ and she jumped up again to pace.

"Lill, don't you think you should?"

"What?"

"Talk to Phil," Valerie said to her back.

Lillian turned, wide-eyed. "I'm going to tell you something. You promise not to say anything?"

Valerie pursed her lips and locked them with a key.

"Reese is planning to sell the company."

She sat up. "He can do that?"

Lillian nodded nervously. "I listened in on a call. They pulled a trick on Bob so that they get all the money. He has no idea that they're so close to doing it."

"Well, Phil must know that."

"He does," Lillian replied. "He said that there's nothing we can do. They got Bob to sign off when Professor Maltbie was away."

Valerie shrugged at Lillian then smiled strangely, suddenly amused by the goings-on.

Lillian fought the image of Lutz smiling at bug pictures on the Internet and wished Phil was there to calm her. "And why are you moving out, Val? This is all too creepy for me. Why don't you stay here until this is over?"

"Lill, I told you. I need my own place."

"Why all of a sudden?"

"It wasn't all that quick. I've been thinking about it all along. You know I'd like to have guys over."

"They can stay over here," Lillian insisted, with a wave of an arm towards Valerie's bedroom.

Valerie shook her head in a way that convinced Lillian to drop it.

***

Bob sat on the edge of the bed rocking, his head in his hands, still at home at eight o'clock in the morning. "I took it up to a hundred milligrams before I went to bed."

Pat massaged his back with the meat of her palm in firm, supportive strokes; the way a stronger mate will instinctively rub at weakness. "What happened last night that you would come home so upset?"

"I don't want to talk about it," he said, and walked to the closet for a moment and came back, not knowing what he intended to find there.

"You tossed and turned all night. You usually settle down after a while. Is it the medication?"

"No. It's my life. It's falling apart." Valerie, Miss Hussy-Flaunt, flashed in his ever-racing mind: she was swooshing her hair at Reese in some kind of bird-like, pre-copulation ritual. "I have to get out of this." His yawn jimmied his jaw before expanding. "And I keep having these weird dreams. I feel like I've been working all night. I wake up exhausted."

"Are they nightmares?" Pat said.

"No. They're busy-like. I'm always working on something important, but I can never get it done. I wake up in a sweat. Beat."

Pat said, "I read about your medication in *RedBook*. A hundred milligrams is a lot. Most people are on fifty." She reached for his hand. "You're not going to hurt yourself, are you?"

"Huh?"

"There was an article about suicides by people on antidepressants."

"No way," he said, and looked at her strangely,

momentarily intrigued by a new option. "I need to take it up to get my mind clear. I need to think of a way out of this." He stood and moved to the bathroom to shave and shower. He started to run the water then stuck his head around the corner. "I haven't been seeing the doctor every week like I said I would. I lied to you."

She got up and walked to him. "Why?"

"And, the IRA money wasn't a loan. I put it into the company. I lied to you about that, too."

He expected a reaction of rage, but she remained calm. "Bob, why?"

He sunk further. "Because, I'm a dirtbag."

SPRINGTIME IN NOVEMBER

Phil said, "Knowing Bob, it would have to be a male." Lillian disapproved of the comment and her eyes told him so. "There are plenty of competent women psychiatrists," she countered.

"Trust me on this. He's seeing a guy."

"So, you can still go." She turned away. "I don't want to do it."

"Lill, they can't talk to anybody about one of their patients, but you're a non-threatening, sweet, young woman. I bet he'll at least agree to hear you out."

"I'm not going to do it," she insisted.

"You have to. If something happens and somebody gets hurt, how will you live with yourself?"

"If he is planning something, it's probably Reese who's going to pay. Why should I do something to help that creep?"

"Hey, I feel the same way. But, this is about Bob, not Reese." He walked to Lillian and gripped her shoulders. "We can't sit on the sidelines and watch him do something that will get himself put away. He's planning something. You told me what was in his notes. We need to step in and stop it before it goes too far."

Lillian broke away, rubbing a hand up and down her arm briskly to erase the goose bumps. "Won't the psychiatrist have to report it to somebody—the cops or something? Won't Bob get in trouble?"

"Not if we stop it in time. We catch it, and they won't have anything to charge him with."

She turned. "Why can't we call his wife and tell her?" Phil made a face to dismiss the idea. "And what's she gonna do?"

"I don't know," Lillian said, as she sat and buried her face in her hands. She looked up suddenly. "What if he's planning to do something to *her*? What if he's going to poison her with bugs or something?" She put her face back in her hands and rocked. "This is oh so creepy."

"It's Reese, hon. It has to be."

She looked up after a moment. "I'm not doing it."

"Lill, you have to."

"I'm not, I'm not, I'm *not*."

"Baby," Phil said, moving in for a convincing hug. "You have to."

***

While Phil continued to work Lillian, Reese had just entered Lutz' office and sat and grinned at him while he talked on the phone with another uncooperative VNA gatekeeper. "I understand," Lutz said, with his voice barely above a whisper. "Do you think she'd see me if I came down there and sat in the lobby until she had a few minutes?"

"Sir, you'll have to speak up. I didn't hear what you said just then."

He stood, nodded at Reese and pointed over his head at the door. When Reese got up to close it, Lutz disconnected from his party but kept talking—substantially louder. "Well, Judy, I look forward to our next meeting on Friday and I'm *so* excited about the prospects, too. We're going to make a great team together. Yeah, the VNA and iCare. I can't wait until the

Boston Globe runs a full pager on this." He fanned through his notebook and took out a freshly sharpened pencil. "Tell me the address again for the gala." He scribbled. "Give my best to your husband, Charlie. Yes, tell him I'll see him on Saturday night. Ha, ha, ha, ha. Yes." He put the phone down and grinned. "Boy, things are popping."

"What the *fuck* are you doing?" Reese said.

"Huh?"

"A little late for the VNA, wouldn't you say?"

"Hey, Jack, we're moving forward. Why are you being so negative?"

"You're too late, Sparky." He smiled broadly at Lutz. "Do you know what yesterday was?"

"What?" Lutz said. He knew exactly the gist of Reese's query.

"November 1." Reese leaned forward, quieting his voice for emphasis. "And do you have the twenty VNAs signed?" He looked at Lutz with a taunting grin. "I believe you're fucked. The new preferences kick in."

"So?" Lutz looked away, acting like it was no big deal.

Now up a decibel, Reese said, "Do you perchance have a turd stuck in your ear? I said the new preferences have kicked in. Read the agreement again. If you don't sign twenty VNAs by November 1, we get the first twelve million of a deal and forty percent of everything over and above. And..." Reese put his fingers to his mouth in mock surprise. "Guess what happened? Someone wants to buy us."

"Jack, I agreed to that clause because you made me. It wasn't meant to be taken literally."

"No? Then why don't you lob it over to your literal lawyers for a look-see, dickwad, and see what they think." Reese followed with a victory guffaw.

Lutz sat expressionless, his mind working. *There's got to be a way I can get some money out of this.*

Reese continued, "Lutz, do you know what a *domestique* is?"

"In what context?"

"In the 'Oops, I fucked up and lost my company' context."

Lutz shook his head.

"In the Tour de France, each racing team has a bull moose that can ride like the wind. Well, the event is so physically grueling that the moose can't do it alone. So they rotate guys to the front to pull him along. When that guy gets worn out, they put another rabbit up front to draft. You know, to make it easier on the moose."

Lutz said, "I, ah, never followed biking, but that makes sense."

"Do you know what the French call the grunt in the front doing all the work?"

Lutz shook his head.

"A *domestique.*"

"So?"

"So, Sparky, you're going to be my *domestique.* You'll draft for me so that we can get this deal done."

"What do I have to do?"

Reese grinned. "Nothing."

Lutz jerked his head once, not understanding.

"Don't queer the deal. Cooperate and I'll make it worth your while." Reese leaned forward. "All you have to do is stay away from Hinckel. Don't let him know about the changes in the preferences. The buyer wants him as part of the deal; plus the engineers. You play ball and we can come to some accommodation on the money you put in."

Lutz sat up. "You'll give me the two hundred thousand back?"

Reese nodded. "We'll write up a side deal. No one will need to know."

Lutz was fighting to contain a smile. "And your partner agrees to this?"

Reese smiled. "He insists you get every penny back."

"Let me think about it," Lutz said.

Reese stood and moved to the door. "Don't think about it too long. You've got until tomorrow morning to give me your answer. Then we should pull everybody into the conference room early next week to tell them. The buyer, a German company, will be here next Thursday to look at the system and interview Hinckel and his team. This deal could get done in two weeks."

"Okay," Lutz said. "Tomorrow morning."

Reese opened the door and started to exit, then turned with a smile. "Oh, I'll throw in a little bonus if you agree to go along. Get yourself a room at the Westin. Tell your wife that you have to go out of town. I'll send a couple of cheerleaders over to drag their titties across your chest." He laughed, slapped his knee and brayed like a hunting dog as he left.

Lutz sat back, smiling. *Two hundred thousand.* He stood, walked to the window and stared out at the parking lot. There was the little red rocket. He'd get to keep it. He smiled. It grew. *Cheerleaders.*

***

It was just before midnight and Reese was in his apartment talking with Shanes in London. "He's spineless. You should have seen him gloat when I told him about the two hundred. The guy looked like he wanted to give me head."

Reese took his shirt off and threw it to the floor and began to unbuckle his pants.

With the phone pressed in his ear, Reese shook his head. "Sumner—for crissakes! Don't worry, he'll take it. I already had the lawyers draw up the document for the side deal. We'll pull everyone into the conference room early next week and announce it. I'll give him the document before we do that so he knows it's a done deal. I also have them drawing up a new document with the updated preferences. He'll sign. He doesn't have a choice."

"I took it to this point," Shanes said. "The ball's in your court. Go gettum. *Ciao*."

Reese was exhausted from an evening of dancing and playing with a new one from the escort service. He went to the dresser to put on his favorite teddy, then to the nightstand to turn out the light, and flopped onto his back.

Though it was the second day of November, it was springtime in apartment 204. Earlier in the day, the first mantis pod split in the Bug House and the fruit flies clustered, moving en-masse in search of a defensive corner, finding none. Some of the larvae remained in the bathroom tissues ready for transfer to a host. Reese hadn't yet used a tissue though a sleepover had used one to wipe many inches below her nose. The first assassin bug had made its way onto the couch where it settled on the corner of a cushion while its counterpart in the bedroom was well into its journey, moving slowly across the bedspread towards the snoring Reese.

THEY ALL STAY WITH US

Dracunculus medinensis: Guinea worm. A parasitic
worm found in remote African villages. Will grow
to three feet in length in one year then migrate to
the surface of the body, typically from the feet.
-Center for Disease Control
Division of Parasitic Diseases

*H*e was into his second hour of full concentration, extended
on elbows and knees, twirling the worm slowly around the
stick. He smiled, placed the stick down carefully and got to
his knees. "Pop, I knew you were here; I could smell you."

*His father stood in the entry wearing a red and green plaid
shirt—a bright raspberry handkerchief flowered in the pocket— and
a one-piece mustard-colored slicker with shoulder straps. He held a
fireman's hat at his waist in one hand and a glass in the other. A
shock of white hair gleamed against his soot covered face. "Bobby, I
don't smell the fire no more." He took a sip and shook his head. "It's
the other smells I can't get rid of."*

*"You're still drinking Canadian Club? I got stuff that's a lot
better." He got to his knees and stretched the tightness in his back. "Let
me get you a snoot-full of some good scotch; you should be drinking
that."*

"Bobby, what are you doin down there?"

*Bob looked back at the woman writhing on the floor. He had less
than six inches of the worm extracted after working on her for four*

hours. The screaming had muted to a soft moan as she chewed the towel he had placed in her mouth—the gnashing of ivory teeth pressing sweat from her forehead. "I just got started on this one. I have to roll it real slow around that chopstick there or it'll break off."

The old man stepped forward and grimaced at a circular gash that was bigger than a silver dollar and as red and tender looking as ground sirloin. "Geez, Bobby, did the worm eat at her foot like that?"

Bob went back down and leaned over the woman, his hand hovering inches above the wound. The old man stepped closer to view what looked like a piece of kite string protruding from the top of the foot. "Yeah, this one's been inside her about a year and just decided to come out. I worked on a young boy from the Sudan last week; did his in under three days. You break 'em and they'll recoil back in and cause all kinds of infections." He looked back at his dad who was nodding with admiration. "They come out of the ankles and feet mostly; sometimes they'll head for an ear and drive a person insane."

The old man stepped back. "Bobby, I ain't got much time. You and me should talk."

Bob patted the woman's head and smiled at her then got to his feet. He took a glass from a coffee table. "Ma said you were pissed at me."

"Don't listen to her. A woman don't know what goes on between a man and his son."

"Yeah, I suppose." Bob was pensive for a moment then smiled. "Pop, do you ever see your old buddy, Frankie Callahan?"

"All the time." He smiled and looked at his Timex. "He went to see his boy today, too." He looked up at his sorrowful son. "It's a woman or a bottle that makes a man that low. What's makin you put your shoulders down like that?"

Bob sighed into his drink. "I made mistakes."

The old man chuckled faintly. "Does your Ma know about it?"

"She's in the hospital." Bob sniffed his drink then sipped. "She told me I'm no good."

"Bobby, you was a kid. She can be nasty like your grandma. She don't know any better."

"Pop, I'm sorry."

"For what?"

"For not talking to you. I was busy with my things. Some of those bugs I collected... well, you could only get them at certain times." He nodded at his father to emphasize the importance of working within the seasons. "I had to stay focused."

The old man looked down at his boots. "And I'm sorry I squashed your frog. You know, that really got to me." He looked up and his eyes shined. "When I woke the next morning, I knew what I done. I didn't know how to tell you I was sorry. I never got trained with words."

"It's okay, Pop. You don't need to be sad anymore."

His father nodded, drained his glass then held it out. "Guess I could try one of yours. Two fingers."

Bob took it and moved to his desk.

His father said, "What's doin it to you?"

He answered as he poured. "I did some things that didn't work out. I lost a bunch of money and lied to Pat."

"She's a good woman, Bobby. You need to be nice."

Bob turned. "I have a chance to get my money back. All I gotta do is cooperate."

"So, why don't you?"

He felt immediate hope from his father's query. "It would be a side deal. All the other employees would get nothing. But they'd get nothing anyway." He went to his father—twirling a release of aroma—and gave him the glass before returning to sit. He looked over at the woman when her moaning intensified and watched the stick turn slowly as the worm moved back in.

"So you'll get somethin and the others won't?"

He glanced quickly at his father then looked away.

His father drank and nodded his pleasure with the barrel-aged whiskey. "What'd you lie to Pat about?"

"Mostly about money. And I got sidetracked over a woman." He sipped. "A much younger girl."

The old man said, "You been doin the 'how d'ya do' with her?"

He turned to smile at his father's speech. "Nah, I think she's got a new boyfriend."

"Like I said, only a woman or a bottle."

"Pop, I've been having a problem concentrating. I have to get things done but my mind won't shut off. And there's a guy who invested in my company. Well, he's a mean one…and I think he's the one the girl's interested in. I saw them together."

"So let them be. Why you need another woman when you already got a good one? She don't sass like your mother. Where'd you meet this other one?"

Bob shook his head with disapproval. "Brad got himself in a jam again." He raised a palm to his father. "I know, I know. I just stepped in to help; then got mixed up with her myself."

The old man shook his head. "You been coverin for your pal since you two were little ones. He's a grown man now, Bobby; let him be, too."

"I know." He put down the glass and studied his father. "Why are you still wearing your boots?"

The old man looked down at them and smiled. "We all do… still. We're always ready to go." He patted a huge silver badge that was pinned to his shirt. "Once you get into this business, you're always prepared."

"So, the other guys are with you, too?"

He saw the most genuine smile his father had ever worn. "Callahan got there first; six other guys plus me have joined since. We keep the kids with us."

"What kids, Pop?"

The old man's face expanded again. "The little ones that didn't make it. They all stay with us."

He remembered the picture on the front page of the newspaper: his father coming down the ladder with a blanket—a small leg dangling underneath.

The old man walked to the desk, put the empty glass down and turned. "So, whatcha gonna do, son?"

"I need the money."

"For what?"

Bob looked up with pride at the twelve foot ceiling bordered by hand-carved moldings thick with glossy stain. "This kind of detail is expensive."

"Bobby, I never had no money...and I never had to lie."

"But things are different now, Pop."

The old man moved his head back and forth slowly. "No they ain't. You need to be a nicer fellow. Do it for me." He glanced at his watch. "Take care of your woman then take care of those folks at work." He began to leave then stopped. "And be nice to Petey. He's a nice boy. Tell him you're proud of him. He'd like that." The old man put on the fireman's hat; his lower lip quivered with pride. "All that time you spent studyin those bugs has paid off. Now you can use that to help others." He flicked his chin at the woman on the floor. "You should get back."

He swelled at his father's acknowledgement. "I like to help people; just like you, Pop." He stood. "Hey, you don't swear anymore?"

He adjusted his hat and tapped the badge. "Nah, the kids got after me about it."

He was back on his knees attending to the woman. He grabbed the stick and slowly applied enough tension to arrest the Guinea worm's progress when he saw a boil the size of a goose egg just below her knee. A spiracle in search of oxygen poked from a tiny hole in its center. "Shit, 'Dermatobia homonis'." He leaned forward to stroke her cheek gently and whispered, "You got a botfly, too?" Her chest sunk as she nodded with fright, her big dark eyes rolling back to pink. He rose slowly to get the book and brought it back, sat, and leafed through his notes: 'There are three cures for botfly infestation. You can start with matatorsalo bot soap which will kill the larva but keep the corpse inside or put airplane glue into the hole and cover it with an inner tube patch to suffocate it (squeeze out the dead larva a couple of days later) or put a piece of raw meat over the hole so the maggot burrows up.' He looked over at the goose egg and saw another spiracle poke through the skin. He turned the page. 'If in pairs, they will likely inhabit the same egg. It only hurts the host when they squirm as you shut their oxygen off'

"Huuuuuuh! Jesus Christ!"

"What!?" Pat bolted up and went for the lamp on the nightstand.

"Jesus Christ!" He kicked at the covers and jerked forward—drenched and shivering.

She grabbed his shoulders and moved in to comfort him. "Was this one a nightmare?"

FARAWAY LOOK

Utethersa ornatrix: the butterfly sports a bright,
aposomatic coloration which makes it highly
conspicuous to visually hunting predators.
-Science Magazine

Phil was in Lutz' office probing for more information, getting none. "I'm telling you, Phil. I don't know anything about it." Lutz looked at his watch—"Shit!"—grabbed his keys and rushed out. He ran to his car and headed out of the lot for his appointment with Felton. A car started a few rows away and followed him.

***

They were halfway through the session, with Dr. Felton observing a calmer and more articulate patient. Lutz was less fidgety; no picking of fingers or bouncing of legs. His sentences were longer and carefully crafted.

Lutz spoke as he looked away. "Sometimes I wish I were absolutely in love. I miss that feeling." He frowned at the doctor. "Whatever happened to romance?"

"I believe it to be very much alive," Felton said.

"I miss it." Lutz gazed into the face of an imaginary lover. "I'd make her pearls out of the dew."

The doctor sensed that another Golden Oldie was about to redirect their discussion.

"It's a Ricky Nelson song," Lutz said.

"I don't recall it."

"*You* wouldn't," he said with a new tone of respect. I assume you led a pretty structured life—didn't have time for pop music." Lutz slapped a palm with the back of his hand. "Gotta hit the books!"

"Why would you think that?" Felton said with amusement.

"Well you ended up a shrink. It must have always been your plan."

Felton shifted and crossed his legs. "I always wanted to be a physician but I didn't decide on psychiatry until quite late."

"Well at least you had a plan." Lutz became transfixed on a spot on the ceiling, studying it as though it were an insect that had escaped all previous discoveries. He sighed and returned to Felton—his eyes misty. "I left something sweet back in my childhood. I was a happy kid once; in awe of my parents—how they knew so much. But they didn't figure out things at all; they just went through the motions. Then something happened to them: they suddenly talked little and laughed less. My mother developed a faraway look."

Felton gauged the emergence of melancholia as a sign that the drug was finally taking hold. "When did that happen?"

"When I was ten. There was always music in the house, something on the stove, and my old man would pinch her butt when he went by. '*Oh my Papa*'. My mother loved that song."

Felton smiled. "I remember it."

"I had a teacher who taught us to be observant, so everyday she would move something in the classroom. One day she called on me: 'Bobby, what changed today?' I said, 'my mom'."

"How so?"

"One day she stopped laughing altogether." Lutz snapped his fingers. "Just like that! And I never understood why until it happened to me. That's the look you get when you realize you're trapped. You finally know that things aren't going to get any better. It's just happened to Pat; she's now got the look."

Felton waited until he found his patient's eyes. "Don't be so tough on yourself."

"I'm a carrier," Lutz said, and turned away to wipe a tear on the bend of a thumb. "I've broken her spirit. She used to be carefree...much like Valerie. I wore her down." He looked over at Felton's desk and noticed that the pretty woman's picture was gone. He returned to gaze at the doctor. "It's uncanny how we slowly morph into the old man: walk like him, complain like him and eventually laugh like him. Imagine if Popeye had a son, with all of that arf-arf-arf stuff going on." He forced a smile, and a new tear appeared and raced after the first. "I miss my dad," he said. "All these years I was angry with him because he didn't pay attention to me. He couldn't. The poor guy was so plagued by images. He didn't know anything other than being a firefighter."

"It's not too late to have him back as someone you feel a deep affection for. You certainly have the capacity to forgive."

Lutz spread his hands. "Look what I've done. I've alienated Pat. I didn't pay attention to the fine print and I've lost our savings. Now, I'll cause people to lose their jobs because I moved too quickly without thinking it through."

Felton was quick with support. "Your brain was operating on imagery and emotion—not judgment and reason. That's where you were through all of this."

Lutz said, "I never increased the dosage."

Felton stiffened, stood instinctively and moved briskly to his desk. On the way, he turned back awkwardly with a slight trip. "Have you been taking the fifty milligrams all along?"

Lutz lied. He had stopped the medication altogether after

that first night with Valerie. "Yes," he said to the doctor's back. "But I never took it up the times you told me to."

Felton turned again. *"Why?"*

"I wanted to have a shot at Valerie, if it came to that, and didn't want a rubber ducky. A few weeks ago, I took it to seventy-five, then last week to a hundred—like you wanted me to."

Felton returned, sat with the folder and fumbled papers to the floor. "I brought you to one-hundred because you weren't responding to the increase to seventy-five." He collected the papers back into the folder and put it aside. "I waited a month before moving you up. You shouldn't have doubled the dosage in such a short period. How are you responding?"

"I have really weird dreams. Mostly in color. All in incredible detail. Kind of freaky how they're about helping others. My dad's in a lot of them." He smiled weakly at the doctor. "But no snakes in his boots."

"Any other changes?"

Lutz thought about it then nodded. "Ever hear of the Utethersa butterfly?"

Felton hadn't. "Another part of your collection?"

"Yeah. It has such beautiful coloring." Lutz brushed a knee. "In fact, so beautiful, predators will leave it alone. I guess they figure something that colorful must be poisonous. If it gets trapped in a web, it folds up in display and waits to be cut free by the resident spider."

"You're about to fold your wings?"

"Yeah," Lutz said. "I don't see any options." He gazed absently around the room and returned to look sheepishly at the doctor. "He made me an offer."

"Reese?"

"Yeah. He said he'd add an incentive equal to my IRA money if I cooperated and didn't queer the deal."

"Don't they owe you that money anyway? Wasn't it a loan?"

"No. When Broadline put their money in, Reese let me turn it into an investment. I figured if they were getting in cheap, so should I." He puffed his cheeks and released a stream of defeat. "I lied to Pat; told her it was a loan. I messed up again."

"Will you take Reese's offer?"

"Why shouldn't I? The employees and other investors get nothing anyway. Why shouldn't I at least recover my savings? Plus, I just found out I have to pay taxes on that withdrawal. That's another eighty grand that I don't have." Lutz looked away. "There's nothing illegal with the payment. It would be on the up and up."

"Would it?" Felton said.

"You know what I mean," Lutz countered, wanting badly for Felton to endorse the possibility. "They'd note the payment as a change to the distribution agreement. It would come out of their cut." He palmed his thighs before repeating his rationale with a shrug. "The employees get nothing, anyway."

"Why would Reese do this?" Felton said. "What could you do to prevent him from consummating the deal? What's he afraid of?"

Lutz twitched a shoulder. "He wants me to deliver the head engineer."

"I don't follow."

"He doesn't want me to spook the buyer."

"Could you?" Felton asked.

"Well, there is one other thing I could do." He started to speak then hesitated, not sure how much he should tell.

Felton looked at his patient with anticipation, hoping that Lutz had more leverage than he thought.

Lutz continued, "I bugged his apartment."

Felton reacted immediately with a shift and a headshake. "That's illegal in this state. You can't tape somebody without their knowledge."

"No, I *bugged* it—real bugs—insects. It's our apartment. The company pays for it. I didn't break in. I walked in...and planted insects."

Felton was bewildered by such infantile behavior and sat up. "Why?"

"It happened on my lower dosage. I wasn't thinking straight. Wanted to make him uncomfortable; to get back at him." He was relieved that the doctor seemed intrigued. "I figured maybe he'd get sick, go back to Pittsburgh and leave us alone. The girls at work were upset with him."

Felton furled his brow. "Sick? Why would he get sick?"

"Oh, I meant uncomfortable," Lutz said, and bent down to work on a pant cuff. He wasn't sure how much he could tell without the doctor having to report it to authorities. He sat up. "Did you know that a cockroach's sense of taste is so advanced that it can tell the difference between food and poison by sampling a single molecule of a substance?"

Felton didn't respond outwardly though his grip tightened on the arm of the chair. It was the second time that Lutz had mentioned poison.

"And it has a reflex action of one-fiftieth of a second; that's faster than a human's response by a factor of five."

"You put cockroaches in his apartment?"

"No. I was going to, but I didn't want him to start spraying and kill off my other friends." *Shit.* He had slipped, so quickly abandoned the cockroach story to share a portion of his real plan. "I disguised an insect farm in a plant in his apartment; put some praying mantis larvae and bedbug eggs in it. It wouldn't hurt him; just make him uncomfortable." He wouldn't volunteer information about the blowfly larvae and the kissing-bugs. "So, I'm about to leave when I decide to have a look around." He shifted to the edge of the seat and leaned forward with a tug on a trouser leg. "I open a drawer in his nightstand and I find this envelope with pictures in it. Weird stuff. Shots of him with women handcuffed, red balls in their mouth, fannies all red. You know, S&M stuff. Then I find all kinds of ladies wear in another drawer. You know, leather panties and garter belts...stuff he's wearing in other pictures."

"You're not thinking of blackmailing him?"

"No, no," Lutz said. "You asked me if there was another possibility to block this deal and that's what I got."

Felton flicked the back of his hand as he sat back and crossed his legs. "You can't act on this," he told him staunchly. "There's a question of illegal entry. I'm not a lawyer, but it doesn't sound legit...you doing something with those photos."

"I don't have them. Where can you have copies made of that stuff, anyway?"

Felton studied the ceiling. Lutz could sense the gears moving. The doctor was pondering possibilities. A minute passed before he leaned forward. "Bob, I've got one for you."

Lutz sat up in anticipation, hopeful that the doctor had discovered an out.

"Did you know that alligators see the world as horizontal?"

Lutz knew all about crocodilians and nodded. "So?"

"Let's say that a woman is standing on the bank of a creek and an alligator surfaces in front of her. Her legs, vertical images, won't map to the alligator. *But,* if she happens to be walking her daschund. Well, *that* little fellow will be mapped *and* responded to."

"I don't follow," Lutz said.

"What else did you find in his apartment? Perhaps there was something you saw that didn't register as important at the time."

Lutz looked away and tapped underneath his chin. He returned to Felton with a smirk. "Well, I did have time to look in other places." He straightened and leaned in with the moves of a gossip. "I found another stack of photos in his dresser drawer."

The doctor tilted his head in anticipation.

"In one of the photos, Reese is lying on a bed wearing a black, cocktail dress. *And*, he was wearing ladies' hose." He spread his thumb and forefinger about four inches. "And the highest heels I've ever seen; all hussied up—he even wore a string of pearls." Lutz shook his head in disgust. "Ridiculous: a buffed guy with high heels and pearls, in a cocktail dress." He paused for a reaction from Felton and got none. "In another photo, there's a picture of a topless blond smiling down at him. He must have taken the picture because—the way she's holding her arms—well, she appears to be on top of him."

Felton furled his brow. "How were those photos different from the rest?"

Lutz looked off to the side momentarily to gather an explanation then smiled at Felton. "She's a Southern girl who works in a massage parlor. I happened by the place, some time ago. Maybe she can do something against Reese to help me out. You know, 'scratch a lover and find a foe'."

Felton jerked his head to the side, not understanding. "You said that she was smiling in the photo and was likely having sex with Reese. Why would she want to get back at him?"

Lutz continued, "Well, you know how a camera puts a date on a photo?" Felton nodded as Lutz broke out in a full grin. "According to the date on these, ah...I think Reese may have given her the crabs."

***

Immediately after Lutz left, Felton was at his desk writing notes in his patient's folder when the phone rang. He studied the caller ID—it wasn't the thug—and answered to a young, female voice.

"Dr. Felton. You don't know me but you should. One of your patients is in danger."

"May I have your name?" Felton said.

She was calm, but firm. "No, I'll tell you when we meet."

"Miss, I am not at liberty to confirm whether a person is or is not under my care."

"He is. I saw him go into your office an hour ago. Want to stop playing games and listen to what I have to say?"

Felton said, "Young lady, I don't like the gist of this discussion. It's neither ethical nor professional." He knew, however, that if Lutz was truly in danger, he was compelled to listen. He waited. "Go on."

"Can I trust you?"

"Certainly, but I repeat that I cannot confirm any relationship with your alleged patient." He turned in the chair, looked at the remaining painting now centered on the wall and blew a stream of defeat.

"So," she said. "When can I come in?"

THE OATH

The following Tuesday, Lillian rushed through the lab slapping the back of the engineers' chairs. "Let's go, let's go. Now!" Hinckel looked over at her and continued to type. "What's so important?"

"Come on," she said. "He wants us all in the conference room for an announcement." She bit at her lower lip, afraid of the meeting's outcome.

Hinckel groaned as he pushed out his chair.

***

Phil was in Lutz' office pacing, then moved in to confront. "What's this all about? What are you going to announce to them that you can't tell me first? Listen Bob, I know they're planning to sell. *And*, I suspect you've made a deal to go along."

Lutz sat back and shook his head. "I might have done that if he hadn't talked to me."

"Who?"

"The most magnificent role model a kid could have."

"What do you mean?" Phil demanded. "What's going on?"

Lutz stood, opened his door and walked down to Reese's office and stood in the doorway. "They're just about ready for us."

Reese came out rubbing an eye and nestled in close. He motioned to his desk. "You haven't signed yet."

Lutz shook his head.

"Jerk," he muttered, then leaned in with a scowl. "Don't fuck this up. Remember to emphasize that some of them will still have jobs." Reese looked at the stream of people walking casually to the conference room. Hinckel was plodding behind at the rear of the entourage behind Valerie, who was laughing and poking at a shy engineer. Reese looked over at Lillian who was sitting at her desk with blotches of red on her beautiful white skin. She was straightening papers, trying to look busy. She would not make the cut. Reese smiled at Phil. He'd be out the door, too.

All employees were in the room when Lutz entered, trailed by Reese. Lillian stood in the back flanked by Phil and Hinckel. She was fighting back tears. Valerie stood on the side of the room against the wall oblivious to the goings-on, wagging her tongue at a guy across from her.

Lutz started. "This will be brief. We reached preliminary agreement with a formidable German company that will buy the assets of iCare and use their resources to implement our solution in Europe. This is good news for many, and not so good for a few. They plan to retain most of you to continue our work." He looked down and sighed. "Some of you will be laid off and given a week's pay." Reese stepped forward to speak; Lutz waved him off and continued. "But before I take questions, I'd like to say something that captures how I feel." His lip quivered as he took in Lillian, who was standing against the far wall, rapidly losing it.

"I talked to someone a few days ago. He visited me and we had the most wonderful discussion. Mostly about people and how we need to be nice. This man used to swear a lot, but doesn't anymore." He wiped at a tear. "He used to be my dad."

Phil leaned into Lillian and whispered. "What's he talking about?" She shook her head, swallowed deeply, and moved a step away.

Lutz pointed at Reese. "But that man, there. He's not nice. In fact, years ago, my Pop would have called him something snappy and to the point. He would have called him a Guinea worm cocksucker." Gasps came from the room's perimeter. Reese bolted forward, wanting to silence him with a punch then stopped.

Lutz continued, "He was not only a great man; he was a proud man. He would have wanted me to say something to all of you." Lutz stood at attention, his arms stiffly to his sides, and began: "I promise concern for others. A willingness to help all those in need. I promise courage—courage to face and conquer my fears. Courage to share and endure the ordeal of those who need me. I promise strength—strength of heart to bear whatever burdens might be placed upon me. Strength of body to deliver to safety all those placed within my care. I promise the wisdom to lead, the compassion to comfort, and the love to serve unselfishly whenever I am called."

Hinckel leaned towards Lillian and whispered, "That's the Firefighter's Oath." She began to sob.

Lutz continued, "We tend to go through life in search of the wrong things. We chase money and fame at the cost of integrity. We'll ignore loved ones to advance our own cause and will turn away from a child's joy to focus on that which makes only ourselves happy." His speech was stolen by another rush of emotion and he wiped another tear. Lillian wiped at one also. "I haven't seen my daughter in three months; haven't even talked to my little girl because I've put my whole heart and soul into this company. I've brought it to where another firm sees its true potential to help the aging. I cannot continue that journey any longer, but know in my heart that I gave it my best and, like those brave firefighters, I have endeavored to deliver each of you under my care."

Phil leaned in to Lillian. "Is he on drugs or something?" She back-handed his thigh and rushed from the room.

Lutz pointed at Reese. "This man here. This low-life equivalent of the assassin bug. He offered me money to lie to you. He offered me money to cooperate."

Reese lunged towards Lutz and was grabbed from behind by Hinckel and shoved against the wall. Reese turned with a raised fist to pummel the head engineer then, understanding the repercussions, stopped.

Lutz glared at Reese and pumped his chest. "I don't want your money. I will cooperate because these fine people require that I do."

Someone coughed and went to the door feigning a need for water. Two more followed, and after a moment, the rest filed out. Reese moved out next leaving Hinckel and Phil with Lutz.

Phil went to him and put an arm around his shoulder. "Are you okay?"

"Yeah, finally." He looked ashamedly at Hinckel. "You can either go along with them or quash the deal. The buyer wants you."

Hinckel said, "I know, Bob. I know what's been going on. I'll work with them. My people need their jobs. I don't need much money, anyway."

Lutz put out his hand. "You're nice to people, Hinckel."

"Thank you," he said. "That means a lot, coming from you."

THE RABBIT'S GOT THE GUN

The following week, Reese sat in the conference room beaming at Lutz. Two copies of a legal document were on the table with red stickums marking the pages to be signed.

"Ready to start?"

Lutz looked down in defeat and nodded faintly. "I guess."

Reese pushed the first document across. "That stupid fucking speech last week cost you two hundred grand."

Lutz shrugged, took a pen from his pocket and looked over at Reese, who sported a swollen, yellow eyelid, ripe with infection. *I bet one of the bugs got him.* But Lutz was too emotionally spent to gloat.

Reese said, "The document spells out the new liquidity preferences that kicked in when you failed to sign the VNAs. You and *F Troop*, that crack team of engineers Hinckel recruited, get this:" He formed a zero with a thumb and finger. "Nada, zilch, shitstick."

"So, there will be nothing for the employees?" Lutz asked, already knowing the answer.

"That's right, BooBoo. Page six, paragraph three: "proceeds from a sale of all or substantially all assets shall be distributed to Broadline Ventures up to the sum of twelve million dollars before any distributions shall be made to other classes of stock." Reese didn't have to read the document to quote the terms. He snickered at Lutz. "You're lucky to come out of this with your house."

Lutz, his eyes pleading, said, "Is there any chance that Professor Maltbie can get some of his money back?"

Reese sneered. "About as much chance as Miss Afghanistan winning the swimsuit competition." He slapped his knee, delighted with his spontaneous quip.

"So, we all get nothing."

Reese beamed anew.

Lutz reached for the document and began to read.

"You're shitting me? You're doing due-diligence now?" Reese rolled his good eye at the ceiling. "For crissakes, Maltbie and Hinckel have already signed."

Lutz looked up from the document and glared across the table. "This time I read— word by word by word."

Reese stretched back in his chair and shook his head, then lurched forward quickly when a heavy voice boomed in the lobby. "Where!?"

"I *told* you, he's in a meeting." The receptionist's little voice strained for command

"Where!?"

Reese stood and looked over the head of Lutz at a huge black man planted in the lobby—in jeans and a Harley-Davidson tee shirt—hands on hips, glaring at the conference room. Next to him was a portly guy in a striped grey suit, sizes too small. "There must be a circus in town," Reese said with a shake of his head and a snicker.

Lutz turned in his chair to see Satch striding briskly towards them with the pot-bellied guy hurrying behind with a briefcase. Satch burst into the room with a big burgundy smile and glared at Reese. "You are one sad motherfucker, Elmer Fudd." He held a Zip disk and shook it. "The *rabbit's* got the gun!"

Reese turned to Lutz. "Who is *he?*"

Lutz said, "Satch, what are you doing?"

Reese said, "You *know* him?"

"Yeah, he's the dart guy."

Reese thrust an arm at the block of black muscle and said, "Leave!" Satch countered with a menacing sneer and feigned a quick advance, stumbling Reese back into the chair.

Satch moved to a computer sitting on a table off to the side. "I'm from 'Blockbuster'. We have a new program: we bring the movies to you." He turned to Reese with a grin that seemed to suck air from the room. "And a new policy, Elmer—no late fees." He inserted the disk, clicked on an icon and turned, winking at Reese as a video started.

Lutz saw the iCare logo at the bottom of the screen. "Hey, that's our GrannyCam." He looked at Reese and watched his face contort.

Satch smiled. "Nice product, Mr. Lutz." He backed away from the monitor towards Reese, sat, and put a huge arm around his shoulders. "The rabbit's got the gun, Elmer." He stomped his foot. "The *rabbit's* got the *fucking* gun!" He put his face into Reese's. "You a bad motherfucker, huh? You want to slap me? Slap my black ass; pull my hair?" Reese sunk in the chair.

The video started. A young woman was sitting on a couch. She pointed the remote at the TV, rose and went to the door and opened it. A man wearing a ski-mask lunged at her, grabbed her hair, twisted violently and put her to a knee. She swung wildly, landing the back of a fist on his thigh. He kicked the door closed behind, put a hand over her mouth and dragged her to the couch. She fought to stand. He pushed her down and slapped her. She kicked at him, the blows from her pointed-toe shoes finding his shins repeatedly. He picked her up and threw her back on the couch, a knee pressed into her abdomen. She rolled off, got to her feet and swung at his face landing consecutive blows.

"My *God*," Lutz said.

Satch looked over at him. "It gets better." He tightened his arm around Reese, who was rubbing a knuckle into his eye.

The intruder lunged again and ripped the buttons from her blouse, grabbed the bra and yanked, exposing her breasts. The GrannyCam zoomed in.

Lutz leaned forward and squinted at the monitor. "Valerie," he said.

She fought; slapping—pushing him away. He grabbed her hair, dragged her back to the couch, threw her down and got on top. She opened her mouth and whimpered. He appeared to whisper something and she went limp, the fight gone. He moved to his knees to unbuckle his pants and she attacked, thrusting a fist into his stomach and grabbing for the mask, lifting it. It was Reese.

Lutz lunged across the table at Reese. "You fucking animal!"

"Whoa...whoa...whoa," Satch said, with a thick wrist and meaty hand warding off Lutz. "There are some *po*lice who want first crack. He tightened his arm around Reese. "Want to meet some *po*lice?" He stood and went to the computer and stopped the video. "No need to take Mr. Lutz through the rest of your game, Elmer."

"This is bullshit," Reese said. "She's into rough sex. She told me to do that." Beads of sweat reappeared.

"Just like that broad at the Charles Hotel, huh?" The briefcase guy stood at the end of the conference table, his arms folded around the worn valise now resting on his paunch. Lutz squinted at him.

"Who are *you?*" Reese said.

"Miss Quinn's attorney." He stepped forward and handed Reese a card. "And you might be interested in these." He took two sheets of paper from the briefcase and handed them to Reese. "A police report and a Rape Confirmation Report." He pointed to the signature of the emergency room physician. "Seems you did quite a job on my client." A finger wiggled over the page. "The Doc says there that there was forced penetration. The photos of the bruising on her whazoo are being held by the hospital. You sure whacked it pretty good."

Reese said, "You're an attorney and you talk like that?"

The attorney bit his lower lip and moved in with a raised fist. "How'd you like a habeas-corpus sandwich, asshole?"

Satch extended a muscular arm and pushed him away. "Back off, Esquire."

"She wanted me to do that," Reese said to the room. "Told me to wear the mask. It was consensual."

"Sure looked like she was fighting back to me," Satch said. "Raise your pant legs."

Reese closed his legs. "Huh?"

"You pull 'em up, Elmer, or I'll do it for you. That cuff there (he kicked at Reese's ankle) would fit might nice around your neck."

Reese pulled them up and exposed a pair of purple shins. Lutz stood to look across the conference table and gasped.

Satch grabbed Reese's face and squeezed. "And where'd you get that beautiful eye? The *po*lice sure would sure like to see how consensual you look." He let go and stood.

"Something bit me, an insect." Reese put a fingertip to his lid. "I got some salve for it." He fumbled in a pocket to produce it for Satch.

Lutz glared at Reese. "How could you?"

Satch stood and walked to the attorney while addressing Reese. "Well, Mr. Fudd, seems we got a distraught young lady at the hospital who, at this time, is unwilling to cooperate with the *po*lice." He spun— "AT THIS TIME."

Reese cowered.

"Seems she's concerned for her fellow employees…what a scandal might do to the company."

"Yeah?" Reese said.

"Yeah (Satch nodded to the attorney). And she would be willing to get amnesia if you agree to help out the team."

"What do you mean?" Reese said.

Satch looked over at Lutz. "You best leave the room while we do some paperwork. We'll ask you back to sign some things."

Lutz shook his head. "I'd rather not."

"Leave!" Satch bellowed.

Lutz jumped up, tiptoeing into a slight bow as he backed through the door. "Just let me know when you need me."

"Mr. Reese." Satch moved to the attorney, flicking his fingers in a 'gimme' motion. "Mr. Elmer-Fucking-Reese. It is my understanding that you have signatory authority for Broadline Ventures."

"Who told you that?"

"Why, Miss Quinn," Satch said, as the attorney produced a document and pointed to a page.

"That cunt," Reese muttered to himself.

Satch spun. "Did you say something?"

Reese shook his head.

"This is going to cost you big, Mr. Fudd."

Reese held a balled tissue in his fingertips and patted his eye—his hand visibly shaking.

"How about two million big?"

Reese sat up. "Two million dollars for what?"

"To stay away from your new boyfriend in the house. You'd sure make somebody a fine bitch. But first (he pointed at Reese's shins) you gotta clean up those legs." Satch roared and punched his thigh as the attorney snickered into his sleeve. "You like rough sex, Elmer?" He moved back into Reese's face. "Motherfucker, you're going to a Disneyland where you can ride all night for free." The puss-soaked ball sprung from Reese and dropped to the table.

Satch looked at the attorney who was rubbing his top gums briskly with a finger. "Esquire, please." The attorney reached into the briefcase.

"Miss Quinn's attorney has prepared a document. And he already filled in your personal account info for you. *Pro bono,* of course." He turned. "Are you following this, Mr. Fudd? We're talking about your *personal* account." He took the sheet from the attorney and walked it over to Reese. "See there." Satch pointed to a line: *'in the amount of two million dollars ($2,000,000.00)'.* "The attorney also filled in the routing numbers so you don't get all confused when you get down to your bank. Oh yeah, you need to sign the release." He turned to the attorney. "Esquire?"

Reese said, "What release?"

"The 'holds harmless release'. In case you ever have a change of heart." Satch smiled. "Not that you got one."

The attorney put the release on the table in front of Reese and handed him a pen then sneezed and wiped his nose with a suit sleeve that stretched over his forearm inches from his elbow.

Satch said, "You don't sign, Miss Quinn files charges and you're on your way to meet your new boyfriend."

Reese signed and put down the pen.

"If your personal funds don't show by five tomorrow, you might want to go shopping for a new prom dress." Satch turned to the attorney. "Get Lutz."

The attorney came back with Lutz and closed the door behind him. Satch said, "Sit," and looked at Reese. "Tell Mr. Lutz the good news."

Reese shrugged. "What?"

"How you've had a change of heart and want the team to have a bigger piece of the pie." Satch looked through the iCare document while addressing Reese. "Where's the preferences section?"

Lutz answered. "Page six, paragraph three."

Reese glared across the table at him.

Satch picked up the document and turned the pages. "Oh yeah," he said. "It's right there," and pointed at the paragraph. "Look at this, Esquire." He walked it over to the attorney. "If we change that word there from *twelve* to *four* and have Elmer initial both copies, I believe we're done for the day." He looked over at Reese. "The attorney wants to get down to the hospital to check on his client."

The attorney sniffed a slick of ooze back into his nose. "Will we have time to stop for a cocktail?"

"Yes, we will, Esquire." Satch turned to smile at the attorney. "I believe we will." He looked over at Lutz. "You don't mind if Elmer recovers his initial investment?"

Lutz shook his head and smiled.

Satch walked the document to Reese who crossed out the larger number and wrote *four,* initialed it, and did the same to the other copy. Satch pushed one across the table at Lutz. "Make sure the other board members initial, too." Lutz took it and held it to his chest.

Satch said to Reese, "You keep one to show your partner

how kind you are?" He kicked Reese's chair. "Let's go. I'll escort you to your car. And don't forget to leave a nice smile for Miss Prettyface in the lobby on the way out."

Reese stood, put the papers in his briefcase and walked out between Satch and the attorney.

When they got outside, Satch grabbed Reese's elbow, squeezed and took the briefcase. "Let me help you." Reese opened the car door and entered. Satch put the briefcase on his lap and leaned in. "Five o'clock," he whispered, before putting his tongue in Reese's ear. "That be five o'clock, bitch."

TO BELIEVE AGAIN

D r. Felton was smiling into the phone. "Yes," he said. "I'll see you there." He chuckled. "It's okay. I don't need to play the ponies; we'll do the casino again." He laughed heartily before saying, "That would be nice. I'll see you then." He hung up, opened the file drawer, found Lutz' folder and placed it on his desk.

Bzzzzzzzzzz.

He waited a few moments before going to the door.

"Hello, Doctor Felton."

"Nice to see you, Bob." The doctor smiled with surprise. Lutz was accompanied by a nervous stick of a woman in a blue, polka dot, A-line dress. She was blushing firetruck red. Bob wore a huge smile. "This is my wife, Pat."

"How very nice to finally meet you." Felton extended a hand to hold hers then placed his other on top. "Bob has told me so much about you."

She looked down. "That doesn't make me feel so good. I'm quite the witch, huh?"

"Not at all, Mrs. Lutz. Your husband is very fond of you. Come in." He guided Pat through the door with Bob trailing, his smile broadening.

"Call me Pat," she said to the floor.

Bob headed for his normal position and stopped. "Oops. We'll probably need the sofa." He looked at Felton, who nodded at the couch. They sat while Felton grabbed Bob's usual chair and moved it over to sit in front of them.

"I wanted Pat to meet you."

"I wanted to thank you personally for being such a big help to my husband," she said, working to contain tears.

Felton stood and retrieved a box of tissues and handed it to her. She took one, dabbed each eye and put the box on the floor. "Sorry," she said.

Felton nodded and smiled his support, his eyes darting to Bob.

"I can't believe how all of this has worked out," Bob said. "A German company is going to purchase iCare for fifteen million. The professor, the founder and Broadline get twelve." He beamed. "Guess who gets the rest?"

Felton's eyes grew.

"The employees," Lutz gushed.

Felton gasped. "Congratulations." He bent forward. "How were you able to accomplish that?"

"Well, let's just say that I found a last minute glitch in the contract that worked in our favor."

Pat beamed at her husband, then at Felton. "He's so smart doctor," she said, locking her arm in her husband's. "We're going to get our savings back."

"Plus another half million, honey," Bob said, and nuzzled her cheek.

Felton said to Bob, "What an abrupt turn-around. When you left two weeks ago, there was little hope."

Bob nodded, and for Pat's benefit said, "I guess the new attention skills I learned in this office have paid off. And, I have you to thank."

Pat sniffed. "Yes, doctor," and pressed the tissue to pursed lips. "Thank you for giving me my husband back," she said, with the end of her declaration moving up an octave. Bob patted her hand.

"Mrs. Lutz, your husband is a very courageous man. He worked hard on his wellness."

She nodded. "I'm so proud of him." She reached for Bob's hand and squeezed.

Bob looked around the room. "I learned so much in here. I can breathe again. So many years wasted." He looked at Felton with admiration. "And it took one of the oldest institutions to get me to believe again."

Felton smiled.

"Medicine," Bob said. "If it weren't for the integrity of you and your profession, who knows what would have happened to me?"

Felton looked down with humility. "Thank you."

"No, thank *you*. You're the one who brought me back."

Pat said to Felton, while nodding approval at her husband, "He's taking his brother on a fishing trip and promised to stop swearing."

Felton smiled at her then said to Bob, "Always remember that little frog. How you can often achieve more by chirping less."

Pat twisted back to take in her husband. "What frog?"

Bob patted her hand again. "I'll tell you about him on the way home, honey." He looked at Felton. "I think I'm done."

"Sorry?" Felton said.

"With therapy."

Felton shrugged. "Well, that's certainly your choice. But I recommend that you continue your medication. Call to check in." He smiled encouragement. "So I can hear how you're doing. I'll call in your prescription."

"Thank you," Bob said.

Felton said to Pat, "Could I spend some time with your husband?"

"Oh...sure," she said, and reached down for her purse.

Bob walked her to the door. "Sit out there, honey; we'll only be a few minutes." She waited until she was out of Felton's view to motion outside and put two fingers to her mouth. "Yes, go for a smoke, sweetie," he whispered. He came back in the office and returned to the couch, recapturing his earlier exhilaration.

Felton stared at him. "So, what happened?"

Lutz rolled his eyes as he clasped his hands behind his neck and sat back, unable to respond.

"How did you get Reese to part with his money?"

After a moment, he freed his hands and shifted forward. "It was the weirdest thing," he said, shaking his head.

Felton studied him with an anxious gaze, wanting to hear how a dire situation could be so dramatically reversed.

"Valerie did it. She set him up."

Felton sat up.

Lutz was now in full grin. "She found out that Reese was a perv, so she met him for drinks and set him up."

Felton moved his head side to side slowly, obviously not understanding. "How?"

"My assistant, Lillian, knew that Reese was about to get all the money and told Valerie—they were roommates. Valerie moved out and had her new place wired with a camera—in fact, one of ours. Remember that guy in the bar I told you about? The dart guy."

Felton nodded with a grimace.

"He used a GrannyCam that Valerie got for him. He watched it happen on the Internet, downloaded it to disk, and the rest is history."

"What happened?" Felton said.

Lutz shook his head. "Brutally rough sex."

Felton cringed. "My *good*ness."

"He did a number on her."

The doctor's eyes widened with concern. "Is she okay?"

Lutz shrugged. "I haven't seen her. But her lawyer had the medical reports. Said Reese worked her over pretty good."

"Lawyer?"

"Yeah, some scrappy looking ambulance-chaser was in our office first thing the next morning to confront Reese with reports from the hospital."

Felton did little to hide his bewilderment. "What did Valerie get from all of this?"

Bob shrugged, perplexed himself. "You know, that's the weird part. She only worked for us for a couple of months. She put herself in harm's way for stock options worth a stinking thousand bucks and hasn't asked for a penny more. Do you believe that?" Lutz shook his face in his hands then looked up with pride. "I told you she was different. I can't believe she would do that for me."

Felton said, "She's obviously a very caring person."

"Yeah," Lutz replied, with a sniff.

"Where is she now?"

"She was released from the hospital last Friday. At five o'clock. She didn't want to see anybody. Went back to New Hampshire. Lillian said she might go back to school." Lutz looked suddenly embarrassed. "You know, the time I met her at the bar in New Hampshire and drove her home? I never went up to her apartment that night."

"I know," Felton said.

Lutz' eyes widened. "How did you know that?"

"Because I know your character. You wouldn't do such a thing."

"Phew." Lutz shook his head. "Unbelievable. You guys see everything."

Felton, pleased, nodded in agreement.

"Professor Maltbie was absolutely delirious when he found out about the last minute change and would be getting a nice return on his investment."

Felton said, "I would imagine so."

"He said I'm his new go-to guy." Lutz smiled. "Said the next company he invests in; he wants me to run it."

"Will you?"

"Maybe, down the road. But I need to take some time off to re-charge my batteries." He sniffed again. "And re-discover Pat."

Felton glanced at the waiting room door. "She's a nice lady. I'm glad I got to meet her."

"Yeah. I'm a lucky guy. So many people care about me."

They sat and smiled at each other. Lutz dropped his eyes then looked up and let them wander around the room. The picture of the beautiful young woman was back on Felton's desk. He sat up. "You brought her back!"

Felton turned to look over his shoulder. "That's my daughter. Sometimes you love somebody so much that it can be distracting. I took it home. But I missed her."

"Yeah, I miss mine, too," Lutz said. They sat serenely, smiling at each other. "Do you think it's a good time for me to stop therapy?"

Felton smiled. "Just practice some of the things you learned in here." He nodded at his patient. "I think you're ready."

"Me, too."

Lutz began to rise. "I'll go get Pat."

"Wait." Felton motioned for him to stay. "Have you heard anything from Reese?"

"No."

"Well, he did sign that document under duress. Couldn't he come back at you and un-do the agreement?"

"He won't," Lutz said. "His partner called me with instructions for wiring the Broadline proceeds after the closing. He didn't seem particularly put out; was very professional."

Felton shook his head. "What an amazing turn of events."

"Yeah," Lutz said, and stood. "Can we get Pat now?"

Felton nodded.

Pat was standing, spraying breath freshener into her mouth when Bob opened the door. They returned, holding hands, and sat. She was still beaming and dabbed at her eyes. Bob looked at his wife. "I've been less than a terrific father these past few years."

She patted his hand. "Honey, you were busy providing."

"It's no excuse," he said.

Pat's eyes searched the doctor for support.

"Don't be so hard on yourself," Felton said. "Mrs. Lutz, I explained to Bob how trauma can be so profound that it can become hard-wired in one's neurology. Recurrence of an event can be triggered by smells, words, even songs."

"Oh, *you*," she tapped Bob's knee. "That's why you always sing those silly songs."

Bob smiled at her and squeezed her hand.

Felton continued, "Our actions are driven through neurological channels—tiny synapses manage our reaction to events. What would appear to be involuntary is actually a response that is chemically encoded. The passing of Bob's father two years ago could have triggered a re-emergence of a childhood trauma."

Bob said, "They're circuits, hon; we all have them.

"My-my," she said. "Now isn't *that* interesting." She stared at Felton with eyes big and pink.

Felton continued, "Some of those synapses can repeat continuously, like a do-loop in mathematics. It's an insidious affliction, Mrs. Lutz, and not until the last twenty years or so has pharmacology been able to provide some relief."

"You poor, poor man," she said to her husband who was nodding softly, a fresh gloss to his eyes.

Felton said to Pat, "It is important that Bob continue his medication."

She nodded at the doctor then looked at her husband, who acknowledged her before nodding at Felton.

"So," Felton said. "This has been quite an experience for you both. I'm very happy for the two of you."

"Three," Bob said. "We miss our daughter." Pat went down for the tissue box. "I haven't visited her on campus since she went away. Pat's been to see her twice. I was always too busy." He looked at Pat. "I want to go see her. I miss my little girl."

Pat sat up. "Oh, can we go?" she said.

"No, I want to go alone and take her some place nice. Talk to her alone. Then the two of us can go see her again and be together as a family." Pat honked into the tissue.

Bob rose and moved towards Felton. The doctor extended his hand. Bob took it in his two and said, "Thank you." Pat stood and put an arm around her husband and started to thank Felton, then turned away to honk again. They left with an arm around each other's waist.

I MISSED YOU, LITTLE GIRL

The bumpy Ocean Airways flight arrived precisely on time. He walked briskly through the airport, anxious to get outside, and stood in line patiently, tilting one side of his face to the afternoon sun, then the other. He sniffed the air for the wonderful floral scents that abandon Boston by November.

He entered a cab. "The Atlantis."

Minutes later he walked across the hotel lobby towards check-in. The gentleman at the front desk smiled at him. "How nice to have you back so soon."

"It is nice to see you again, David."

"We put you in the same suite as last time."

"How nice. Thank you so much."

"And your daughter?"

"Yes?"

"She will be staying longer also?"

He smiled. "For the week."

"Wonderful." The clerk handed an envelope with room and mini-bar keys across the marble counter. "She has checked in and awaits you."

He was anxious to see her.

"Will there be luggage?"

He lifted a carry-on bag. "Just this. I'm all set."

"Very good," the clerk said with a slight bow. "Enjoy your stay."

He loved the Bahamas. They came three weeks ago—just for the weekend—to discover each other and plan. She lifted his heart with her playful mood and childish ways. He hated to leave that Monday morning.

He walked to the elevator, entered, and put the plastic penthouse key into the slot and pushed the button for "PH".

He walked the length of the hall to the ocean-facing corner suite and tapped on the door. "Room Service," he said.

The door opened to a wonderful little girl smile. "We got the same room as last time," she said, bouncing with excitement. She grabbed his wrist and pulled him in. He put the bag down—the door closing behind—and placed his arms on her hips and studied her face.

"I missed you, little girl."

She buried her cheek into his chest. "I missed you too, Daddy."

He lifted her face with a finger, stroked her cheek tenderly and studied her features. "He worked you over pretty good."

"Hey, I can take a few punches for the big bucks."

"Teeth okay?"

"Yeah." She moved her tongue over her front teeth and smiled.

"Did you bring the money?"

"Yes (she nodded at her suitcase). Your cut's in there; cashier's check like you said."

"Great. They'll cash that in the casino." He smiled at her. "You're a gutsy little kid."

"And you're a big, smart man. You signing that rape form in the emergency room really convinced Reese."

He stepped back and wagged an admiring finger at her. "If you hadn't called me and come in, we never could have planned this." He shook his head and laughed. "I wish I could have seen that deviant's face."

"And Satch," she said, thrusting out her arms. "He *bought—a new—Harley!*"

He smiled. "Good for him."

She nodded at him, full of herself. "I was right that Lutz would give up. That we had to step in."

"The man's incapable of sustained action," he said, leaning back to take her in. "Blamed his father."

She shook her head. "My father was a jerk, but it made me stronger."

"In this case, he was the jerk." He poked her playfully. "A natural born jackass."

"Yeah, I saw it the minute I met him. I had him set up but, within days of working there, I knew he didn't have much dough." She walked to her suitcase, got the cashier's check and brought it to him. "Got any wealthy patients we can work on?"

He snapped the check with approval and grinned. "One comes immediately to mind. Let's work on it this week."

She laughed and brought her hands together in one loud clap. "*Ha!* Don't you think it's hysterical? You must see it every day."

"What?"

She snickered into her fingertips. "How men think."

He answered while moving to the door. "I have dinner each month with a couple of my psychiatrist friends. Lutz barely made our Top-Ten Buffoons list." He opened it and hung a small Do Not Disturb sign on the knob.

"You had him on some pretty powerful stuff, huh?"

He started back to her. "A hundred milligrams. I couldn't figure out why he wasn't responding. He wasn't *taking* it. I was about to take him up again. One-twenty-five could make a horse sing *Melancholy Baby.*"

She furled her brow. "*What* was his problem?"

"Bad circuits, my love."

"But he's a smart guy."

"Not smart enough to change his behavior."

"Geez, I feel kinda sorry for him."

He gripped her shoulders then leaned in to nuzzle her. "Don't," he whispered.

She stepped back. "Why?"

"Because he's had a character-bypass. Add a case of acute pettiness to that and you can see the extent of my challenge."

"You're so curt," she said, and poked his stomach.

"And you're so cute." He drew her near, kissed a freckle on her nose and put his tongue gently in her mouth. He leaned back to look at her. "Let's order champagne."

She smiled and nodded across the room at an ice bucket. "I already did. *Cristal.*"

He shook his head on the way to the bucket. She was always thinking ahead. "He told me yesterday that he never went up to your apartment the night you met him in New Hampshire. Looked me right in the eye and lied."

"*Hah,*" she said. "I told you I worked on him for a solid hour but he couldn't get it up."

He turned holding the bottle. "Well, little girl, that won't be a problem here."

She let her robe fall to the floor. She was wearing light pink panties—the push-up bra he bought her the last time they were here—and a white silk garter belt held her lavender hose. He loved everything about this young woman: how her face lit at each insight; how she pulled her ponytail to the front when she wanted to flirt; and how she moistened her lips with each sexual innuendo. If he could bottle her, he'd put Pfizer out of business.

"Get in your chair," she said.

He put down the bottle and walked to the formal Victorian chair facing the ocean and sat.

She came over and knelt in front of him, loosened his belt and found his erection. She started to go down, then stopped to look up at him. "Oh," she said, maintaining her grip, "I gave Frosty ten grand for posing as my attorney."

"Seems fair," he said.

She took him in her mouth.

One leg was out straight as the other bounced on the ball of his foot. "Go slow, Val."

She moved the pearl around the base of his penis then flicked slowly up the shaft, stopping suddenly to look up at him. "I bet I can make you come in two minutes."

He winked. "I wouldn't touch that bet. You're too good. I'll give you ninety seconds."

"Okay. Ninety seconds."

"How much?" He said.

"Ten thousand."

He checked his watch. "You're on."

She took him in her mouth again.

His eyes fluttered at the ceiling. "Who's your daddy?"

She came off him and smiled as she continued to stroke his hardness. "You're my daddy, Daddy. Look at me," she said, and went back down to moan softly, staring up at him with her ten thousand dollar eyes.

"Baby, slow down," he said. "Play fair."